OPERATING SYSTEMS
Structures and Mechanisms

OPERATING SYSTEMS
Structures and Mechanisms

Philippe A. Janson
IBM Forschungslaboratorium Zurich
Rüschlikon, Switzerland
and Université Libre de Bruxelles
Bruxelles, Belgium

1985

ACADEMIC PRESS, INC.

(Harcourt Brace Jovanovich, Publishers)

London   Orlando   San Diego   New York
Toronto   Montreal   Sydney   Tokyo

Framingham State College
Framingham, Massachusetts

ACADEMIC PRESS INC. (LONDON) LTD.
24–28 Oval Road
LONDON NW1 7DX

United States Edition published by
ACADEMIC PRESS, INC.
Orlando, Florida 32887

British Library Cataloguing in Publication Data

Janson, Philippe
   Operating systems.
   1. Operating systems (Computers)
   I. Title
   001.64'25   QA76.6

ISBN 0-12-380230-X

Library of Congress Cataloging in Publication Data

Janson, Philippe.
   Operating systems

   Bibliography: p.
   Includes index.
   1. Operating systems (Computers) I. Title.
QA76.6.J364   1985   001.64'25   84-20391
ISBN 0-12-380230-X (alk. paper)

PRINTED IN THE UNITED STATES OF AMERICA

85 86 87 88   9 8 7 6 5 4 3 2 1

Contents

Chapter VIII. Addressing and Naming

Chapter IX   Protection and Security

Part 6
SYNTHESIS
Chapter X.   System Design

List of Figures

Preface

1. Objectives

This text constitutes the material of an elementary course introducing students in computer engineering to the structures and mechanisms of operating systems. It aims to provide the reader with a basic understanding of operating systems principles and techniques. It explains what an operating system is, what kinds of operating systems exist, what problems they try to solve, and how they go about solving them. It is designed both as a guide to assist a lecturer in preparing and organizing classes and as a set of lecture notes offering detailed information to help students.

In the field of operating systems, any single book cannot claim to be complete and self-contained. Every work covers different aspects of the subject in its own fashion. The best way to acquire an even and wide knowledge of the field is not to limit oneself to one source, but to learn from each source what it teaches best. This volume focusses on two aspects of operating systems:

1. First, emphasis is put on the *organization* of operating systems. Knowing what an operating system does for its users and how it operates is not sufficient to understand all the issues facing its designer. In other words, it is not sufficient to describe operating systems as sets of algorithms and tables. It is necessary to put these components in perspective and to see how they are related to one another. It is essential to have some knowledge about the modular and structural aspects of operating systems.

Most commercial operating systems were designed with efficiency as their main objective. Many shortcuts were taken to gain development time, to save space and to optimize run time. As a result, these systems are not well organized and are extremely complex to understand and to change. A recent need for provably correct operating systems also has stressed the importance of having well-organized operating systems and has fostered an interest in techniques for structuring an operating system. This book tries to communicate the essence of this work.

2. Second, this book stresses the *practical aspects* of operating systems. There does not exist a complete theory in the field of operating systems as there exist theories in the various fields of mathematics, physics, chemistry, or even electronic devices and circuits. Operating system theory is restricted to certain performance problems and only a few theoretical principles have proved useful in practice.

The study and design of operating systems remain very pragmatic areas, where practical experience and a sound sense of engineering are the best tools for success. Thus, stating general principles and describing algorithms in an abstract way without explaining how they can be implemented gives a one-sided view of operating systems.

This book stresses the mechanical and operational aspects of operating systems. Mechanisms for solving each problem are evaluated and classified according to their advantages and disadvantages.

To illustrate these mechanisms, the book refers to case studies and existing systems. The diversity among operating systems is so great that one cannot learn about the subject without studying some of the most representative or most famous examples of real systems. An effort is made to integrate these discussions with the rest of the material at least by using a unified terminology. Thus, systems that have been described in their own technical jargon in the literature will be presented here in the same words as the rest of the text to stress the similarities and differences that may exist.

It is also useful to stress the difference between this and other texts on the subject:

In the past decade, several books have been published, some of which are rather interesting in their own way. Most of these offer high-level descriptions of operating system principles and concepts and define algorithms and functions in a very abstract way. They are meant as general reading. By contrast, this course devotes relatively less attention to basic principles and spends more effort on practical aspects, as suggested earlier. The style is often dense and concise, leaving little room for basic definitions and relying on the figures to explain the details of mechanisms. The text is not meant as general reading but as support material for lectures, allowing students to refresh their memory about details, while assuming that they have attended class or read other more general texts that devote more time to introducing basic concepts.

On the other hand, some books have been published that offer many more details or more specific information than the present one. Such books discuss operating systems for very specialized audiences: operating systems for a specific computer; operating systems for system programmers; operating systems for data processing managers; operating systems for users, seen from a run-time environment and control language viewpoint. These approaches are completely orthogonal to the present work, which is addressed to a wide range of students in computer engineering.

Other books have stressed more advanced and theoretical aspects of operating systems, in particular their performance and modeling aspects. By contrast, this book offers a qualitative rather than quantitative view of systems. Performance aspects are mentioned only briefly here, as they do not belong in an introductory course. The same is true for reliability problems. These are fundamental issues in operating systems, but they demand an already intimate understanding of the field and are emerging as a new discipline in its own right. They receive only a brief treatment here.

Other books have been devoted almost entirely to one specific operating system problem, most notably multiprogramming and process synchronization, at the cost of neglecting almost entirely other important and basic issues. This course gives as equitable a treatment as possible to all fundamental operating system components.

The most recent classification of computer science subjects published by the Association for Computing Machinery mentions under the heading of Operating Systems some topics that are not covered in this text, e.g., data organization, terminal management, networking, and communication (architecture and protocols). While these topics definitely belong in an introductory course and are not unrelated to operating systems, they do not belong primarily in an operating system course, a fact acknowledged by the ACM classification. Data organization belongs more in a course on data base and data management. This book discusses directory structures, file access, and the mapping of files in process address spaces, but leaves out higher-level aspects involving the internal organization and the semantics of file contents. Similarly, all aspects of operating systems related to network software, virtual terminals, communication protocols, and network architecture belong in a course dedicated to computer communication and data networks. Discussion of communication issues in the present course is limited to problems of interrupt handling, message queueing, and buffer management.

To conclude, this book looks at operating systems more from a mechanical and structural point of view, as engineers or designers would look at them, rather than from an algorithmic or theoretical point of view, which already has been done in the existing literature. As a result, the book focusses on the low levels of operating systems, where software and hardware interact in rather complex ways to realize the kernel mechanisms. It leaves out descriptions of higher level functions, such as command language processors, network access methods, data base management systems, and related operating system utilities.

2. Required Background

In attacking this book on operating systems, the reader is assumed to be knowledgeable in the areas of computer *architecture* and organization, and *programming* languages and techniques.

1. Knowledge in the hardware field is necessary to understand how processors, memory, devices, and communication equipment work, what their limitations are, how they interact with system software, and what the gap is between their possibilities and the expectations of user programs.

2. Knowledge about programming languages and programming techniques is necessary for two reasons. First, operating systems are collections of programs. As such, what they can do and how they can do it is limited by what programming languages and techniques allow. Second, the purpose of an operating system is to serve as cement between the raw hardware of a system and the programs written by the users of that system. Therefore, what that cement must achieve, i.e., the functionality it offers to users, is partly dictated by the demands of the languages in which users write their programs.

Notice that a common practice in courses on operating systems is to illustrate problems by writing small programs. While this technique may have its advantages, we avoid it as much as possible. We believe that it is distracting to describe a problem or its solution by showing a program that exhibits that problem or realizes its solution. The reader tends to spend more time on deciphering the semantics of the program than on thinking about the true nature of the point it illustrates. Hence, knowledge about programming is required only insofar as we expect the reader to be familiar with the data and control structures most frequently used in programming. Knowledge about any particular programming language is not assumed. When necessary, a Pascalgol notation self-explanatory to any programmer will be used.

Some books on operating systems require and use a substantial knowledge of probability theory and calculus. The interest of mathematical models for analyzing the behavior of operating systems is important. However, modeling the performance of operating systems in a useful and realistic way is not easy and demands great experience. Many scientists have been carried away by the elegance of mathematical tools and have ignored typical operating conditions of real systems. For these reasons, and as suggested earlier, it would be premature to attack this topic in an introductory course. Thus, this book does not discuss it and does not expect the reader to be an expert in these mathematical tools.

3. Method of Approach

The book focusses primarily, though not exclusively, on general purpose *time-sharing* systems. This deliberate choice was made because general-purpose time-sharing systems are in the center of a spectrum of operating systems ranging from batch to remote batch, to time-sharing, to personal and real-time systems. By studying general-purpose time-sharing systems, one essentially studies the most complete systems. Any problem encountered in any system is encountered in one form or another in a general-purpose time-sharing system. Thus, by studying general-purpose time-sharing systems, the reader will acquire the basic tools for studying almost any other kind of system.

However, while general-purpose time-sharing systems play a central role from a *pedagogical* point of view, their practical importance for the future will be moderate. They have been the center of interest for the past decade and will still be produced and used for many years to come; but, as batch systems before them, they are on their way out because of recent technological advances.

Time-sharing systems were designed in the late 1960s and early 1970s to reconcile a need for general-purpose interactive computing with a need to share hardware to achieve the economies of scale called for by the high cost of computing then. Today, with the decreasing cost of microcomputer technology, there is evidence that terminals of yesterday are being replaced by intelligent workstations. In this scenario, the human interface support and front-end software that general-purpose time-sharing systems provide today will be off-loaded to the workstations. Because of the ever-increasing need for computing, storage, and communication, central machines will still be needed. However, the function of such shared resource controllers will change from one of time-sharing to one of dedicated data repositories and batch "number crunchers."

Thus, while today's world is still dominated by time-sharing systems, it will slowly evolve toward a world dominated by personal computing systems using dedicated resource controllers, such as data base systems and file servers, where operating system issues are very different. This trend towards *personal computing* and *distributed systems* is reflected in the book by digressions stressing the key differences between personal computing systems and time-sharing systems.

In reading various books on operating systems, one notices that no two of them present the mechanisms composing an operating system in the same order. Furthermore, in reading any particular book, one notices that no chapter is self-sufficient. Every chapter contains references to later chapters, leaving many loose ends upon the first reading. This phenomenon is probably due to the complexity of operating systems themselves. Because operating systems are complex, they are hard to understand. Being hard to understand, they are hard to describe. Existing descriptions lack organization, just as most operating systems themselves lack organization.

This book tries to avoid as much as possible complexity due to lack of organization and resulting forward references. (To be sure, it has not completely succeeded!) Operating systems are described in such a way that every chapter is based solely on material presented in previous chapters. As will be seen in Chapter X (please excuse this forward reference!), this organization of the text corresponds to an organization of operating systems that has been proposed recently to make them easier to understand, to maintain, and to verify, if not more efficient to use. (This latter point has yet to be demonstrated.) The whole book thus reflects the organization of an operating system. As the course progresses, a model operating system is developed from the bottom up.

4. Outline

In Chapter I, we present basic concepts in *operating systems*. We define operating systems and classify them into various categories. We briefly describe the main roles of an operating system. We also identify the major components of an operating system. We discuss key aspects of *distributed systems*.

In Chapters II and III, we discuss the basic mechanism of an operating system, i.e., that of *multiplexing* physical processors among several users and allowing the program written by such users to *communicate* with one another in a smooth fashion.

In Chapter IV, we deal with computer *input/output*. We review what kinds of I/O architectures exist. We present techniques for synchronizing user programs with I/O devices and for managing queues of I/O requests. We also review some buffer management problems.

In Chapters V and VI, we study mechanisms for *memory* management. We examine how the information can be addressed and how it is stored into information containers called segments or pages. We also show how it can migrate between levels of memory represented by main memory and peripheral storage devices to multiplex the main memory among all users.

In Chapter VII, we study mechanisms for *file* management. We first show how the information stored in a system can be filed away for later retrieval. Some attention is devoted here to the problem of reliable storage. We then see how files can be addressed by user programs.

In Chapter VIII, we discuss the problem of *naming* objects (files) and we explain how the operating system can interpret names and translate them into addresses that it can use to actually refer to the information in main memory. The operation of mechanisms called linkers is described. All the types of names, addresses, and identifiers that can be found in a system are put in perspective and their properties and objectives are reviewed.

In Chapter IX, we study mechanisms for *protecting* information from access by unauthorized users. We define the means for controlling access to information and for authenticating users. We explain how these means can be implemented in a practical system.

In Chapter X, we present guidelines for *organizing* operating systems. We explain why systems should be well organized what is meant by organizing a system, how a system can be organized, and how all the mechanisms of the model operating system described in earlier Chapters fit together from a bird's eye viewpoint.

Acknowledgments

"Getting education at MIT is like getting a drink from a fire hose" says a famous quote at the Institute. However uncomfortable either may be, the flow that the Massachusetts Institute of Technology dispenses has been an essential ingredient for this textbook on operating systems. I feel very much indebted to the Faculty of the Computer Systems Research Group that provided me with a very challenging environment for learning about systems. I also feel indebted to the designers of Multics, in its time the Rolls-Royce of operating systems, as they produced a system that is at least pedagogically outstanding, having all imaginable gadgets and then some, while being anything but a toy!

A word of acknowledgment is in order for the many authors of previous textbooks on operating systems. Writing the first book on this subject must have been an unrewarding job. My job was much simpler as I benefited from their mistakes and could build on their successes. This work was definitely influenced by their contributions, although any of its defects are my sole responsibility.

I am also thankful for the help offered by the Academic Press reviewers and editors, who provided constructive ideas on the overall content and organization of the text as well as on its style.

Special thanks are due to Liba Svobodova for the merciless comments and insightful criticisms she offered on a draft of the text. Her remarks had a substantial impact on the final appearance of the manuscript.

I thank the IBM Zurich Research Laboratory for having provided me with a designer's help, secretarial support, a personal computer at home, and permission to use central facilities, over the course of several years, to prepare this manuscript.

I am indebted to the University of Brussels, which provided a framework, an incentive, and the financial support to develop a course on operating systems.

In all fairness, I must express my gratitude to several generations of students at

IBM's ESRI and at the University of Brussels, who really played Guinea pigs for this course and offered many suggestions and comments to improve it.

Last but not least, I wish to thank my wife for the many nights and weekends of time-off she gave me in the past few years, and for the moral and secretarial support she offered in the last year of this writing marathon.

Part 1

INTRODUCTION

Chapter I

Operating Systems

1. Resource Management

The operating system of a computer can be defined in several different ways, depending on the viewpoint adopted. In this chapter, we examine two of the most significant definitions. The first one, discussed in this section, views the operating system as a monolithic resource manager. The second one, discussed in Section 2, views the operating systems as an extension of the hardware, providing the user with a virtual machine.

As pointed out by Denning (1982), the second definition evolved from the first one in the course of operating system history. The view of operating systems as monolithic resource managers prevailed in the 1960s. Then the viewpoint of operating system designers evolved, and the virtual machine definition seems to prevail today.

The definition of operating systems as *resource managers* corresponds to the view of a computer as a set of resources such as processor, memory, devices, and files that have to be multiplexed among competing tasks or jobs.

In this context, the main problem solved by the operating system is the orderly sharing and protection of resources: offering competing tasks the ability to share the use of and access to common machine resources while guaranteeing the necessary protection of the tasks from one another. Control of sharing and protection is based on the maintenance of detailed status information about resource usage. This status information must be constantly updated by the operating system, which keeps track of all resources within one large monolithic program.

As computer power grew and computer resources required more sophisticated management, the maintenance and synchronization of resource usage and status information became more and more complex. Operating systems designed as monolithic resource managers became more and more intractable, hard to understand, hard to maintain, and hard to test. Sometime in the 1970s, designing operating systems as gigantic resource managers became so impossible that new design techniques were needed, leading to the definition of operating systems as virtual machines.

2. Virtual Machines

The evolution of design techniques and of the corresponding definition of operating systems stemmed from the realization that a computer can no longer be regarded as an unordered collection of resources all managed together by a monolithic operating system. Instead, a computer has to be treated as a structured collection of classes of resources, where each class of resources is managed by a separate set of programs. Each set of programs completely hides the details and the complexity of maintenance and synchronization problems associated with the corresponding resource class. It exposes to other programs composing the operating system only a very abstract, idealized, and simplified view of the resources it manages.

Modern operating systems invariably recognize four generic classes of resources, some of which are further divided into subclasses, as pictured in Fig. 1. A first distinction is made between active and passive resources. Active resources are those that trigger and/or support the evolution of computing tasks and jobs. Passive resources are those manipulated by the active ones as directed by the evolving computations.

A second distinction is made between central resources and peripheral resources. Central resources compose the heart of the computing equipment. They are often located in the same cabinet or in the immediate vicinity of one another. Peripheral resources allow the central ones to communicate with the outside world. They are generally physically separated from the central complex by communication lines and can be located at a distance from it.

These two dividing lines cut the set of computing resources into four types: central active resources, peripheral active resources, central passive resources, and peripheral passive resources. Let us consider each of these separately.

Central active resources are the physical processors. Physical processors are the engines of computers without which any activity is impossible. They interpret software instructions, thereby causing computations to make progress.

Peripheral active resources are the communication devices allowing external agents such as human users, sensors, control devices, or other computers to interact with the central processors. These communication devices can be further divided into terminal devices, such as keyboards, printers, displays, pointing

CENTRAL RESOURCES	PERIPHERAL RESOURCES

ACTIVE RESOURCES PROCESSORS	COMMUNICATION DEVICES
	
	• TERMINALS: KEYBOARDS
	         PRINTERS
	         DISPLAYS
	         POINTERS
	
	• NETWORK: REMOTE
	        LOCAL
	
	ETC.

PASSIVE RESOURCES MEMORY	STORAGE DEVICES • DISKS • TAPES • DRUMS • MASS STORAGE ETC.

Fig. 1. Computing resources classification.

devices, meters, and gauges, and networking devices, such as I/O channels, local networks, telephone lines, and satellite links.

Central passive resources denote main memory and cache memory devices, where the central processors and communication devices just discussed may store data they are manipulating in the short term.

Peripheral passive resources denote all types of storage devices, such as paging devices, disks, tapes, and mass storage devices.

For each of these classes and types of resources, modern operating systems provide a piece of software that hides the details of the management of the resource while offering to the rest of the operating system, as well as to user software, an idealized, abstracted view of the managed resource. Thus, the operating system turns every real resource into one or more virtual resources. These virtual resources exhibit a behavior much like that of the real resources but do not require the complex multiplexing and protection mechanisms that the operating system needs to implement for the real resource. For example, writing into a real memory area requires making sure that no other computation is writing in the same area at the same time. This necessary protection can be guaranteed by

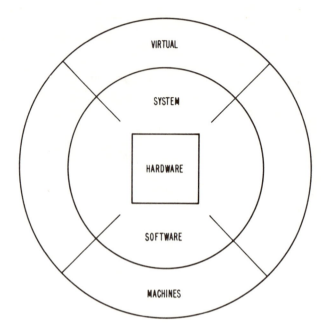

Fig. 2. Virtual machine definition.

the operating system so that a user program may write in an area of virtual memory knowing full well that that area is by definition private at least for the moment.

Generalizing from the view of the operating system as a collection of software modules that turn real resources into virtual ones, one can view the whole operating system as one piece of software that turns the real computer, including all resources, into one or more *virtual machines** composed of virtual resources. This is pictured in Fig. 2. With this perspective, the operating system is nothing more than a software extension to the computer hardware that makes the hardware more amenable to user programming. In fact, a recent trend that is bound to become prevalent as technology advances tends to regard and indeed to implement more and more of the operating system as firmware or microcode rather than plain software.

In summary, the definition of operating systems has evolved from one of managing resources to one of making raw resources more convenient to deal with in user software.

---

*This loose definition of virtual machines is related to but distinct from that supported by IBM's VM/SP operating system, discussed in Chapter X (Meyer and Seawright, 1970; Pamerlee *et al.*, 1972).

3.   Software Layers

3.1.   Levels of Abstraction

Figure 2 shows a computer system to be composed of three layers. At the innermost or lowest layer, one finds the hardware or real resources of the computer. At the second or middle layer, one finds the *operating system* software. At the outermost or upper layer, one finds the user software.

The operating system software uses (i.e., runs on) the hardware resources of the real computer. In turn, the operating system turns the real machine into virtual ones, so that user software uses (i.e., runs on) virtual resources.

Thus, the view of the operating system as an extension to the computer hardware transforming real resources into virtual ones casts a layered structure upon the whole computer system. In other words, viewing the operating system as providing a layer of abstraction in resource management divides the total computer software into two parts: system software and user software.

Clearly, it does not take much thinking for any observer to make the same division without resorting to concepts of abstract resources. However, it is interesting to note that the concept of abstract resources leads to this same division of the total software into two distinct layers that can be treated individually. Modern software design techniques pursue the idea of abstract resources further to arrive at a much finer subdivision of the system software, where each layer of abstraction is so thin that it is fully tractable as one entity by a single person.

3.2.   User Software Layers

As pictured in Fig. 3, the user software itself is often divided into *application software* and *utility software*. Application software is that software written by or for the individual user to solve a particular problem. Utility software is usually written by or for the computer manufacturer to go with a particular operating system. It comprises such software tools as command language interpreters, programming language translators, debuggers, and common scientific or business packages.

Just as the operating system transforms real resources into virtual ones that are easier to use, the utility software transforms the virtual resources offered by the operating systems into yet more convenient to use resources. The difference between operating system and utility system is the type of ''convenience'' they offer. The convenience provided by the operating system is aimed primarily at solving multiplexing issues to protect resources from users and users from one another. The convenience provided by utility software is aimed more at making resources functionally richer and more meaningful to human users.

For instance, the operating system turns one real processor into a collection of

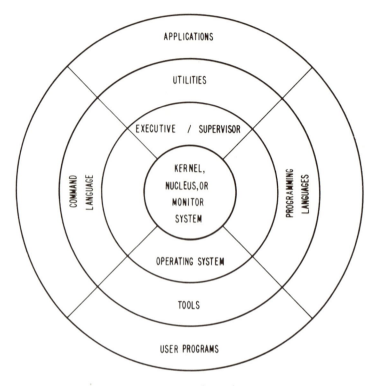

Fig. 3. System software layers.

virtual ones that are well protected from one another. However, the virtual processors, in addition to operating system calls, understand only the same machine language that real processors understand. By contrast, the instruction processors seen above the utility level understand high-level programming languages and command languages.

3.3. Operating System Layers

Further subdivision of software into finer sublayers is not restricted to user software. The same phenomenon can be observed for operating system software, as shown in Fig. 3. The latter is often divided into two layers: the *supervisor* or *executive* software and the *kernel* or *nucleus* software (sometimes called monitor software).

While both layers of abstraction are concerned with the safe multiplexing of system resources, they differ in the functional richness they offer. Kernel processors are few and expensive in memory requirement, whereas supervisor processors are plentiful and demand less memory and fewer privileges. As for communication resources, the kernel supports byte- or block-level communication but, unlike the supervisor, has no notion of structured messages. Similarly, for storage devices, the kernel supports disk record access, while the notion of structured files as collections of records is not supported below the supervisor level.

Now that we have contrasted the concepts of executive or supervisor system with kernel or nucleus system, a word of caution is in order. These concepts are rather fuzzy in the literature, as in most systems. Different people give various meanings to the concepts. The context in which they are used generally clarifies the situation. Even if one adopts the definitions we have proposed above, it is not easy to identify the mechanisms corresponding to each of the concepts in a real system, as there exists no clear-cut boundary between them. It is often a matter of personal judgement.

3.4. Kernel Resource Layers

Even the finer subdivision of system software into kernel and supervisor software is not sufficient to reach software modules of a complexity manageable by one programmer, or by one student for that matter. Thus the kernel and the supervisor are themselves further subdivided into more tractable entities.

With this finer layering, every layer corresponds to one class of resources. The order of the layers is governed by what class of resource uses what other class of resource. More details about this finer layering and its justification are given in Chapter X on system design. For the moment, we just describe what resources are managed at which layer by way of introduction to the later parts of this volume.

The kernel provides primitive forms of the four resource classes. At the bottom layer, it offers a form of abstract processor, called a *virtual processor*. The bottom layer multiplexes the real processor(s) into a multiplicity of virtual processors and allows these to communicate with one another in a rather primitive way. It also hides interrupts from the rest of the operating system by mapping them into more amenable communication primitives between virtual processors.

This bottom layer, sometimes called kernel itself, is a key element of the nucleus of an operating system: by turning the real processor(s) into a multiplicity of virtual processors, it allows the operating system designers to use one such virtual processor to manage each different type of operating system resource. As a result, what used to be designed as a monolithic resource manager running on a real computer can be broken into nicely structured programs, each managing one type of resource within a dedicated virtual processor.

The second kernel layer offers a primitive form of abstract I/O device, where each *virtual device* is implemented using a virtual processor. At this level, all I/O devices, whether communication or storage devices, are managed in pretty much the same way. The kernel I/O software gives the illusion to its users of byte or block oriented devices that all support fairly analogous operations such as setup, input, output, and shutdown.

Given virtual processors and virtual I/O devices, the third kernel layer is in a position to offer memory management. Note that main memory management alone does not require the use of virtual processors and virtual devices. However, the trend in operating system design is clearly towards *virtual memory,* a concept that does require the use of virtual processors and storage devices, as will be explained in the chapter on multilevel memory management.

The three kernel layers briefly described above are studied in detail in Parts 2, 3, and 4.

Building upon the primitive resources offered by these three layers, the rest of the operating system adds a number of layers as part of the supervisor. The exact number of layers depends very much on the level of sophistication and the application for which the operating system is destined. There are many different types of operating systems, as explained in Section 4, and each type has to meet very different requirements. Some operating systems may not offer anything beyond the kernel. Others may offer more layers of processor management, memory management, storage device management, and communication management. While high-level communication management falls in the realm of a computer networking course, other supervisor resource management issues, such as file storage, address spaces, and data protection, are discussed in Part 5 of this book.

4. Operating System Types

Figure 4 represents an attempt at classifying operating systems according to their function. The function of an operating system determines in a very large measure the functional, structural, performance, and reliability requirements it has to fulfill.

One dividing line is provided by the distinction between on-line and off-line systems. Off-line systems are systems where the user is not interacting with the system while his program is being executed. Off-line systems include so-called batch and remote batch systems.

4.1. Batch and Remote Batch Systems

Batch systems draw their name from the way in which work is submitted to them. Work is submitted in batches of cards. A batch of cards defines a job. A job consists of a related set of tasks, for instance, the compilation, loading, and

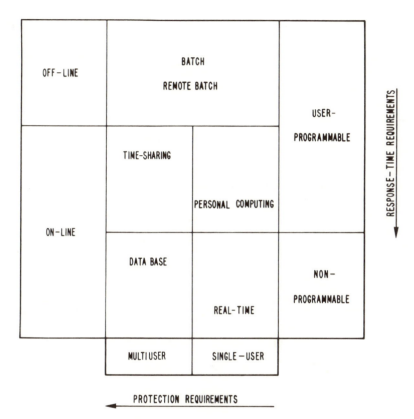

Fig. 4.   Operating system types.

execution of a program. Typically, a batch of cards includes control cards and program cards. Control cards are commands to the operating system that tell it what to do about the program cards that follow, for instance: compile, load, and execute; or load and execute; or compile only and punch the results; or pass as input to some application program residing in the file system.

Remote batch systems are distinguished from batch systems by the simple fact that the jobs (decks of cards) are submitted not at the site of the computer but at a remote card reader that is connected via leased or switched high-speed lines to a batch system. A remote card reader is usually installed together with a remote printer so that the results of the jobs that were submitted from that remote card reader can be printed on the associated remote printer.

In early batch systems, batches of work were submitted sequentially, one at a time, for the computer to process. When one job was processed, the operator was informed and allowed to deposit the next job in the card reader. This caused great delay in the sense that reading a deck of cards is an I/O intensive task, meaning it does not require much thinking on the part of the computer but it takes time because card readers are slow. During the time a deck was read in, the main processor of the computer was doing nothing else.

One of the first and essential improvements of these early batch systems was the introduction of *spooling*. With spooling, while the computer is processing one job it simultaneously devotes a very minimal amount of its power to reading in one or more batches of work and writing them out to disk. This allows future jobs to be read in while current work is in progress. Thus, when the current job is completed, the computer can rapidly retrieve another batch of work from its disk and proceed. It need not even take spooled batches in the order in which they were read in.

Nowadays, most batch systems are of the remote type. Furthermore, jobs are submitted not in the form of card decks but rather in the form of terminal input representing a card deck. Terminal input is of course performed on-line. The off-line aspect of the system is restricted to the processing of the input, not to its collection.

Off-line systems are meant to be used for large computations where the expected response time is so long that the user will not want to sit on-line at his terminal waiting for results to be computed. Because such computations are so large and so time-consuming, they demand very powerful computers with large memories and much computing power. Given the cost of such computers, batch systems are normally not dedicated to a single user. Instead, they are shared among a community of users for economic reasons.

4.2.   Interactive or Time-sharing Systems

Among the on-line systems, one must distinguish between shared *multiuser* systems and private *single-user* systems on one hand, and between *user-programmable* and *non-programmable* systems on the other hand.

In the first category, shared and programmable systems, one finds so-called interactive or time-sharing systems.

The term *interactive* comes from the fact that the user interacts with the system directly via a private terminal composed of a keyboard for input and a slow printer or CRT screen for output. The user submits his job not in one batch but rather step by step, for instance, by typing in his program, then editing out the mistakes he has just typed, then compiling the program perhaps several times until the compilation succeeds, then trying to execute the program and perhaps debugging it with the help of the system, and finally moving on to some other work like proofreading and editing some text. By comparison to a batch job, a single interactive transaction, such as editing a line of text, is very short, as the user expects an on-line response very fast.

The term *time-sharing* means that the processor time is shared among all
users. The processor jumps from one user to another as the users interact with the
system and need a fast response. In fact, the term time-sharing could be used for
any system that serves several users at a time. Even batch systems may be time-
shared. However, the rate at which an interactive system jumps from one user to
another is perhaps 10 times higher than the rate at which a batch system switches
between its users. A large batch system may execute up to a dozen jobs at a time,
and switches from one job to another every few seconds so that short jobs do not
have to wait indefinitely for longer ones to complete. A large interactive system
may serve hundreds of users at a time, and switches from one to another on every
interaction, perhaps every fraction of a second. Thus, historically, when interactive systems were first designed in the 1960s, they were often called time-sharing
systems because of the relatively high user-switching rate of processors. The
name has remained since.

This book is deliberately oriented towards the study of general purpose time-
sharing systems. General purpose time-sharing systems are time-sharing systems
that accommodate between 10 and 100 users and allow these users to do all kinds
of computations, in particular program development (typing, editing, compiling,
debugging, execution of programs) and also interactive text editing, dynamic
modeling and simulation, interactive scientific calculations, graphic design, interuser communication, etc.

Among existing time-sharing systems, some stand out as milestones in the
history of the field and represent interesting pedagogical examples that are
quoted often in this book. These include the Multics system (Corbato *et al.*,
1972; Organick, 1972); one of its descendents widely used in academic and
scientific circles, Unix (Ritchie and Thompson, 1974; Unix, 1978); IBM's
VM/SP (Creasy, 1981), a descendent of CP/CMS (Meyer and Seawright, 1970;
Pamerlee *et al.*, 1972) that was itself largely inspired by CTSS (Corbato *et al.*,
1962), the first time-sharing system built in the 1960s; and CDC's Kronos
system, DEC's VAX/VMS system, and the earlier TOPS-10 and TOPS-20 systems that were partially inspired from the experimental Tenex system (Bobrow *et
al.*, 1972).

4.3.   Personal Computing Systems

In the second category of on-line systems, private and programmable systems,
one finds all *personal computer* operating systems. Such operating systems offer
interactive tools very similar to those found in general purpose time-sharing
systems. However, they are much simpler in that the multiuser aspect has disappeared, with some of the protection and multiplexing issues it raised in time-
sharing systems. At the same time, since an entire processor can be dedicated all

the time to a single user, the user interface support offered by a personal computing system can be much more responsive and better tailored to that individual.

4.4. Data Base Management Systems

In the third category of on-line systems, shared but not user-programmable systems, one finds *data base* systems. Data base systems offer their users the ability to manage large collections of data pertaining to some specific application, such as airline reservations or banking.

These systems share with interactive systems their time-sharing capability, which requires corresponding interuser protection and multiplexing facilities. They often meet more demanding response time requirements in that they typically support more interactive users than a programmable time-sharing system. However, they differ from interactive systems because they are not general purpose systems. Data base systems are programmed for a specific application and cannot be used by their users (usually clerks not trained as computer programmers) to write further programs. Thus, a lot of data protection can be provided by the data base application itself and need not be included in the operating system.

4.5. Real-time and Embedded Systems

The fourth and last category of on-line systems, single-user (or rather single-application) nonprogrammable systems, includes *real-time* systems, such as message switching or process control systems. These systems share their non-programmability with data base systems and share their dedication to a single task with personal computing systems. In such systems, the on-line user is usually only a control operator. The system monitors signals and sensors of all kinds and reacts by adjusting controls and logging events pertaining to whatever application it is aimed at. In such systems, data protection requirements are almost absent, whereas response time requirements may be very strict.

So far, we have distinguished basically five types of systems. As we warned readers to beware of the exact distinction between supervisory system and kernel system, we must warn them again to beware of the distinction between batch, interactive, personal, data base, and real-time operating systems.

It is not unusual to find that an operating system designed for one purpose is actually used for a different one or even for several different purposes at the same time. For instance, a small time-sharing system may very well be used as a basis for a personal computing system. A real-time kernel may be used as a basis for a data base system. Very often, time-sharing systems are used to provide interactive services in the foregound, i.e., when they are demanded, while offering batch services in the background, i.e., when there is no interactive work to do. They may even offer data base services at the same time to a wider set of users.

4.6.   Distributed Systems

In the preceding sections, we have classified operating systems into five distinct categories. Cutting across all dividing lines between these categories, one may further divide operating systems between *shared-memory* systems and *distributed* systems.

Shared-memory systems, which have been assumed so far, are operating systems designed to run in environments where all code and data reside in a central memory that may be accessible by one or more physical processors. A distributed system is composed of a multiplicity of shared-memory systems interacting through communication lines. Thus, in distributed systems, code and data by definition reside in disjoint memory systems, to each of which one or more physical processors may be attached.

The essential difference between shared-memory and distributed systems lies in the way programs may interact with one another inside the system. In shared-memory systems, information may be exchanged between programs using the shared memory as a transmission medium. In distributed systems, exchange of information between programs running on different shared-memory systems requires the use of communication lines for transmission.

Due to the profound differences in the quality and quantity of information that can be communicated through these two transmission media, distributed systems have to cope with several hard problems not found in shared-memory systems. As we proceed through this book on operating systems, we will discuss those aspects of systems where the distinction between shared-memory and distributed systems is most important. Special attention is given to distributed systems in Chapter II, where we discuss interprogram communication in general and a problem known as deadlocking; in Chapter VII, where we discuss file systems and their integrity; and in Chapter IX, where we discuss protection issues.

Though it is not addressed within the scope of this volume, another area of systems that is directly affected by distributed systems is the communication software for controlling transmission lines. While transmission lines are not new to operating systems, they were used strictly to communicate with human users and the outside world until the advent of distributed systems. Since then, however, they are used also to communicate with other computers, which requires that they be managed in rather different ways. The interested reader is referred to a text on network architecture for more information (e.g., Tanenbaum, 1981).

Distributed systems have become technically conceivable because of the ever decreasing costs of computing versus communications. Computing hardware used to be so expensive that it was desirable to concentrate it as much as possible to achieve economies of scale. As a result, it was necessary to use communication lines to tie the human users with the centrally located computing resources. Nowadays, though, computing hardware has become relatively inexpensive compared to communication lines. Thus, it has become economically feasible to install smaller computers closer to where the users are, to save on communication costs.

However, in spite of the advent of distributed mini- and microcomputers, the need for communication has not disappeared. It has only changed its aspects. Typically, individual computers need to be tied into distributed systems for sharing and communication.

By pushing the distribution of computing power to its limit, one arrives at systems of personal computers interconnected by some network. In such a system, users may each have enough power to do whatever computing they want. However, computing requires more than just processor cycles and memory space. Users may need to communicate with peers through electronic mail. They may want to use programs or data, such as a data base, that need by their very nature to reside on some centrally available, shared-access computer. They may want to use a service, such as file backup and archival security, which is provided centrally to a large community of users. Finally, they may want to use a piece of hardware, such as a laser printer or a high-speed tape drive, that they do not want attached to their own personal computer because it is too expensive, too large, too noisy, or generates too much heat.

Then, in spite of their economic feasibility, why are distributed systems desirable, given the inherent need to communicate and share? Distributed systems present an autonomy advantage over shared-memory systems.

Users of a central, shared computer are fully dependent on that computer for service. If the computer crashes, they are denied the use of their tools. If the computer is overloaded with too many users, they will observe a degraded service time. If the computer does not offer some facility or service that a user would like, e.g., fulfillment of some special information protection requirements, that user might have a hard time finding or building the facility he wants and persuading the computer center manager to install it.

By contrast, if a user has a personal computer or a departmental computer, he is much more in control of things. If the computer crashes, the user may promptly restart it or borrow another personal computer, or forward work to another departmental computer while it is being repaired. Certainly, there are computations for which a personal computer is not powerful enough, in which case one may want to ship work to be performed on some central "number cruncher". However, for most interactive tasks, such as text editing, drawing, and program testing, a personal computer provides adequate computing power and much better response with a richer functional interface than a central time-sharing system.

In summary, as a corollary of increased autonomy, distributed systems may offer higher availability and better performance than shared-memory systems, thanks to parallelism.

It is worthwhile pointing out that the need to communicate and share on one hand and the desirability of autonomy on the other hand often conflict in a distributed system. In fact, in most existing distributed systems, one can detect a bias towards one or the other objective.

Distributed systems stressing communication and sharing are recognized by the homogeneity they exhibit (Apollo, 1981; Luderer *et al.*, 1981; Popek *et al.*, 1981; Rashid and Robertson, 1981). In such systems, participating computers are all treated as peers, and users can be attached to any of them. They are often of identical manufacture, or at least hide their differences as well as possible. They run the same or similar operating systems. They present a unified and homogeneous interface to all users. They offer what is often called location transparency: a user attached to one computer cannot tell whether a program he just called or a file he just referenced resides on his computer or on some other remote computer.

Systems of the other kind, favoring autonomy, do not exhibit such homogeneity (Clark and Svobodova, 1980). They typically bring together computers of very different caliber. One often differentiates the server computers, shared resource controllers managing large disks or expensive printers, from the user workstations, personal computers. These various computers often are of different manufacture and run different operating systems. Different server computers may present radically different interfaces to their users. Different users sitting at different personal computers may have totally different views of the system as a whole. Some may use their workstation as a terminal attached to some server computer, while others may use it most of the time as a stand-alone computer. Location transparency is the exception rather than the rule.

Distributed systems of the former kind were designed right from the beginning with integration as an objective, whereas systems of the latter kind grew from a haphazard aggregation of heterogeneous systems. For certain systems, however, it may be hard to say which side of the dividing line they are on.

Suggested Reading and Classics

On monitor, supervisor, and operating systems:

Rosin, 1969
Denning, 1982

On CP67/CMS, the precursor of IBM's VM/SP interactive system, one of the best illustrations of the concept of virtual machines:

> Meyer and Seawright, 1970
> Pamerlee *et al.,* 1972
> Seawright and McKinnon, 1979
> Creasy, 1981

On Multics, a sophisticated time-sharing system including most of the mechanisms discussed in this text:

> Corbato *et al.,* 1972
> Organick, 1972. An in-depth book about the Multics design.

On Unix, a time-sharing system very popular in scientific and academic circles:

> Ritchie and Thompson, 1974
> Unix, 1978. A collection of papers on the Unix design.

On distributed systems in general:

> Scherr, 1978. A taxonomy of distributed systems.
> Saltzer, 1979b. Research topics in distributed systems.
> Clark and Svobodova, 1980. On the conflict between autonomy of individual systems and cooperation towards common objectives.
> Lampson, 1981. An advanced course on distributed systems.

On specific distributed systems and prototypes:

> Jones, 1977. The Cm* multiprocessor system.
> Wilkes and Needham, 1980. The Cambridge distributed model.
> Apollo, 1981. The Apollo domain commercial system.
> Luderer *et al.,* 1981. Unix distributed around a virtual circuit switch.
> Popek *et al.,* 1981. Locus, a fully distributed Unix.
> Rashid and Robertson, 1981. Accent.
> Birrell *et al.,* 1982. The Grapevine electronic mail system.

Further Reading and References

Books about operating system principles:

> Brinch Hansen, 1973a. Stresses particularly the processor dispatching and interprocess communication aspects.
> Madnick and Donovan, 1974. Offers an IBM-oriented view of operating systems with very practical information about implementation, particularly concerning I/O.
> Habermann, 1976; Shaw, 1974. Interesting treatments in file management.
> Tsichritzis and Bernstein, 1974; Calingaert, 1982. Fairly basic and evenly good introductions to high-level concepts and principles of all components of operating systems.
> Deitel, 1983. A text of particular interest for its case studies and examples.
> Peterson and Silberschatz, 1983. A complete and up-to-date introduction to all aspects of operating systems.

Books about time-sharing:

> Watson, 1970
> Wilkes, 1975

On operating system theory:

Coffman and Denning, 1973. Recommended for the theoretical aspects of processor and I/O scheduling, as well as virtual memory paging.

A bibliography:

Bunt and Tsichritzis, 1972. 113 annotated references.

Historical papers about Multics:

Corbato and Vyssotsky, 1965
Glaser et al., 1965
Vyssotsky et al., 1965

On other landmark time-sharing systems:

Corbato et al., 1962. The CTSS.
Bobrow et al., 1972. The Tenex system.
Stephens et al., 1980. A history of the Emas system.
Rees and Stephens, 1982. The kernel of the Emas system.

Part 2

PROCESSOR MANAGEMENT

Chapter II

Multiprocessing Issues

1. Definitions

In beginning our study of operating system mechanisms, we assume that the reader knows nothing about them. In particular, in studying processor management, we assume that the reader knows nothing about storage management. It is possible to talk about processor management without knowing anything about storage management, because the mechanism that manages the processors executes in an environment such that storage management is not necessary (and not available): All the code and data necessary to implement the *processor management* mechanism are resident, meaning that they are premanently stored in main memory, readily available to be executed; and their operation does not require, if they are well designed, the allocation or release of main memory areas. Why such code and data are resident can unfortunately not be explained until Part 4*.

A computer may contain one or more *physical processors* that are often fairly similar if not identical and can execute independent instruction streams in parallel. Each physical processor contains an arithmetic and logic unit that implements the various mathematical operations supported by the hardware. Each physical processor also contains a control unit that performs the sequencing and branching instructions in hardware. The control unit typically contains an instruction counter, an instruction register, various index registers defining the environment of execution of the procedure being executed, and last but not least the wires, gates, and potential microprogram store that control the sequencing of events within each instruction cycle and chain instruction cycles together.

---

*This is one unavoidable reference forward to yet unexplained material. Until then, the reader is asked to accept that all the code and data to be described here are (must be) resident.

Two objectives of an operating system are to *multiplex* the resources of the system among all users and to allow these users to *share* information. In the context of processor management, these objectives mean multiplexing the physical processors among users and allowing user computations to interact with one another.

Physical processors are multiplexed over time. From a microscopic point of view, time slots are allocated to each user in some sequential manner. This is called *time-slicing*. From a macroscopic point of view, however, each user has the impression that he executes on a processor of his own in parallel to other users. What really happens is often called *pseudoparallelism*. This form of processor multiplexing is called *multiprogramming*. As a result of multiprogramming, each user sees what is called one (or more) *virtual processor(s)*. A virtual processor is an abstract processor that implements a unit of parallelism, a locus of control that evolves through a user instruction stream. While the term "virtual processors" is preferred and will be further used in this text, virtual processors are often called *tasks* or *processes* in other contexts.

A virtual processor appears to its user as a physical processor with a somewhat different instruction set (Fig. 5). A physical processor has a few *privileged hardware instructions,* which a virtual processor normally cannot exercise. They are, for instance, interrupt masking and unmasking instructions and I/O instructions, among others*.

On the other hand, a virtual processor has a few "software instructions" that a physical processor does not have, namely the set of software primitives composing the processor management mechanism. These "instructions" are programs that run on the physical processor, but the virtual processor regards them as atomic primitives that it can use in exactly the same way as it uses regular hardware instructions. They hide the effects of multiprogramming from virtual processors.

Thus, the processor management mechanism, which is a software program resident in main memory, can be regarded as a true extension of the hardware of the system that makes the few physical processors look like many virtual processors. In fact, some advanced physical processors today are being built with a hardware sufficient to make them look like many virtual processors, i.e., with a microprogrammed processor management mechanism.

In a system composed of several physical processors, one refers to the problems dealing with communication and *concurrency control* among these parallel physical processors as multiprocessing issues. Since virtual processors, as we have defined them, are so similar to physical processors, we will also use the term *multiprocessing* to cover all issues related to communication among parallel

---

*Selected virtual processors belonging to the operating system itself may, however, have access to a restricted set of privileged instructions, as is illustrated in Chapter IV.

PHYSICAL
REPRESENTATION

LOGICAL
REPRESENTATION

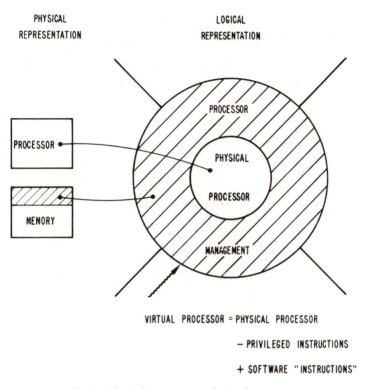

VIRTUAL PROCESSOR = PHYSICAL PROCESSOR

— PRIVILEGED INSTRUCTIONS

+ SOFTWARE "INSTRUCTIONS"

Fig. 5. Physical processors and virtual processors.

virtual processors, i.e., parallel or pseudoparallel physical processors. Multiprocessing is the topic of this chapter.

Since virtual processors are the result of multiprogramming one or more
physical processors among a multitude of users, one might think that it is essential to understand multiprogramming before talking about communication between virtual processors. In fact, if interprocessor communication mechanisms
are well designed, they should not make any distinction between parallel and
pseudoparallel processors. Thus, all of what will be said in this chapter can be
interpreted in the context of truly parallel physical processors, and it naturally
will become clear in Chapter III on multiprogramming that the same mechanisms
are applicable to pseudoparallel processors as well. In fact, if one proceeds the
other way around, by describing mechanisms designed for pseudoparallel processors first, one discovers that these mechanisms do not generalize easily to
truly parallel processors. Thus, it is better to envision true parallelism in the first
place as the right framework for describing interprocessor communication
mechanisms.

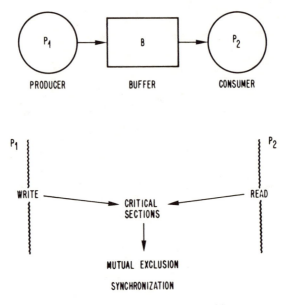

Fig. 6.   The producer–consumer problem.

2.   Mutual Exclusion

2.1.   Statement of the Problem

Multiprocessing issues cover all problems dealing with the synchronization, cooperation, and communication between parallel (or pseudoparallel), asynchronous processors. In a system providing multiple processors, it is often desirable to coordinate the activities of two or more processors. To illustrate this need, we consider a classic multiprocessing situation known as the *producer–consumer problem*. This will help us understand the first of several multiprocessing problems.

In the producer–consumer scenario (Fig. 6), a processor $P1$ writes information into a buffer B while a process $P2$ takes it out of the buffer and processes it in some way.

If the actions of $P1$ and $P2$ were not coordinated, $P2$ could read B while $P1$ writes into it, which would clearly lead to inconsistencies in passing information. This illustrates a first multiprocessing problem, namely the need for *mutual exclusion*. The sections of code in which $P1$ writes into B and $P2$ reads from B are called *critical sections*, meaning that they are mutually exclusive. Only one of $P1$ and $P2$ can be executing its critical section at any one time.

2.2. Dekker's Primitives

One mechanism to enforce mutual exclusion consists of using *Dekker's primitives*. It involves (Fig. 7) the use of two boolean flags $L1$ and $L2$ that ensure mutual exclusion and a toggle switch T, which avoids non-productive waiting, as explained below.

In the following discussion, i stands for the index (1 or 2) of one of the processors in the producer–consumer problem, while j stands for the other.

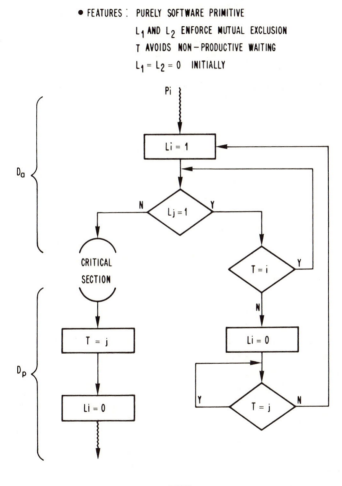

- FEATURES : PURELY SOFTWARE PRIMITIVE

  L_1 AND L_2 ENFORCE MUTUAL EXCLUSION

  T AVOIDS NON – PRODUCTIVE WAITING

  $L_1 = L_2 = 0$ INITIALLY

- DRAWBACK : BUSY – WAITING

Fig. 7. Dekker's primitives.

Mutual exclusion is guaranteed because *Li* is always true when *Pi* requests permission to enter its critical section, which prevents *Pj* from entering its own critical section.

When given the task of implementing mutual exclusion, the unaware programmer will almost invariably produce a solution where mutual exlusion is indeed guaranteed but where productive work is unfortunately not guaranteed under all circumstances. The layman's solution to mutual exclusion typically allows unproductive waiting to occur when *P1* and *P2*, for fear of entering their own critical section at the wrong time, wait for the other to take initiative, in a characteristic "After you, Sir.—No, please, after you!"

In Dekker's primitives, unproductive waiting is impossible because *T* is not affected by the *Da* code of either processor. Thus, if both processors enter the *Da* part of their code simultaneously, one will go through to the last test, setting its *L* flag to false and looping until *T* changes value. The other will loop on the first test until the partner's *L* flag is changed and then go through its critical section, which changes the value of *T*.

A problem of Dekker's primitives is that they force *busy-waiting* of a processor locked out of its critical section. Processor cycles are wasted testing *T* or *Li* over and over again instead of allowing inactivity until the critical section can be entered. Of course busy-waiting would not be a problem in a multiprocessing system offering true parallel physical processors to each user. However in a more realistic system, multiplexing a small number of physical processors among many pseudoparallel virtual processors, all physical processor cycles wasted through busy-waiting by one virtual processor are wasted for all virtual processors. For this reason, Dekker's primitives are mainly of academic interest but are rarely found in real systems.

2.3.   Interrupt Masking

In monoprocessor systems, and only in monoprocessor systems, mutual exclusion can be achieved by inhibiting or *masking interrupts*. In our earlier example of the producer–consumer problem, if *P1*, for instance, masks interrupts before entering its critical section and keeps them masked until leaving the section, it can be guaranteed exclusive access to *B*. Indeed, to enter its critical section, *P2* needs a physical processor to run on. However, the only physical processor of the system is used by *P1*, which does not give it up and has made itself noninterruptible.

As stated above, the first limitation of interrupt masking is that it implements mutual exclusion only on monoprocessor systems. In a multiprocessor system, masking the interrupts on one of the physical processors cannot prevent a virtual processor running on another physical processor from entering its critical section.

Second, allowing user processors such as *P*1 or *P*2 to mask interrupts is inefficient and even potentially dangerous. A user processor could keep the interrupts masked for so long that the system would actually lose events (e.g., I/O interrupts); he could also monopolize the processing resources by accidentally or maliciously keeping other user processors out for much longer than just a critical section. In practice, on multiuser systems, interrupt masking instructions are among the privileged instructions that can be used inside the processor management mechanism but are not visible to virtual processors.*

In spite of the above limitations, interrupt masking is a very important tool for implementing mutual exclusion. On multiuser systems, while it cannot be used by virtual processors, it is used extensively inside the operating system itself as illustrated in several of the following sections. In many monoprocessor, single-user systems, particularly real-time and embedded systems, it often is the main mechanism for mutual exclusion.

2.4. Locks

In multiprocessor systems, the most basic mutual exclusion mechanism is based on hardware instructions called *locks* or *test-and-set* (TAS). There are many variations of TAS operations (e.g., COMPARE-AND-SWAP in the IBM S/370), but all have the same general flavor illustrated by the following example.

A TAS primitive takes three parameters: a test value, a set value, and the address of a word of memory (Fig. 8). When a processor performs a TAS operation on a word *L*, the content of *L* is set to the set-value if it is equal (or superior, or inferior, etc.) to the test-value. Otherwise, it remains unchanged and the processor may retry the TAS operation at a later time.

TAS primitives can be used to implement mutual exclusion because they test and set the value of a word in one atomic operation. The action is atomic, meaning indivisible, both from the memory-access point of view and from the interrupt point of view.

From the memory-access point of view, if several processors try to test and set the same work *L* at the same time, the memory protection mechanism, which arbitrates all references to memory, will hold the action of all but one of the processors. That processor will be allowed to test and possibly set *L* before any other processor is allowed even to test it. Thus, the value of *L* is guaranteed not to change between the time it is tested and the time it is set if the test succeeds.

From the interrupt point of view, interrupts are disabled from the start of the test operation to the end of the set operation (if it takes place) so that the virtual

---

*Certain virtual processors belonging to the operating system itself may, however, have access to restricted interrupt masking facilities, as is illustrated in Chapter IV.

• ATOMIC <u>HARDWARE</u> INSTRUCTION TO TEST AND
  CONDITIONALLY SET A MEMORY CELL

• USES INTERRUPT MASKING IMPLICITLY

LOCK (L, †, s) :   [TAS]

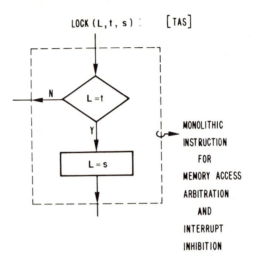

MONOLITHIC
INSTRUCTION
FOR
MEMORY ACCESS
ARBITRATION
AND
INTERRUPT
INHIBITION

• DRAWBACK: BUSY-WAITING

Fig. 8.   Locks.

processor executing TAS cannot lose the physical processor it runs on between the test and set operations.

In the case of our earlier producer–consumer problem, locks would be used as follows. A conventional word L, called the lock, is associated with B. By convention, $L = 1$ *implies that B* is accessible, while $L = 0$ implies that some processor is already accessing B and any other processor should wait. Before a processor Pi tries to access B it must successfully execute TAS(L,1,0). By doing so, Pi is said to lock L and B. Thereafter, no other processor will access B since TAS operations will fail. When Pi has finished accessing B, it simply writes a 1 back into L, thereby enabling later TAS operations to succeed. This is called unlocking L and its associated data base B.

If it were not for atomicity, mutual exclusion could not be guaranteed. Indeed, if $P1$ and $P2$ tried to test and set L with regular instructions, they could both test it when $L = 1$. They would both deduce that B is not being accessed, set $L = 0$, and enter their critical sections at the same time.

Locking suffers from the same busy-waiting problem that Dekker's primitives present.

In conclusion, blindly using TAS instructions in user programs presents a danger, as it can lead to busy-waiting. What is needed for user programs is the ability to stop when encountering a locked critical section. This is a synchronization problem discussed in Section 4. However, for system programs, inside the kernel of an operating system, where busy-waiting times can be kept short, locks are frequently used, as will be seen in the following sections.

3.   Serialization

3.1.   Statement of the Problem

Serialization is a second multiprocessing problem that is found particularly in data base systems. Serialization is similar to but stronger than mutual exclusion.

Consider the classical banking system problem where a processor $P1$ wants to transfer money from an account A to an account B, while a processor $P2$ is trying to compute the sum of A and B. Clearly, $P1$ and $P2$ will want to lock A and B while using them to guarantee mutual exclusion. However, this is insufficient to guarantee correct operation.

Imagine that $P1$ locks A while subtracting the necessary amount from it, then releases it, then locks B while adding the said amount to it. Further imagine that $P2$ locks A while adding its content to the total, then releases it, then locks B for the same purpose. It may be that $P2$ reads A after $P1$ has decremented it and B before $P1$ has incremented it. Thus, $P2$ will effectively "miss" the amount of money involved in the transfer carried out by $P1$. In certain applications, this may not be acceptable.

What is desired here is called *serialization*, i.e., that $P1$ and $P2$, while operating in parallel, preserve the illusion that they operate in series, so that they each see a consistent snapshot of the portion of the data base they are interested in.

3.2.   Two-phase Locking

The solution to the serialization problem is called *two-phase locking*. Two-phase locking states that a processor involved in some data base operation, and wanting to preserve the illusion of serial access to the data base, must hold all locks it acquires until it releases any of them. Thus, lock manipulation occurs in two phases, one during which locks may be acquired but not released, the other during which locks may be released but no further lock may be acquired.

Two-phase locking guarantees serialization, because a data base record locked by a processor remains locked until the processor has acquired all the records it needs. This is then equivalent to having locked the entire data base right from the beginning, which clearly would guarantee a consistent view of it. At the same time, two-phase locking allows multiple processors to act on the data base in parallel, as long as they do not access the same records.

4.   Synchronization

4.1.   Statement of the Problem

In the producer–consumer problem described earlier, mutual exclusion is necessary but not sufficient to support proper operation. Mutual exclusion guarantees that either $P1$ or $P2$ but not both will enter the critical section at any one time. However, $P1$, for instance, may succeed in entering its critical section when $P2$ has not even had time to read the last message that was deposited in B. Furthermore, while one processor is in its critical section, the other can do nothing but wait in a busy cycle. Unless $P1$ and $P2$ alternate in accessing B, $P1$ can fill the buffer and overwrite it before $P2$ has a chance to process the information in B. Or, $P2$ could try to process the content of B while $P1$ has not yet written anything useful into B.

A mechanism is needed to enable $P1$ and $P2$ to communicate and synchronize themselves so they will know when to wait and when to restart. This section and the next one will discuss a series of mechanisms for *interprocess communication and synchronization.*

4.2.   Semaphores

One of the earliest and most famous synchronization mechanisms consists of two *semaphore primitives.* Such primitives are known as P and V after the Dutch notations used by their inventor, E. W. Dijkstra. They are sometimes called wait (P) and notify, post, or signal (V).

The P and V primitives are designed to manage variables called semaphores. A semaphore is a cell of memory that resides inside the processor management mechanism and is accessed only by the primitives for handling semaphores. The simplest semaphore is a boolean or a one-bit *binary semaphore.*

Semaphores were first implemented in the THE system (Dijkstra, 1968b). Different varieties of semaphores have been implemented under different names in many later systems, such as DEC's VMS, where each virtual processor can have as many as four groups of 32 semaphores, some of which are private.

Semaphores (Fig. 9) may in fact be viewed as software implementations of locks without the disadvantage of busy-waiting. (Thus, semaphores may be used instead of locks to achieve mutual exclusion while avoiding busy-waiting.) The P(S) primitive works like a LOCK instruction. It tests semaphore S and sets it to 0 if it now equals 1. Otherwise, it puts the name of the executing (virtual)

P (S) :

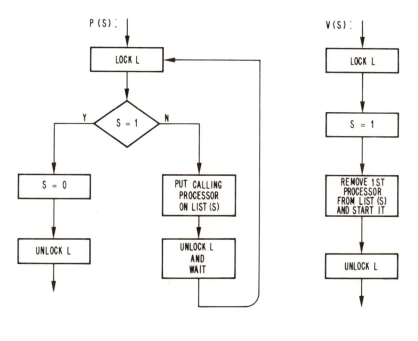

V (S) :

- SOFTWARE IMPLEMENTATION OF TEST – AND – SET
  WITHOUT BUSY – WAITING

- CAN BE EXTENDED TO COUNTING SEMAPHORE

Fig. 9. Semaphores.

processor on a waiting list associated with S and stops it. A later invocation of the
V(S) primitive would then restart the stopped (virtual) processor and reset the
semaphore to its initial value.

The implementation of semaphore primitives is itself based on the use of locks
and interrupt masking inside the processor management mechanism. Indeed,
since P and V use normal processor instructions to manipulate S and its associated list, problems would arise if two processors invoked the primitives at the
same time. In other words, the P and V primitives, which are part of the
processor management mechanism, are themselves critical sections that may not
be executed by more than one processor at a time. They are thus protected by a
common lock L.

In order to minimize the amount of busy-waiting that could result for processors locked out of the semaphore primitives (as well as to avoid other problems that shall remain hidden for the moment), the primitives are even made
atomic by keeping interrupts masked between locking and unlocking time. Thus
a virtual processor traversing P or V is guaranteed not to lose its physical

processor in the middle of either primitive, which keeps the traversal time to a minimum (typically between a few microseconds and a few milliseconds, depending on the operating system and the hardware).

If busy-waiting is a real issue, for instance in a real-time system, recent work has shown several solutions to reduce it. They are all based on using several locks rather than one and implementing the semaphore operations in microcode rather than in software so that they are faster.

Semaphores eliminate the problem of busy-waiting: a processor trying to enter a critical section when it should not is stopped. This may not mean much in the case where that processor is a physical processor, but in reality, when it is a virtual processor, stopping it means that the physical processor can do something else. Thanks to this ability to stop virtual processors with P and restart them with V, semaphores can be used to signal events between processors, as illustrated by Fig. 10 for the producer–consumer problem. In this example, two semaphores R and W are used, where W allows $P2$ to signal $P1$ when it may produce a message, while R allows $P1$ to signal $P2$ when it should consume the message.

The concept of semaphores has been generalized in various ways to suit various problems. First, imagine that B is a buffer capable of holding not one but several messages of a fixed size, that there are several processors like $P1$, which add messages to B, and several processors like $P2$, which remove messages from B (Fig. 11). To coordinate all processors, *counting semaphores* can be used. With counting semaphores, a V operation increases the semaphore by one. A

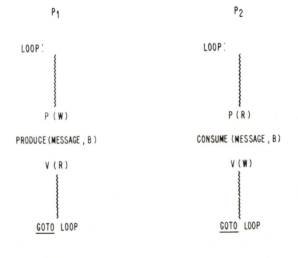

Fig. 10. Exploitation of semaphores.

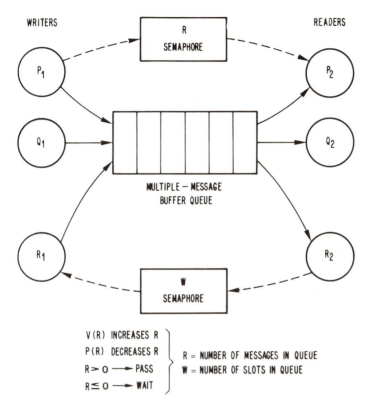

Fig. 11.   Counting semaphores.

P operation decreases the semaphore by one if that semaphore is strictly positive. Thus, in the above example, a semaphore R may be used to indicate the number of messages in B. It is increased by every writing processor, and is decreased by every reading processor when possible. A semaphore W can be used to indicate the number of free message slots in B for the writing processors to fill in. It is increased by every reading processor and decreased by every writing processor when possible.

At all times, while no processor accesses B, $R + W$ is equal to the total number of message slots in B. When $R + W$ differs from the total number of slots, the difference is equal to the number of processors accessing B. Readers and writers must use additional variables to keep track of who uses which slot in B so that no conflict will result.

A second extension of semaphores follows. Imagine that there are several buffers $B1, B2. \ . \ . \ , Bn,$ where multiple producers deposit messages, and imagine that processor $P2$ needs one message from each buffer to perform its task.

Then it is necessary for *P2* to do a P operation on the *R* semaphores of all buffers at once. Similarly, it should perform V operations on all the *W* semaphores at once. For these purposes, P($S1$, $S2$. . . , Sn) and V($S1$, $S2$. . . , Sn) are defined.

There are many more forms of semaphore primitives—multiple-value multiple-semaphore primitives, bounded-value semaphore primitives, etc.—but we will not review them all and study their implementation here. The basic principles are always the same: P operations are used to cause processors to hold processing while waiting for events; V operations are used to notify waiting processors of the occurrence of events.

As mentioned above, semaphore primitives are part of the processor management mechanism. They are the first example so far of the "software instructions", mentioned at the beginning of this chapter, that are added to the instruction set of a physical processor to constitute the instruction set of a virtual processor.

The main disadvantage of semaphores as synchronization primitives is the number of variables they require. As stated earlier, the processor management mechanism knows nothing about virtual memory and is completely resident in main memory. Thus, semaphores that are part of it consume primary memory space. The real problem is that the amount of memory consumed is variable because the number of semaphores is variable. As buffers are created and destroyed in the above example, more or fewer semaphores may be necessary. Thus, when the operating system is generated it is impossible to accurately predict the maximum amount of primary memory that will be required to hold all the semaphores that the processor management mechanism will ever need to maintain at any time.

In spite of this problem, semaphores are found in many operating system kernels. Most of the time they are used by other internal mechanisms of the operating system so that it is possible to get an estimate of how many semaphores are going to need room in main memory. While they have been described here exactly as Dijkstra conceived them, semaphores are usually implemented differently in practice. According to Dijkstra's definition, on a V operation all processors on the waiting list are released at the same time and, coming out of their wait state, immediately loop and try again the P operation that caused them to wait in the first place. Obviously only one of them will succeed in acquiring the semaphore, while all others will be forced to wait again. In practice, upon a V operation not all processors are released. Only one is selected and allowed to proceed immediately.

4.3. BLOCK and WAKEUP

The BLOCK (B) and WAKEUP (W) primitives solve just the problem that semaphores present. They require only one bit (more realistically, one word) of memory per virtual processor. Since the maximum number of virtual processors is always limited in practice, the number of bits (words) required is also limited and known in advance.

The B primitive simply stops the processor that invokes it and puts it on a global list of waiting processors. The W primitive takes one argument, the name of the processor to be restarted. The processor management mechanism keeps a list of all blocked processors. Like P and V, B and W are mutually exclusive. They are executed under a lock L to protect the integrity of the list of blocked processors (Fig. 12). They are also executed under interrupt mask to minimize execution time and therefore reduce busy-waiting by processors looping on lock L.

The reason that one bit (word) per processor is necessary follows. Imagine that processor $P1$ is slow relative to $P2$. This is easy to imagine for two different physical processors. If $P1$ and $P2$ are virtual processors sharing the same physical processor, their relative speed depends on the fraction of the physical processor's time they each run. If $P1$ gets less, between the time it awakens $P2$ and

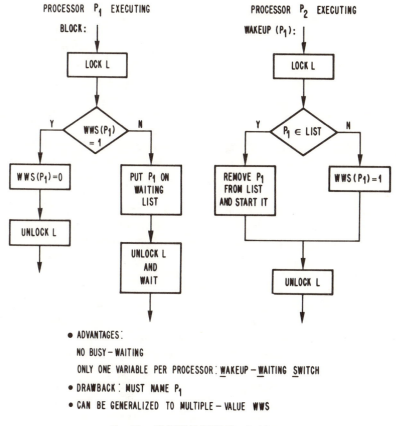

Fig. 12. BLOCK/WAKEUP primitives.

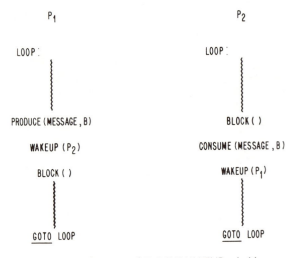

Fig. 13.   Exploitation of BLOCK/WAKEUP primitives.

the time it goes blocked, $P2$ may have emptied B and awakened $P1$. Since $P1$ is not yet blocked, the $W(P1)$ operation would have no effect. Then, $P1$ and $P2$ would both go blocked, never to wake up again. The problem is that the wakeup signal from $P2$ to $P1$ would have been lost. In order not to lose it, a bit called a *wakeup–waiting switch* (WWS) is associated with $P1$. (A similar bit is associated with $P2$.)

Just as the concept of a binary semaphore can be generalized to that of a counting semaphore, the concept of a binary WWS can be generalized to that of a counting WWS. The above WWS bit is replaced by a whole word, which is incremented by one by the W primitive and decremented by one by the B primitive. This allows several pending wakeup signals to be recorded.

The B and W primitives are a second example of software instructions implemented by the processor management mechanism. They are very frequently found in operating system kernels.

In the case of semaphores, waiting was associated with a particular semaphore and thus with a particular event. Here, processors do not wait for events; they just wait and expect their partners to wake them up in due time when an event of interest to them has occurred, as illustrated in Fig. 13 for the example of the producer/consumer problem. Thus, partners have to know one another's identity as opposed to knowing semaphore names. This constitutes a disadvantage of the B and W primitives: it is always necessary to name the processor to be awakened, which may not be practical in all real cases. For instance, if $P1$ fills a buffer that can be emptied by any of a number of processors like $P2$, $P1$ cannot guess which of all the $P2$ processors is free and should be awakened to process the contents of B.

To remedy this problem in a system offering B/W primitives as the basic synchronization mechanism, one can use the B/W primitives to realize P/V primitives. The "wait/start" instructions found in our definition of P/V primitives are implemented as B/W primitives. The details of such a design are left to the reader as an exercise.

4.4.   Event Counts and Sequencers

Event counts and *sequencers* are much more recent and more powerful synchronization mechanisms (see Fig. 14). The idea behind event counts and sequencers is to synchronize access to a shared resource by multiple processors in a way similar to that used to synchronize access of customers to the shopkeeper in a busy store. When customers enter the shop, they take a ticket from a distributing machine. All tickets are numbered in increasing order and determine the sequence in which the customers will be served. Customers then wait for their number to be called out by the shopkeeper when he can serve them.

```
TICKET (T):  T = T + 1
             RETURN (T)

AWAIT (E, N):  IF  E = N  THEN  RETURN
                         ELSE  WAIT ( E = N )



ADVANCE (E):  E  =  E + 1
                    START ( PROCESSOR  WAITING  FOR  E = N )

READ (E):    RETURN (E)
```

ADVANTAGES :

- • T FORCES STRICT SEQUENCING
- • NO MUTUAL EXCLUSION BETWEEN AWAIT AND ADVANCE
- → NO NEED FOR SHARED MEMORY COMMUNICATION
- → POTENTIAL FOR DISTRIBUTED SYSTEMS

DRAWBACK :

- • STARVATION IF ONE PROCESSOR CRASHES

Fig. 14.   Event counts and sequencers.

To realize such a mechanism, two variables are needed: a sequencer T used to sequence processors, and an event count E used to synchronize them. Both are defined as up counters. Their initial value is zero. In theory, their upper bound is defined by the number of bits they occupy. In practice, this number of bits is chosen to be large enough to avoid overflow within the life of the application where they are used. To manipulate T and E, one operation is defined on T and three on E: TICKET(T), AWAIT(E,N), ADVANCE(E), AND READ(E).

The *TICKET*(T) operation models the ticket distributor operation. Every time it is invoked, the sequencer T is incremented and a corresponding ticket numbered N ($N = T$) is returned to the requesting processor.

The *AWAIT*(E, N) operation models the customer's action when he waits for the called out number E to reach the ticket N he was assigned. When calling AWAIT, a processor may be put to wait until the condition $E = N$ becomes true. The notation WAIT($E=N$) means that the processor waits after storing the name of E and the value N into a private wait condition variable.

The *ADVANCE*(E) operation models the action of the shopkeeper who calls out the next customer. A processor calling ADVANCE increases the value of E and restarts the processor that was waiting for E to reach the value (N) it just acquired.

The *READ*(E) operation models the action of the impatient customer who looks up the number of the customer being served to evaluate the time that remains to be waited. Read just returns the current value of E.

With these primitives, it is clearly possible to realize the equivalent of semaphore or WWS primitives. For instance, the effect of the P primitive can be achieved by invoking TICKET and then AWAIT. The effect of the V primitive can be achieved by invoking ADVANCE.

Then what are the difference between event counts and semaphores or WWS?

1.   One difference is that P/V or BLOCK/WAKEUP primitives do not in principle impose any sequencing, although specific implementations may do so. Their definition does not specify that a list of waiting processors must be ordered in any particular way, in a chronological order of arrival for instance. By contrast, the use of sequencers clearly implies that processors stopped as a result of invoking AWAIT will be restarted in the order in which they invoked TICKET.

2.   The second difference results from the use of two variables instead of one. With semaphores, the only variable S is a boolean or an up–down counter. It can take only a bounded number of values. Within its bounds, it is modified in opposite directions by P and V. The same is true concerning a WWS in the case of BLOCK/WAKEUP primitives. By contrast, with event counts the evolution of one variable within fixed bounds is replaced by the constant tracking of one variable (T) by another (E). As a result, neither of the variables is ever tested

before it is updated, and each is updated by only one primitive, always in the same direction.

These two differences result in an essential property of event counts and sequencers that other primitives seen so far do not have: beyond the need for atomic LOAD, and INCRement hardware instructions, TICKET, AWAIT, ADVANCE, and READ are not mutually exclusive primitives. They do not even require a TAS instruction. They can be executed in parallel without any risk of conflict.*

With semaphores (WWS primitives), since invocations of P and V (BLOCK and WAKEUP) compete to read, test, and eventually set S (WWS) in opposite directions, S (WWS) must be accessed under the protection of mutual exclusion (realized by the lock L in our earlier definitions). In addition, the maintenance of waiting lists in the case of semaphores requires mutual exclusion. By contrast, for event counts and sequencers, atomic LOAD and INCRement instructions are sufficient to guarantee that parallel invocations of primitives will not return erroneous values or lose increments to the variables.

Not having to rely on any mutual exclusion mechanism is a key feature of event counts. First, it implies less contention and thus less busy-waiting on locks such as those protecting semaphores or wakeup–waiting switches. Second, the necessary condition that semaphores or wakeup–waiting switches reside in a memory shared by all processors does not hold for event counts. In particular, event counts can be used in distributed systems, where each processor has its own memory and all processors communicate through some network.

In such a system, one processor can be assigned the role of ticket distributor and hold the sequencer. Each processor participating in the application requiring synchronization may hold its own copy of the event count. Every time some processor performs an ADVANCE operation on the event count, it increments its local copy of the counter, then broadcasts the update to all other participants. Such a casual replication of the synchronization variable on all participating processors would be very hard with semaphore (WWS) primitives, because P (BLOCK) operations would need to lock all copies of the variable at the same time.

The main drawback of event counts is the possibility of a processor's dying between the time it acquires a ticket and the time the event count is signalled to have reached the value of that ticket. This is equivalent to a customer in the busy store taking a number and then leaving the room, so that nobody shows up when the missing number is called out. Vulnerability to the problem is particularly high in distributed systems, where different virtual processors tend to run on remote physical processors that are likely to fail independently. Time-out mecha-

*It has even been shown that atomic instructions are not necessary if load and increment operations are carried out with some care (Reed and Kanodia, 1979).

nisms can clearly be added to remedy the problem, but they complicate an otherwise elegant scheme.

5.   High-level Mechanisms

5.1.   Convenience

So far, this book has presented a set of concurrency control primitives for implementing mutual exclusion, serialization, and synchronization. These primitives are of a very basic level in the sense that processors programmed by the users are responsible for the correct usage of these primitives. Failure to properly use the primitives may result in loss or destruction of shared data, or inconsistencies in the shared data.

To remedy these problems, many mechanisms of a higher level have been proposed. They all attempt to make the control of concurrency more convenient, i.e., foolproof against user ignorance or carelessness. In general, these mechanisms have been invented in the context of parallel programming languages. And they are usually implemented as part of some high-level language support. However, parallel programming has become central to operating system design, and high-level parallel programming languages are used more and more inside modern operating systems. Furthermore, the realization of these high-level synchronization mechanisms now uses the low-level primitives seen earlier and, with time, is likely to be cast more and more in microcode. Thus, a discussion of these primitives, however brief, is relevant to the subject of operating systems.

5.2.   Critical Regions

Critical regions were designed to make mutual exclusion implicit and relieve the user from the need to worry about it. This is achieved by explicitly declaring to the compiler which variables or data structures are shared so that every time the user attempts to reference shared data, the compiler can insert code to guarantee mutual exclusion.

This is shown in Fig. 15 for the producer–consumer problem. By explicitly declaring the buffer B to be a shared variable, the programmer can direct the compiler to insert "hidden" statements to enforce mutual exclusion wherever his program accesses B. Accesses to B can, for instance, be protected by acquiring and releasing a test-and-set lock associated with B.

The limitation of critical regions is of course that they express only mutual exclusion, but no synchronization. Thus, in the example of Fig. 15, unless the programmer has declared additional shared variables (not shown here) to keep track of the state of B, $P1$ could enter its critical section to write into B when B is

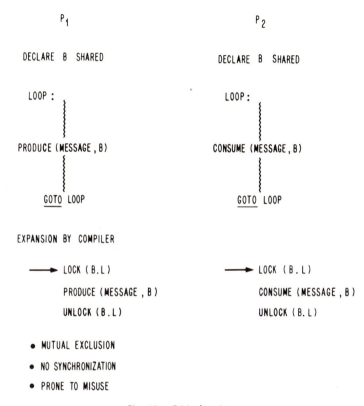

Fig. 15.   Critical regions.

in fact still full. Each additional shared variable declared for synchronization purposes calls for a separate critical region. Furthermore, the critical region concept is still subject to misuse in the sense that the user may forget to declare what data are shared and how synchronization should occur.

5.3.   Conditional Critical Regions

Conditional critical regions are an enhancement to critical regions aimed at allowing the user to couple reference to shared data with reference to associated synchronization variables. A processor will enter its critical section only if the associated synchronization variable is in the proper state.

This is shown in Fig. 16 for the producer–consumer problem. The programmer declares as shared not only *B* but also synchronization variables, such as EMPTY and FULL, explicitly associated with *B*. The programmer then writes plain test statements to specify the necessary synchronization. Recognizing the

P₁   P₂

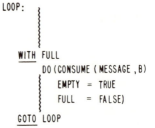

DECLARE B SHARED   DECLARE B SHARED
        WITH EMPTY/ FULL   WITH EMPTY/ FULL
            BOOLEAN   BOOLEAN

    LOOP: LOOP:

        WITH EMPTY   WITH FULL
            DO (PRODUCE(MESSAGE , B)   DO (CONSUME (MESSAGE ,B)
                EMPTY = FALSE   EMPTY = TRUE
                FULL = TRUE)   FULL = FALSE)
        GOTO LOOP   GOTO LOOP

EXPANSION BY COMPILER
        P (EMPTY)   P (FULL)
        PRODUCE (MESSAGE , B)   CONSUME (MESSAGE , B)
        V (FULL)   V (EMPTY)

INITIAL CONDITION   EMPTY = 1   FULL = 0
    • MUTUAL EXCLUSION
    • SYNCHRONIZATION
    • PRONE TO MISUSE

Fig. 16. Conditional critical regions.

association between *B* and its associated synchronization variables, the compiler generates for each processor a conditional critical region, using semaphores for instance. This critical region is conditional because the processor will enter it only if the synchronization condition expressed by the associated variable is fulfilled.

Conditional critical regions add the synchronization feature that was lacking in critical regions but do not solve the problem of potential misuse of the mechanisms. Indeed, the user can still make mistakes in declaring the shared data or in formulating the synchronization conditions associated with their use.

5.4. Monitors

Monitors are a synchronization mechanism based on *abstract data types*. Abstract data types are a concept found more and more, under various forms, in modern programming languages like Pascal, Simula, and their derivatives, including ADA. With abstract data typing, variables cannot be manipulated directly by user programs. Instead, variables of a given type (e.g., strings, arrays, stacks, queues, records, or aggregates of any form) may be manipulated only through primitives provided for that effect by the programmer who designed that data type. The set of all such primitives constitute what is often referred to as the type manager.

Thus, an abstract data type, as it is embodied by its type manager, realizes a fence around its variables, where each of the defined primitives constitutes a gate to the inside domain. The main objective of an abstract data type is to relieve its users from having to know anything about the internal implementation of variables of that type. The type manager *hides information* about the implementation, and variables are accessible only indirectly, through the well-defined and published interface composed of the set of primitives of the manager.

With the concept of monitors, all shared data are regarded as variables of some abstract data type accessed and managed exclusively by the corresponding type manager. However, in addition to simply specifying and hiding the internal implementation of the data, as a plain type manager would do, a monitor also specifies the necessary synchronization conditions for accessing the data. As a first and general rule, primitives composing the monitor are mutually exclusive: each primitive is a critical section, so that only one processor at a time can enter the monitor. In addition, synchronization signals are exchanged inside the monitor by the processors that successively penetrate the fence, through some primitive signalling mechanism, such as the semaphores seen earlier.

Thus, using the mutual exclusion and synchronization primitives seen so far, a monitor, which is a set of procedures callable by any of the processors using it, can cause these processors to be queued at various places, waiting for different events, once they invoke the monitor and enter it.

Processors may be queued and have to wait right after entering the monitor and before doing any useful work because of the mutual exclusion among the various monitor procedures. Any processor trying to invoke any monitor procedure while some other procedure is already active on behalf of some other processor will be queued at the gate into the monitor. Processors may also be queued and have to wait after entering the monitor, if some synchronization condition prevents them from proceeding.

Figure 17 illustrates the use of monitors in the producer–consumer problem. Buffer *B* may be regarded as a repository for abstract objects of type message. By declaring MESSAGE as being a variable of type TYPE, the user imports into his program all the primitives (e.g., PUT and GET) of the MESSAGE monitor, through which he will be able to manipulate messages.

Figure 17 shows how a MESSAGE monitor might be realized using semaphores. Mutual exclusion between the two primitives PUT and GET of the MESSAGE monitor is achieved through the use of the MUTEX semaphore.

P₁   P₂

```
DECLARE MESSAGE TYPE  TYPE        DECLARE MESSAGE TYPE  TYPE
        B       TYPE MESSAGE              B       TYPE MESSAGE

LOOP:                             LOOP:

     MESSAGE. PUT ( B , TEXT )         MESSAGE. GET  ( B ,TEXT )

     GOTO LOOP                         GOTO  LOOP

MONITOR MESSAGE:
     DECLARE  PUT ( B , TEXT ) PROCEDURE    DECLARE GET ( B, TEXT ) PROCEDURE
     BEGIN                                  BEGIN
          P ( MUTEX )                            P ( MUTEX )
          if B. W = 0  THEN  ( V ( MUTEX )       if B. R = 0  THEN ( V ( MUTEX )
                              P ( B. W )                           P ( B.R )
                         GOTO BEGIN )                         GOTO BEGIN )
          PRODUCE ( TEXT , B )                   CONSUME ( TEXT, B )
          V ( B. R )                             V ( B. W )
          V ( MUTEX )                            V ( MUTEX )
     END
          • MUTUAL EXCLUSION
          • SYNCHRONIZATION
          • SAFETY OF USE
          • POSSIBLE  ERRORS  IN  MONITOR  ITSELF
```

Fig. 17. Monitors.

Synchronization is achieved through the use of the two semaphores W and R.

In the original definition of monitors (Hoare, 1974), synchronization is achieved through the use of SIGNAL and WAIT primitives. The implementation of these primitives is not given for any particular machine, but the description of their behavior is similar to that of semaphores, with some restrictions having to do with scheduling. The restrictions are described below.

In Fig. 17, as long as there are only two processors $P1$ and $P2$, the given monitor implementation works. However, if we envision for a moment the case of two producing processors $P1$ and $P1'$, the following problem can arise. $P1$

may start executing the PUT primitive, discover that B is not EMPTY, and put itself on the waiting list for event W. When $P2$, while executing GET, signals the event $V(W)$, $P1$ must reenter the monitor, i.e., reacquire the MUTEX semaphore. However, while $P1$ was waiting on the W semaphore, $P1'$ may have tried to enter the monitor and be waiting on MUTEX. Thus, when trying to reenter the monitor, $P1$ may find itself in competition with a newcomer $P1'$, which has not even waited on W yet. Many ideas can be and indeed have been proposed to solve the problem (e.g., Howard, 1976), which all amount to giving $P1$ a special treatment so that it can be assured to make progress and avoid competing with newcomers.

While this fair scheduling issue is important, it should be kept separate from synchronization, which is the main objective of monitors. However the scheduling issue is resolved, monitors represent powerful high-level synchronization primitives and can be built using P/V, BLOCK/WAKEUP, SIGNAL/WAIT, or any other similar lower level mechanism. In all cases the essence of the synchronization aspects is the same, setting aside scheduling aspects.

The use of monitors guarantees mutual exclusion, proper synchronization, and robustness in the face of user misuse. However, all the burden of providing these features lies on the shoulders of the monitor designers, who must include in their code the appropriate calls to the basic operating system primitives to realize synchronization. As can be seen in Fig. 17, this may be nontrivial even for the simplest problem of a one-message buffer.

Notice that in view of the above definition of a monitor, we can now see that the entire processor management mechanism, as we have described it so far, is itself a monitor. Indeed, primitives such as P/V and BLOCK/WAKEUP are mutually exclusive operations that permit exchange of synchronization signals between processors successively penetrating the monitor. Mutual exclusion is achieved by masking interrupts and setting a global lock (called L in our earlier descriptions). Synchronization is achieved, in the case of semaphores for instance, by moving processors into and out of waiting lists associated with the semaphores.

In most operating systems, although the processor management mechanism was not regarded as a monitor in the formal sense when it was designed, it effectively plays the role of one. In fact, in numerous operating systems, the basic communication primitives offered by the processor management mechanism are very similar in flavor to the PUT and GET monitor primitives described in the above message queuing example. For instance, the RC4000 system (Brinch Hansen, 1970) offered primitives called send-message, receive-message, send-answer, and receive-answer. Similarly, the Tripos system (Richards et al., 1979) supports a queue-packet and wait-packet pair of primitives, where each virtual processor has one private queue for receiving packets. Thoth (Cheriton et al., 1979) also offers such message queuing primitives. The "mailboxes" of DEC's VMS and the "links" found in Demos (Baskett *et al.*, 1977) are yet other examples of message queuing primitives.

5.5. Path Expressions

Path expressions appear to be one of the most powerful and safest high-level synchronization mechanisms proposed so far. As far as the user is concerned, the advantages are identical to those of monitors. There is also the concept of an abstract data type and operations to manipulate member objects. However, path expressions further relieve the designer of the type manager from the potentially complex task of imbedding the right synchronization primitives at the right place in the code of his monitor. Instead, the designer codes the type manager as a plain sequential program. Then, he specifies, in addition to the sequential program, a set of synchronization conditions under the form of regular expressions restricting the order in which the various primitives of his type manager can be invoked.

In the producer–consumer example, illustrated in Fig. 18, the relevant regular expression is (PUT; GET)*, meaning that the sequence of operations PUT then GET can be invoked any number of times. Any other order of invocation implies that the invoking processor must be stopped until the proper sequence can be performed. The regular expression, together with sequential code for reading and writing buffer *B* are fed to the compiler, which could generate code including calls to semaphore primitives, as shown in Fig. 18.

Of course, path expressions assume that the compiler is capable of translating the regular expressions into calls to synchronization primitives at the appropriate places. While no compiler has been implemented to date with this capability, this situation may change in the future. Furthermore, even in the absence of an implemented compiler, path expressions are useful in that they force the designer to produce a concise specification of synchronization constraints separately from his code and allow him to then verify the implementation against the specification.

5.6. Distributed Systems

Aside from event counts and sequencers, all low-level synchronization and communication mechanisms seen in Section 4 assume that processors communicate through a shared memory. Event counts and sequencers are thus the only low-level communication mechanism applicable to distributed systems.

At a higher level, the most common model of interprocessor communication is called *message queues*. Message queues are in fact exactly what the producer–consumer problem discussed earlier implements: a buffer managed as a queue of messages between two processors. As seen in preceding sections, the implementation of a message queue on a shared memory system requires the use of

P_1 P_2

```
DECLARE MESSAGE TYPE  TYPE         DECLARE MESSAGE TYPE  TYPE

       B      TYPE MESSAGE               B      TYPE MESSAGE


   LOOP:                             LOOP:



       MESSAGE. PUT (B, TEXT)           MESSAGE. GET (B,TEXT)



       GOTO LOOP                        GOTO LOOP

   PATH EXPRESSION: ( PUT; GET)*
   POSSIBLE COMPILATION:
   PROCEDURE PUT (B, TEXT)           PROCEDURE GET ( B , TEXT )
       BEGIN                             BEGIN
           P (PUT)                           P (GET)
           PRODUCE (B,TEXT)                  CONSUME ( B ,TEXT )
           V (GET)                           V ( PUT )
       END                               END
```

   • MUTUAL EXCLUSION
   • SYNCHRONIZATION
   • SAFETY OF USE
   • EASE OF IMPLEMENTATION

Fig. 18. Path expressions.

semaphores or BLOCK/WAKEUP primitives. This is precluded, however, in distributed systems.

In distributed systems, message queues are implemented by cooperation between communication software in each of the communicating systems. Typically, a sequenced stream of messages are exchanged between both partners according to a commonly agreed upon protocol. Communication software casts messages in a format suitable for transmission and tags every message with an address identifying the processor it is destined to. It controls the flow of messages between sender and receiver to prevent the former from overflowing buffer space available in the latter. This software is also responsible for the recovery of errors such as messages damaged, lost, or duplicated during transmission.

Chapter IV describes in some detail the structure and operation of low-level communication software. The objective and organization of higher-level software belongs in the field of network architecture and communication protocols. It is not discussed further in this book on operating systems. The interested reader is referred to specialized sources (e.g., Tanenbaum, 1981) for more information on the subject.

Because of the growing importance of distributed systems and their vital dependence on communication mechanisms, the fields of operating systems and network architecture are coming ever closer together. Recently, more and more material relating to communication mechanisms has appeared in the literature normally devoted primarily to operating systems.

Such is the case of a new communication mechanism, called *remote procedure calls* (RPCs). Since individual processors in a distributed system by definition communicate through messages sent over wires or wireless channels, most communication mechanisms implemented to date support the message queue model. However, the most common way for a programmer to implement communication between two programs is procedure calls. Remote procedure calls build upon the procedure call model by extending it across physical machine interfaces. What appears to the caller as a plain procedure call is trapped by communication software, mapped into a message (or a sequence of messages), and sent to the destination, where it is interpreted and translated back into a local procedure call. A similar operation is performed to reflect the remote procedure return on the machine of the local caller.

Of course the very nature of distributed systems is such that many events can affect the operation of a RPC, which cannot occur in the case of a real procedure call. In shared-memory systems, the most catastrophic event is a crash of the physical processor, which wipes out both calling and called procedures, usually making independent recovery of either irrelevant. In some high-reliability, shared-memory multiprocessors, it is possible that one of the partners could crash while the other is unharmed. However, in most systems, the crash of one physical processor often means the crash of the whole operating system.

By contrast, in distributed systems the crash of one processor rarely implies the crash of another. Furthermore, communication links or network switching nodes may crash too. Thus a caller may very well find itself with a pending and unresolvable call. Similarly, a called procedure may find itself with a "nonreturnable" dangling call. Worse yet, neither the calling nor the called procedure can know with certainty what happened to an unresolved call. It could have completed, but the return message may never have reached the caller.

In such cases, the caller must be prepared to exit from a pending call to avoid indefinite waiting. It may also want to retry the call. On the other hand, the called procedure must carefully define the semantics of the calls it supports. It must be prepared to abort a nonreturnable call and to retry it later if requested, without compromising the integrity of the data it manipulates. For example, unless properly implemented, a RPC such as

$$\text{call debit(bank-account-no, amount)}$$

could lead to errors if it completes but the return message does not reach the caller, who then retries it. Publications are beginning to emerge on these issues (Spector, 1982; Birrell and Nelson, 1984).

6.   Deadlocks

6.1.   Statement of the Problem

The foregoing sections on mutual exclusion, serialization, synchronization, and primitives designed for convenience and safety give a fairly comprehensive overview of techniques for allowing parallel or pseudoparallel processors to coordinate their activities. Yet the very use of these primitives may lead to so-called deadlock situations among two or more processors.

Deadlocks, or *deadly embraces*, are situations in which two or more processors, competing for the same set of resources, each acquire a fraction of the resources they want, and doing so mutually block one another, waiting indefinitely for others to release what they have.

Consider as an example the *cigarette smokers' problem* (Fig. 19). Two people (processors $P1$ and $P2$) like to smoke (copy one tape onto another). However, the system contains only one cigarette pack C and one lighter L (two tape drives). If $P1$ grabs C while $P2$ grabs L, $P1$ and $P2$ are each going to wait indefinitely for the other to release what it has, and neither will be able to make any useful progress.

A deadlock may also result from two-phase locking situations. In our money transfer example of Section 3.1, $P1$ and $P2$ are assured to have a consistent view of the data base if they use two-phase locking to manipulate A and B. However, the very use of two-phase locking, namely, holding one lock until they have acquired both, may lead them to a deadlock if they request the locks in reverse order from each other. As illustrated by this example, deadlocks are the result of several circumstances:

1.   The first necessary condition for a deadlock to appear is the need for exclusive use of several resources. In the above example, only one processor at a time may access any one account. Accessing an account constitutes a critical section. The use of the resource must thus be protected by some mutual exclusion mechanism, typically a lock.

2.   The second condition is that multiple critical sections overlap, i.e., that processors need several of the critical resources at the same time. Thus, a

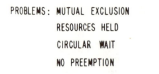

PROBLEMS: MUTUAL EXCLUSION
          RESOURCES HELD
          CIRCULAR WAIT
          NO PREEMPTION

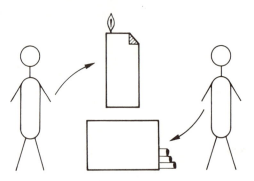

SOLUTIONS:

PREVENTION: RESTRICTS LOCKING ORDER (PREVENTS CIRCULAR WAIT)

AVOIDANCE : STEERS SYSTEM AWAY FROM
             FORECASTED DEADLOCKS

DETECTION : ABORTS WORK WHEN   (BREAKS CIRCULAR WAIT
             DEADLOCK HAS OCCURRED   BY ALLOWING PREEMPTION)
             OR IS ABOUT TO OCCUR

Fig. 19. The cigarette smokers' problem.

processor may be holding one or more resources while it waits for additional resources to become free.

3.   The third condition is that there be a *wait-for loop,* or *circular wait* condition, i.e., that there be a set of processors circularly waiting for one another.

4.   The fourth and last condition is that there be no means to preempt any of the waiting processors, i.e., that it be impossible for an outside processor to break, abort, kill, or otherwise interrupt any of the waiting ones.

While the need for mutual exclusion is intrinsic to the exclusive use of the resources, the latter three deadlock conditions can be relaxed under certain circumstances. Relaxing each of them corresponds to a different technique for fighting deadlocks.

1.   The first method, called deadlock *prevention,* consists of preventing deadlocks by preventing the formation of wait-for loops.

2. With the second method, called deadlock *avoidance*, certain processors may be denied certain resources over a certain time to allow other processors to acquire these resources while they already hold others. Such a policy restricts the occurrence of waiting-while-holding situations.

3. With the third method, called deadlock *detection*, the system lets itself be driven into a deadlock (or near-deadlock) situation and backs out of it by pre-empting and aborting selected processors involved in the circular wait.

Each of the techniques has its drawbacks and limitations. Prevention methods, in general, restrict the amount of parallelism in the system. At the other extreme, detection methods do not restrict parallelism at all, at the cost of occasionally having to abort processors, which is unproductive. Avoidance methods may appear more interesting, in that they allow as much parallelism as possible without going so far as to let the system deadlock itself. However, avoidance methods usually require a fair amount of advance knowledge about resource requirements, which cannot be satisfied by computations whose requirements are data dependent and cannot be predicted. Examples of each method are outlined below.

6.2.   Prevention

The following algorithm, due to Havender, is based on giving every resource a unique number. The deadlock prevention policy then states that processors requiring several resources at a time may claim these resources (and possibly wait for them to become available) only in decreasing (or increasing) order.

In our earlier example of the cigarette smokers' problem, if the cigarette pack number is greater than the lighter number, $P1$ and $P2$ must claim the cigarette pack first and the lighter afterwards. $P1$ and $P2$ cannot end up in a deadlock because neither may claim the cigarettes once it has claimed the lighter. If $P1$ claims the cigarettes before $P2$, $P2$ will have to wait. On its part, $P1$ will successfully claim the lighter, light its cigarette, and then release the cigarettes and the lighter for $P2$ to help itself.

With the locking order requirement, even if a processor knows it needs only a tape drive to start and an additional printer later, but the printer number is higher than the tape drive number, the processor must claim first the printer and then the tape drive. The printer will thus remain unused but locked for the first phase of the processor work, which leads to lower utilization of higher numbered resources.

While the obligation to claim resources in a rigid order, regardless of the order in which they are needed, may be a constraint for certain application programs, it turns out not to interfere with programming inside the kernel of an operating system. Indeed, experience shows that critical resources, such as status tables and control blocks, can often be numbered in an order that mirrors the order in which they are needed along any computational path through the kernel.

6.3.   Avoidance

Perhaps the most classic example of a deadlock avoidance algorithm is Habermann's algorithm, also called the *banker's algorithm.* It assumes that a set of processors (customers) are competing for a set of resources (bank loans) and that all processors are able to announce initially the maximum amount of resources they will eventually claim even if they will not claim this maximum amount right away. Their claims are assumed never to decrease with time. The banker's algorithm was first implemented in the THE system (Dijkstra, 1968b).

In essence, the algorithm consists of using the knowledge about maximum anticipated claims to keep the system away from situations where it could not satisfy any of the maximum claims. In other words, the objective is to guarantee at all times that all maximum claims can be satisfied in some order. This may require temporaily withholding resources from some processor although they may be available, because granting these resources immediately would prevent the system from being able to fulfill any further claim by other processors.

In practice, the algorithm operates as follows. Let $\{Pi\}$ be the processors, $\{Mi\}$ be their maximum claims, $\{Ci\}$ be the resources they currently hold, T be the total amount of resources, and A be the balance of available resources. Then a state of allocated resources is said to be "safe" if there exists a sequence

$$Pk1, Pk2, \ldots , Pkn \qquad (ki \neq kj \quad \text{for } i \neq j)$$

such that

$$Mk1 - Ck1 \leq A$$
$$Mk2 - Ck2 \leq A + Ck1$$
$$\cdot$$
$$\cdot$$
$$\cdot$$
$$Mkn - Ckn \leq A + \sum_{k=k1}^{kn-1} Ck$$

i.e., if the processors $P1$ to Pn can complete their task in the order $Pk1$ to Pkn.

Thus, the problem of deadlock avoidance consists of deciding, every time a processor requests more resources, whether the state into which the system would be driven if the request were granted is safe i.e., if there exists a safe sequence $\langle Pki \rangle$ in which all processors eventually complete their work. A sequence $\langle Pki \rangle$ $(1 \leq i \leq n)$ is said to be safe if all the competing processors are in that sequence and can be completed in the order of the sequence.

Dijkstra has demonstrated that if a state is safe, any safe subsequence starting from it can be extended into a safe full sequence, because completing any processor means returning its resources to the pool, thereby increasing A, which

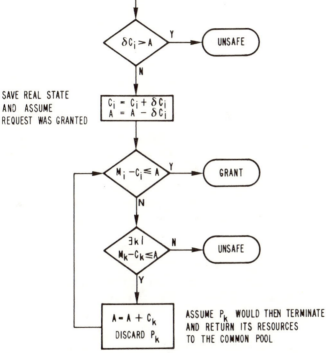

P$_i$ (i · 1, n) PROCESSORS

M$_i$ (i · 1, n) THEIR MAXIMUM REQUIREMENT OF <u>SOME</u> RESOURCE

C$_i$ (i · 1, n) THEIR CURRENT USE OF <u>SOME</u> RESOURCE

T TOTAL AMOUNT OF RESOURCE

A BALANCE OF AVAILABLE AMOUNT OF RESOURCE

δC$_i$ AN INCREMENTAL CLAIM BY P$_i$

$\delta C_i > A$ — Y → UNSAFE

N

SAVE REAL STATE
AND ASSUME
REQUEST WAS GRANTED

$$C_i = C_i + \delta C_i$$
$$A = A - \delta C_i$$

$M_i - C_i \leq A$ — Y → GRANT

N

$\exists k \mid M_k - C_k \leq A$ — N → UNSAFE

Y

$A = A + C_k$
DISCARD P$_k$

ASSUME P$_k$ WOULD THEN TERMINATE
AND RETURN ITS RESOURCES
TO THE COMMON POOL

• SHORTCOMINGS: MONOTONICALLY NON – DECREASING REQUESTS

Fig. 20. The banker's algorithm.

means that finding the rest of the safe full sequence is made easier. Two conclusions follow.

First, in trying to see if there still exists a safe sequence after a given request, it does not matter which processor *Pk* is selected to complete first, because if the state is safe, any safe subsequence starting from it will eventually lead to a safe full sequence. This is pictured in Fig. 20. If, at some point, no *Pk* can be found to complete and not all *Pi* are completed, one can directly assert that the state would be unsafe, without trying other possible subsequences.

Second, one can insert a test ahead of the search for *Pk* to detect the completion of the requesting processor and declare the state safe. Indeed, any subsequence terminating by *Pk* can certainly be extended to a safe full sequence, since the completion of *Pk* will return all the resources *Pk* has, including those it is now requesting.

One disadvantage of the banker's algorithm is that it assumes monotonically nondecreasing claims, which may not be realistic in all practical cases. A second minor disadvantage of the banker's algorithm is that is considers only one pool of resources, say tape drives. Though it can be generalized to heterogeneous resource types, this generalization is not trivial.

6.4.   Detection

a.   The Backup Algorithm

We now come to deadlock detection algorithms. The first algorithm, known as the *backup algorithm,* may appear at first sight as an avoidance rather than a detection algorithm, as it avoids deadlocks by forbidding certain processors from holding certain resources. However, it resembles detection algorithms in their end effect on processors. Processors may be forced to abort and abandon work in progress. In reality, the backup algorithm does not detect real deadlocks but only potential deadlocks.

Like the prevention algorithm seen earlier, the backup technique assumes that each resource bears an order number (Fig. 21). However, contrary to the prevention technique where locking order is restricted, a processor can claim resources in any order. A restriction appears if a processor *P*1 tries to claim a resource bearing a number *j* higher than the number *k* of the lowest numbered resource currently owned by *P*1 and discovers that that resource is not available. Then *P*1 must "undo" all the work it did with resources bearing numbers *i* smaller than the number of the resource *j* it failed to acquire, under the presumption that some other processor *P*2, holding resource *j*, might be waiting for some resource *i* held by *P*1, which could lead to a deadlock. This corresponds to the detection by *P*1 itself of a potential deadlock which it has to back out of.

Undoing work is a problem common to all detection algorithms. Undoing work done with a resource that has to be relinquished is essential to preserve the illusion of serializability. Backing out of a deadlock by releasing locks must return the corresponding resources to the state they were in before locking occurred. Doing otherwise could leave a resource in an inconsistent state.

Detection algorithms may be hard to use, because it is not always possible to undo a computation or to "decompute". For instance, undoing a sequence of writes to a tape is easy: it is sufficient to dismount and abandon the tape, since the writes can be redone later. However, restoring the state of a data base before

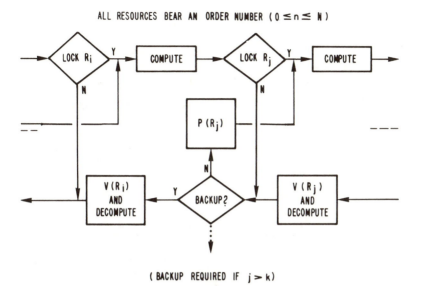

ALL RESOURCES BEAR AN ORDER NUMBER ($0 \leq n \leq N$)

(BACKUP REQUIRED IF $j > k$)

(k = OWNED RESOURCE WITH LOWEST NUMBER)

Fig. 21. The backup algorithm.

it was locked is possible only if one always operates on shadow copies of the data records before actually updating the master copy.

b.   The Loop Detection Algorithm

A first pure deadlock detection algorithm is the *loop detection algorithm*. Figure 22 represents the state of a system involving four processors competing for seven resources. An arrow from a resource Ri to a processor Pj means that the resource is owned by the processor. An arrow from a processor Pi to a resource Rj means that the processor has claimed and is waiting for the resource. With the loop detection algorithm, the system keeps track of all processor claims and maintains an internal representation of such a graph. If and when a loop is detected in the graph, as is the case in Fig. 22, the system preempts some processor in the loop, aborts it, and frees the resources it holds so other processors can proceed.

One problem with the loop detection algorithm is precisely the method used to detect loops. With small wait-for graphs, a human being can readily see loops. However, with large graphs, the decision becomes more difficult. For a computer, the decision becomes really complicated. The system must continuously search the graph for cycles.

Another problem is the choice of which processor to preempt once a loop is detected. While it may sound preferable to preempt the processor that has done

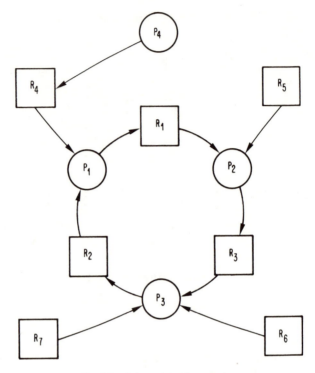

Fig. 22. A loop detection graph.

the smallest amount of work so far, this choice may not always be wise. The system may be in a state where there are several loops in the graph, in which case aborting a single processor that has done a lot of work but is involved in all loops may turn out to be more desirable than aborting three different processors. The choice is never easy for the system. It requires much information on the various processors involved and an exhaustive search of the whole loop to decide which to preempt.

The loop detection algorithm is applicable also to distributed systems. In a system of processors that are physically distributed and connected by a network, processors may want to claim (lock) software resources, such as data base records, residing on other processors. This is typical in distributed data base systems. In such systems, as in the shared-memory systems we have considered so far, it is of course possible to drive a set of processors into a deadlock situation. Deadlocks can be detected by the graphical loop detection method. The operating system of each machine keeps track of the wait-for graph involving local resources and regularly forwards a copy of its graph to all remote processors waiting for some local resource. This allows all processors to reconstruct a global wait-for graph and eventually to detect deadlocks.

c. Time-out Algorithms

Another classic method among early deadlock detection techniques is the use of *time-outs*. Based on estimates of system load, one associates time-outs with processors or with resources. One can put an upper bound on the amount of time a processor may spend doing its task, or one can put an upper bound on the amount of time a resource can be held by any processor. In either case, if the estimated upper bound is exceeded, the system decides that the processor having exceeded the estimated time-out is probably involved in a deadlock, must be aborted, and must return all the resources it owns to the system for others to use.

Like the loop detection technique, this method detects real deadlocks. However, like the backup algorithm, it may cause backing out of situations that are not true deadlocks. They may be situations of starvation, a result of underestimated time-outs, or "livelocks", a result of underestimated system load. *Starvation* occurs when the task of a processor demands so much time to complete that it can never complete before some time-out preempts it. *Livelocks* occur when the system is so overloaded that progress is slower than normal. As a consequence, tasks are preempted, which wastes processing and aggravates system congestion even more, making further preemptions more likely. The system is thus not deadlocked but unproductive, which defines a livelock.

Like the loop detection algorithm, time-out methods lend themselves well to distributed systems. In fact, quite aside from deadlock issues, time-outs are essential in distributed systems. They may be the only way to recover from situations where individual processors or communication links between processors fail, leaving a processor involved in a task it cannot complete because it cannot communicate with the necessary partner.

d. Time-stamping Algorithms

Using *time-stamps* instead of time-outs minimizes to some extent the risk of unnecessarily preempting processors, though that risk does not completely disappear. Rather than being preempted when a time-out expires, processors are preempted only when there appears to be a potential locking conflict.

Time-stamping techniques have been used first in data base systems. Every time a processor starts a new task, called a transaction on a data base system, the processor (or the transaction it performs) is stamped with the time of start, as determined by a clock with a resolution fine enough to guarantee that no two transactions will ever be marked with the same stamp.

Once started, every time it acquires a resource (presumably a data base record or set of records) through locking, a transaction carries its own time-stamp onto the lock. In this way, a resource does not carry any intrinsic number specifying a locking order, as in the prevention or backup techniques seen earlier. However, once locked, it carries a number equal to the time-stamp of the processor/ transaction that holds it. In case of locking conflicts, this number is used, in a way similar to the backup algorithm, to decide whether a potential deadlock exists and whether preemption is necessary.

Two different preemption policies can be found: (1) the *wait–die* policy and (2) the *wait-wound* policy, which are schematically represented in Fig. 23.

1. With the wait–die technique, when a processor $P1$ attempts to lock a data base record that is already in use by $P2$, it compares the time-stamp in the lock (which belongs to $P2$) with its own. According to the DIE part of the rule, if $P1$

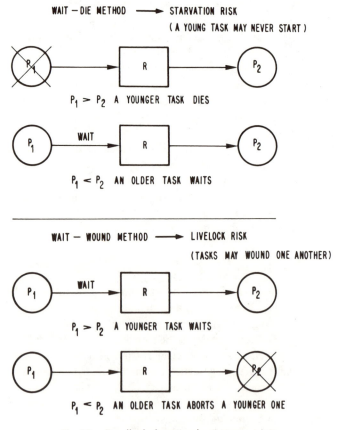

Fig. 23.   Deadlock detection by time-stamping.

is "younger" than $P2$, it commits suicide by preempting itself, on the ground that it may be holding a lock that $P2$ may be waiting on. On the other hand, according to the WAIT part of the rule, if $P1$ is "older" than $P2$, it decides to wait on the lock until $P2$ releases it. Indeed, either $P2$ will complete its transaction and release all locks it holds, or $P2$ will encounter a lock held by $P1$, in which case it will abort, as dictated by the DIE part of the rule.

2.   With the wait–wound technique, the WOUND part of the rule states that $P1$ must "wound" $P2$ if it is older than $P2$. Wounding means telling the system to preempt $P2$. $P1$ can then wait for the resource held by $P2$ to be released. The WAIT part of the rule states that $P1$ may wait on a lock held by $P2$ if it is younger than $P2$, knowing that $P2$ would preempt it according to the WOUND rule if a locking conflict is discovered.

Both policies give priority to older processors over younger ones, thereby guaranteeing that the system will eventually always make progress. The difference lies in the approach to preemption.

The wait–die technique presents a risk of starvation, in that a processor may restart itself several times, and every time request some very busy lock held by an older processor, which causes it to die again. Every time it is restarted, it acquires a younger time-stamp, which makes it more prone to dying. In other words, a young processor may have a hard time "getting off the ground".

The wait–wound technique presents the danger of a livelock. A young processor may have acquired all the locks it needs and be in its final computation phase when an older processor wounds it and causes it to be restarted, with a younger time-stamp of course. Thus the young processor can "get off the ground" but may be preempted until very late in its life.

In some applications, such as our earlier bank data base problem it may be possible to decide in advance which resources will be needed to do the work. In such cases, time-stamping can be improved by *prelocking* all the necessary resources before doing any work and using the wait–wound technique. In a two-phase locking situation, prelocking shortens the first phase to its minimum. Then, a young processor can refuse to let itself be preempted once the prelocking phase is complete, since it knows that nothing else can deadlock it from then on. On the other hand being preempted during the prelocking phase cannot be very wasteful, since no real work has taken place yet. Prelocking has the disadvantage of restricting the amount of parallelism in the system.

Time-stamping techniques are among those most frequently used in distributed systems. In such systems, however, the creation of unique time-stamps is not trivial. First of all, since the systems are distributed, they cannot possibly have perfectly synchronized clocks (Lamport, 1978). More important, even if they had synchronized clocks, time-stamps generated from these clocks would not be unique and therefore could not be used to resolve deadlock conflicts. Unique time-stamps can be obtained by concatenating the serial number or some unique identifier of the issuing processor with a local time reading.

Suggested Reading and Classics

On the definition and significance of the ''process'' concept:

Horning and Randell, 1973

On synchronization issues and primitives:

Dijkstra, 1965. The paper that started the field, including a discussion of Dekker's primitives.
Dijkstra, 1968a. An exhaustive discussion of semaphores and deadlock prevention (banker's algorithm).
Dijkstra, 1968b. On using semaphores to structure a system.
Saltzer, 1966. On block/wakeup and wakeup–waiting switch (among many other issues).
Dijkstra, 1971. Introduces an early flavor of monitor.
Hoare, 1974. The original reference on monitors.
Howard, 1976. On scheduling problems in monitors.
Brinch Hansen, 1972b; Hoare, 1972. Two independent descriptions of conditional critical regions.
Reed and Kanodia, 1979. The event counts and sequencers paper.

Surveys of synchronization primitives:

Andler, 1979. A good critical comparison of primitives.
Lagally, 1979. A more tutorial paper on primitives.

On interprocess communication as implemented in various systems:

Brinch Hansen, 1970. Message queues in the RC4000 system.
Baskett *et al.*, 1977. Links in Demos.
Cheriton *et al.*, 1979. Messages in Thoth.
Richards *et al.*, 1979. Efficient message passing in the Tripos real-time system.
Ritchie and Thompson, 1974. The concept of communication pipes in Unix.

On classical synchronization problems:

Courtois *et al.*, 1971. The multiple readers/writers problem.
Parnas, 1975. The cigarette smokers' problem solved with semaphores only.

On techniques for coping with deadlocks:

Murphy, 1968. A classic on detection algorithms.
Havender, 1968. A technique based on resource numbering as used in IBM's OS/36.
Habermann, 1969. The banker's algorithm and extension.
Coffman *et al.*, 1971. A classic survey of deadlock handling.
Eswaran *et al.*, 1976 On the interference of synchronization and consistency issues in data base systems, including two-phase locking.

On time management and clock synchronization in distributed systems:

Lamport, 1978

On interprocess communication in distributed systems:

Walden, 1972; Akkoyunlu *et al.*, 1975. On examples of interprocess communication.

Feldman, 1979; Liskov, 1982. On language primitives for interprocess communication in distributed systems.

Spector, 1982; Birrell and Nelson, 1984. On remote procedure calls.

Further Reading and References

A survey of synchronization issues in early operating systems, with references:

Denning, 1971

More on synchronization problems and primitives:

Brinch Hansen, 1972a
Brinch Hansen, 1973b
Brinch Hansen, 1978
Brinch Hansen and Staunstrup, 1978
Habermann, 1972
Hoare, 1978
Wirth, 1977

More on implementations of primitives:

Keedy, 1977. An implementation of semaphores.
Lister and Maynard, 1976. An implementation of monitors.

More on deadlocks:

Holt, 1972. A graph model of deadlock handling.
Gray, 1979. Synchronization in data base systems.
Newton, 1979. An annotated bibliography.

Chapter III

Multiprogramming Issues

Chapter II has discussed that part of the processor management mechanism dealing with multiprocessing issues, i.e., problems resulting from the concurrency of parallel (or pseudoparallel) processors. In this chapter, we study the other aspect of processor management, namely, how to multiprogram one or a small number of physical processors to support the abstraction of a multiplicity of virtual processors.

Operating systems for most personal computers found on the market today do not offer any multiprogramming. They are called single-thread systems. The philosophy behind this design is that since such systems serve a single user, all their processing power can be devoted to that user. There is no need to multiplex the processor between several pseudoparallel tasks.

However, in recent years this thinking has been changing, and a trend towards multiprogramming can be expected in future personal computers. There has been a realization that single-user does not imply single-task—that while the user is performing some foreground task, such as editing, he may want his computer to use "think" pauses towards some background task, such as compilation or printing. In addition new system programming styles have arisen that are based on the existence of multiple virtual processors (Brinch Hansen, 1976; Redell *et al.*, 1980).

1. Processor State Description

Virtual processors as well as physical processors are machines that evolve through a succession of *states*. The state of a processor is defined by the content of all the registers (arithmetic, logic, instruction, counter, index, etc.) of the processor. Such a state defines the instruction the processor is currently executing and the environment in which the instruction is executed.

Notice that one can talk about a processor state at various levels. For a physical processor, the state between two instructions is completely defined by the content of the hardware registers. However, in the middle of an instruction, it is necessary to include all internal registers used by the microcode (assuming a microprogrammed processor) to fully qualify the physical processor state.

Similarly, to describe the state of a virtual processor between two of its instructions, it is sufficient to describe the state of its registers. Remember, however, that the instruction set of a virtual processor is not identical to the instruction set of a physical processor. The physical processor may execute certain privileged instructions that are not visible to the virtual processor, while the virtual processor sees software primitives, such as semaphores, as "instructions".

Thus, to describe the state of a virtual processor in the middle of a processor management operation implemented in software, it is necessary to define the current environment and instruction of the virtual processor, as well as the current state of the physical processor executing the virtual processor software instruction, and eventually even the state of the microcode processor. In summary, the description of the state of a processor may require information pertinent to various levels of the implementation of that processor.

2. Multiprogramming

2.1. Principle

Multiprogramming consists of multiplexing physical processors among virtual processors. In order to "do" multiprogramming, one stops a virtual processor $P1$ that is currently running on a physical processor, and one gives the physical processor to another virtual processor $P2$. This is done by freezing the operation of $P1$, storing a snapshot of its state somewhere in (main) memory, and loading into the physical processor registers, from (main) memory, the state of $P2$ that must have been saved at some earlier time. As soon as that state is loaded into the physical processor, the physical processor will interpret it, causing $P2$ to resume execution and evolve to another state.

Processor states are saved in main memory and restored from main memory in a table that is referred to in this book as the *Virtual Processor Table* (VPT). The VPT is used to hold snapshots of the states of virtual processors while they are not running on a physical processor. Notice that the VPT is used to implement all the waiting lists mentioned so far in the P, V, BLOCK, and WAKEUP primitives. Waiting lists consist of threaded lists of entries in the VPT. The lock L mentioned in the various primitives is none other than a global processor management lock protecting the integrity of the VPT.

2.2.   When to Multiprogram

One question concerning the implementation of multiprogramming is, What are the opportunities for stopping a virtual processor? There are two possible answers.

1.   First, a virtual processor may be stopped when it spontaneously asks the processor management mechanism to be stopped, i.e., when it calls a primitive like P or BLOCK. In our earlier description of the P and BLOCK primitives, we explained that the calling virtual processor was put on a waiting list, without further specifying what this implied. Appending a virtual processor *VP*1 to a waiting list is in reality the operation that corresponds to multiprogramming. To append *VP*1 to the list means to save its state somewhere in a list stored in memory and to give away the physical processor to some other virtual processor *VP*2 by reloading the physical processor registers from the previously saved state of *VP*2. The append operation is best viewed as the following sequence:

$$\text{Switch processor} \begin{cases} \text{store state of requesting } VP1 \\ \text{and} \\ \text{reload state of some } VP2 \end{cases}$$

Thus, when a physical processor starts executing a P or a BLOCK instruction on behalf of a virtual processor *VP*1 that has expressed a desire to wait, the physical processor enters the processor management mechanism as an incarnation of *VP*1 but the UNLOCK operation at the exit of the P or BLOCK operation is really executed under the identity of *VP*2. An UNLOCK operation on behalf of *VP*1 will be performed only later, when *VP*1 will in turn come out of the waiting state as a result of someone else's having entered that state. This transition from one virtual processor to another inside a synchronization primitive is pictured in Fig. 24.

2.   Second, a virtual processor may be forcibly stopped if it has had a physical processor for a long time (clock interrupt) or if an event (e.g., I/O interrupt) occurs that demands immediate attention of another virtual processor. This second, nonspontaneous way of stopping a virtual processor is called interrupting the virtual processor—interrupting by time-out in the first case, and interrupting by preemption in the second case. Either type of interrupt needs corresponding software support in the processor management mechanism. This software, which is invoked at the time of the interrupt, can be regarded as a virtual processor "instruction", like the P/V or BLOCK/WAKEUP primitives seen earlier. These instructions are not explicitly called by virtual processors, but their effect is similar to a P or a BLOCK in that the physical processor is passed to another virtual processor.

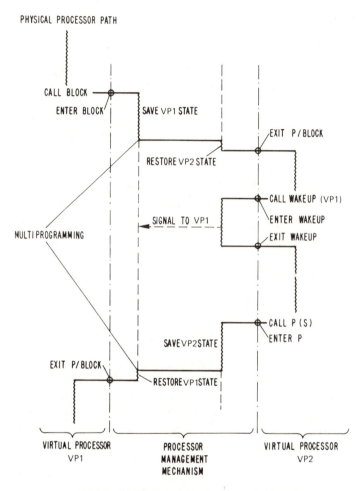

PHYSICAL PROCESSOR PATH

CALL BLOCK

ENTER BLOCK'

SAVE VP1 STATE

EXIT P / BLOCK

RESTORE VP2 STATE

CALL WAKEUP (VP1)

ENTER WAKEUP

SIGNAL TO VP1

EXIT WAKEUP

MULTIPROGRAMMING

CALL P (S)

ENTER P

SAVE VP2 STATE

EXIT P/ BLOCK

RESTORE VP1 STATE

VIRTUAL PROCESSOR
VP1

PROCESSOR
MANAGEMENT
MECHANISM

VIRTUAL PROCESSOR
VP2

Fig. 24. Multiprogramming inside a primitive.

2.3. When to Interrupt

Having described the two possible opportunities for multiprogramming, the second question is, Can a virtual processor be interrupted at any random point in its computation?

A virtual processor may be stopped *only* between two of its instructions, i.e., between non-privileged hardware instructions or between a nonpriviledged hardware instruction and one of the software "instructions" (e.g., P/V, BLOCK/ WAKEUP) constituted by the processor management mechanism. In other words, a virtual processor may be interrupted between any two hardware instructions *unless* those hardware instructions are inside one of the software primitives of the processor management mechanism.

The reason why a virtual processor should not be stopped in the middle of a hardware instruction is purely convenience. Stopping a virtual processor in the middle of a hardware instruction requires more information (about microcode registers) for a complete state description. Thus it is preferable to stop the processor at a time when its state is as simple to define as possible, i.e., just between two instructions.

In addition to the above argument, there are three reasons why a virtual processor may never be interrupted while executing processor management code:

1. The first reason is that there is a fair probability, if a virtual processor is inside the processor management code, that it is already doing a P or a BLOCK operation or is already in the process of stopping following an earlier interrupt, in which case there is no point interrupting it.

2. The second reason was mentioned when P/V and BLOCK/WAKEUP primitives were first defined. These primitives, as all processor management primitives, require mutual exclusion, as expressed by the lock we called L. To keep busy-waiting on this lock to a minimum, it is desirable to mask interrupts while a physical processor holds the lock.

3. The third reason is plainly one of preventing a system deadlock. If a virtual processor were interrupted while holding lock L, it would lose the physical processor. Without that physical processor, it could not complete its software "instruction", and could thus not release lock L. At the same time, the physical processor that abandoned the virtual processor as a result of the interrupt would be busy waiting on lock L. Thus, the system would be deadlocked, since any processor trying to enter the processor management mechanism would find lock L set, and the one virtual processor that held lock L would be interrupted.

To conclude this argument, as soon as a virtual processor invokes a processor management primitive or is interrupted and thus forced to execute some processor management interrupt handling code, the physical processor on which it is executing must acquire the lock L and inhibit further interrupts until completion of the processor management primitive, whereupon the lock must be released and the interrupts unmasked.

2.4.   Saving States

The third question about the implementation of multiprogramming is, What state information must be saved when a physical processor switches virtual processors?

In the case of a P or a BLOCK operation, the virtual processor state to be saved must describe the virtual processor in such a way that it will resume execution at the instruction following the current software "instruction". Thus, the physical processor can find the relevant snapshot in the top frame of the call stack (assuming a stack-based architecture) of the virtual processor, where the normal procedure call mechanism will have dumped it before calling the software primitive.

In the case of an interrupt, the virtual processor state to be saved must describe the virtual processor just before the instruction that was about to be executed when the interrupt occurred. How this snapshot can be obtained depends on how a virtual processor enters the processor management mechanism at the time an interrupt occurs. The description of one possible implementation follows.

An *interrupt* occurs as a bit that goes on in a register called an interrupt cell which is tested at the end of each hardware instruction cycle unless the interrupts are masked. If and when an interrupt is detected, the physical processor masks further interrupts right away, dumps at the very least the content of the instruction counter in some predetermined memory location, and reloads it with an address determined by the interrupt that just occurred. The instructions at that address must invoke a subroutine of the processor management mechanism to dump all registers defining the state of the virtual processor that was just interrupted into the VPT. The physical processor proceeds to mark the interrupted virtual processor as ready for more physical processor time and handles the interrupt.

2.5.   Handling Interrupts

The last question about multiprogramming is, What does it mean to handle an interrupt?

All interrupts may be classified into one of two categories: timer/clock interrupts and all others.

Timer interrupts inform the system that the interrupted virtual processor has been executing for long enough and should be forced to give up the processor for now. To handle a timer interrupt, the system calls the innermost routine of the processor management mechanism, called the *dispatcher*. The dispatcher's task consists of selecting one candidate from the list of virtual processors waiting for a physical processor to become available. Such virtual processors are said to be in the *ready state,* and the list is called the ready list. Like the various waiting lists, it is implemented by threading entries of the VPT together.

Other interrupts inform the system of the occurrence of some event of interest, such as completion of an I/O operation, or failure of some piece of hardware or software instruction. Each such event needs its own software handler. In most operating systems, all these special event handlers were somehow grafted onto the processor management mechanism as subroutines, which made the kernel of the system look like one big aggregate of unrelated subroutines.

In modern operating systems, the handler for every different event is designed to reside inside some virtual processor dedicated to handle that sort of event. The interrupt signalling the event is then interpreted as the hardware equivalent of a WAKEUP operation addressed to the corresponding virtual processor. Thus, that processor is marked as needing a physical processor, and the dispatcher subroutine is entered. It may or may not select the interrupt handling virtual processor to run immediately depending on the urgency of the task.

2.6. States of a Virtual Processor

We have just seen that a virtual processor may be stopped in two different ways, either spontaneously or by an interrupt. In fact there is a third way in which a virtual processor may be stopped. That is by invoking spontaneously a processor management primitive called STOP to indicate that it has completed its task and has nothing more to compute. As a result of STOPping, the calling virtual processor is destroyed, i.e., removed from the VPT, which corresponds to the release of a VPT entry.

Similarly, one more primitive that has not been mentioned so far is called START, which causes a new virtual processor to be created, resulting in the allocation and initialization of a previously empty VPT entry.

When a user requests service from a terminal, a virtual processor is allocated to him to do his work, i.e., a slot in the VPT is assigned to the user and initialized to a state reflecting a fresh virtual processor about to start accepting commands from a terminal. That virtual processor is set in the ready state.

Thus a virtual processor is always in one of four states, as represented in Fig. 25.

1.   Before creation, the VPT is in the *null* or inexistent state, corresponding to a free and empty VPT entry.

2.   After creation, the virtual processor is initially in the *ready* state, meaning that it can use a physical processor to run on as soon as one is available.

3.   The virtual processor will go from the ready state to the *running* state when it is chosen to execute by the dispatcher. In response to an interrupt, the virtual processor stops running and goes back to the ready state indicating that it can resume execution at any time, as soon as a physical processor is available.

4.   If it invokes a P or BLOCK operation, the virtual processor goes into the *waiting* state on a waiting list. It will get out of the waiting list when the corresponding V or WAKEUP signal arrives. At that point, the virtual processor is put back into the ready state. Finally, in response to invoking the STOP operation, the virtual processor returns to the null state.

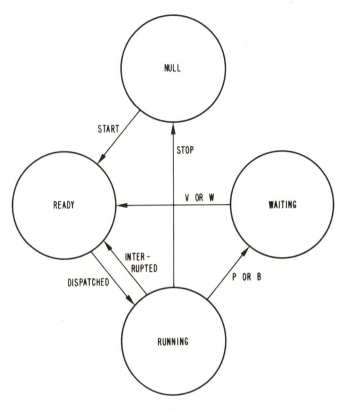

Fig. 25.   Virtual processor states.

3.   Scheduling

3.1.   Definition

Remember that the processor management mechanism which supports the virtual processor concept knows only about main memory. Thus, all the procedures that compose it and the data structures it uses, including the VPT, are resident, as suggested earlier.

Since primary memory is not infinite but is a scarce resource, it is necessary to limit how much of it is used up by the processor management mechanism. In particular, it is necessary to limit the size of the VPT. This implies limiting the number of virtual processors (VPT entries). The number of virtual processors on a system is called its *level of multiprogramming*. While the level of multiprogramming of a system may be limited for different reasons, VPT size considerations are certainly one factor.

On a typical batch system, since the user is not on-line and does not expect a response in real time, no more user jobs need be processed in parallel than the number of available virtual processors. Similarly, on a real-time system, where response time is important, the number of virtual processors necessary to do the job must be kept small enough so they can all fit in the VPT.

However, on a typical time-sharing system, the system can concentrate its efforts on at most as many user jobs as there are virtual processors, but there may be many more users needing service. There may be only 10 virtual processors to serve 50 logged-in users, each user representing at least one different job. Thus, the need is felt for another abstract machine, which we will call a *user process,* similar to a virtual processor from an external point of view but not occupying main memory space from an internal point of view.

3.2.   User Processes

The concept of a user process is supported by a mechanism called the *process management* mechanism. This mechanism is similar in nature to the processor management mechanism seen so far, but sits at a higher level in the software hierarchy of the operating system and implements a higher level abstract machine.

The process management mechanism does to virtual processors what the processor management mechanism does to physical processors: it multiplexes virtual processors among user processes and allows user processes to communicate among themselves. Everything applicable to virtual processors with respect to physical processors can be stated about user processes with respect to virtual processors.

By stating that user processes do not consume primary memory space, we imply that their state may be kept on peripheral storage devices. Thus, to deal with user processes, the process management mechanism must know about peripheral storage. It must use the storage management mechanism. We will not start studying this mechanism until Chapter V. However, for our present purpose it is sufficient to know that its function is to perform management of storage space and to move information between main memory and peripheral storage.

The process management mechanism uses the storage management mechanism to multiplex virtual processors, i.e., VPT slots, among user processes. User processes are of course represented by slots in a table further called the *User Process Table* (UPT), which looks like the VPT but reside most of the time in peripheral storage. The user process management mechanism moves processor states between UPT slots and VPT slots, an operation called *scheduling* and analogous to the dispatching operation of the virtual processor management mechanism.

The equivalent of giving a physical processor to a virtual processor is giving a virtual processor to a user process by copying a UPT entry into a VPT entry. To give up a virtual processor, its state is copied back from its VPT entry to a UPT entry. Copying the state of a user process into a virtual processor is a part of an operation called loading the user process.

Users see only user processes. They never see virtual processors, much less physical ones. The process management mechanism is a second extension to the instruction set of hardware processors; it hides the software instruction set of virtual processors from users behind another software instruction set that offers the same functionality at a lower cost, and with a lower efficiency since there are two levels of multiplexing below the level of user processes.

All the primitives and states that were defined about virtual processors may be defined about user processes. In fact, the waiting–ready–running states of a virtual processor play the role of the running state of a user process. The null state of a virtual processor plays the role of the ready–waiting–null states of a user process. This is shown in Fig. 26.

When a user logs on, a user process is created for him, meaning that an entry is initialized in the UPT and set in the user process ready state. As a VPT entry becomes free at a later time, the user process is loaded into it by the equivalent of the dispatcher for user processes, called the scheduler. From then on, the computation is under the control of the processor management mechanism. As a user process, it is in the running state. As a virtual processor, it is only in the ready state since it does not yet have a physical processor.

Considering Fig. 26, one question must be answered: What do the u and v indices mean on the P/V and BLOCK/WAKEUP primitives? They serve to distinguish operations bearing on virtual processors from those affecting user processes. V/WAKEUP and P/BLOCK operations are addressed to virtual processors or to user processes based on the nature of the event under concern.

System-generated events, which are normally known to occur within some finite amount of time, are addressed to virtual processors, i.e., only virtual processors may wait for them. User-generated events, which may never occur or take an indefinite amount of time to occur, are addressed to user processes, i.e., virtual processors should never call the low-level P or BLOCK primitive if it means to wait for a user event.

A typical system event is a peripheral storage I/O operation. When a physical processor needs a piece of information that is not in main memory, the information must be brought into main memory by a system I/O operation. After the physical processor requests the operation, it puts the running virtual processor into the waiting state until the operation completes, which is known to occur within a short, finite period of time (a few milliseconds for modern disks).

A typical user event is an I/O operation on a communication device such as terminal. When a virtual processor incarnating some user process runs out of work, it requests the process management mechanism to stop it until further work

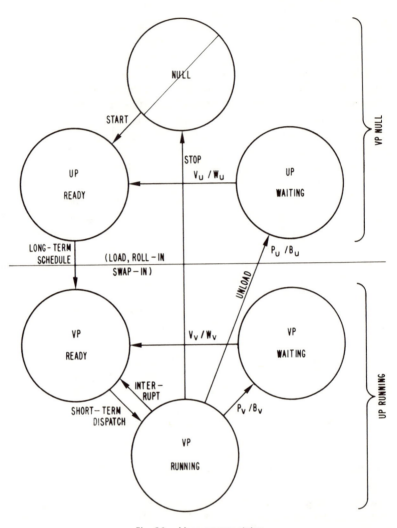

Fig. 26. User process states.

is submitted from the terminal. This is because the virtual processor will not have
any work to do until the user issues a new command at his terminal, which may
take a few seconds, or a few minutes, or forever. It would be a waste to keep the
virtual processor state in primary memory that long. Thus, it is unloaded to the
user process waiting state.

Essentially, the difference between the ready–waiting user process states and
ready–waiting virtual processor states is a matter of time grain. Typically, a
virtual processor may travel around its waiting–ready–running loop between 1

and 10 or even more times per second, while a user process travels around its waiting–ready–running loop between 10 and 1 or even fewer times per minute.

As a result of the above discussion, it should be clear that system events, which are a fixed, well-defined set of events of which we will study the main ones later, are invisible to user processes in that they are not under the control of the user. They occur inside user process instructions.

A virtual processor that is executing inside the kernel system is in full control of the events it generates, receives, and is willing to wait for. In particular, it cannot be stopped at random points by user-generated events. If a user generates an I/O interrupt for his process, for instance by pressing the BREAK, ATTEN-TION, INTERRUPT, ABORT, or some similar key on his terminal, he must wait until his process leaves any kernel system code it might have been executing before the process will see the interrupt.

Doing otherwise might be extremely dangerous, as the process might be put on a waiting list for an indefinite amount of time when it was using and had locked some crucial system tables. In summary, all system kernel code must be ex-ecuted in the context of a virtual processor to mask out user events and protect the system from uncontrolled interference.

Notice that we have defined two types of abstract processors so far: virtual processors and user processes, which are materialized by entries in two different tables, the VPT and the UPT. Each type of processor has four states, where one of the four states corresponds to three states of the other type of processor. In many systems, such as Unix or DEC's RMS, there is the concept of loading and unloading an abstract processor, and there is the resulting six-state diagram. However, all six states are implemented in one table and correspond to a single type of abstract processor. In such systems, each entry in the table contains a minimal amount of information about the state of each existing virtual processor. The complete state description, necessary for running the processor, is loaded and unloaded, together with the processor environment (i.e., the programs and data it uses), when appropriate.

4.   Algorithms

As should be clear from the above descriptions, the function of a scheduler is very similar in principle to that of a dispatcher. Both multiplex a relatively small number of low-level processors among a relatively large number of processors of a higher level of abstraction. A key issue in the implementation of multiplexing at either level is the selection of a higher level processor to run on a lower level processor. To perform this selection, dispatchers and schedulers use algorithms that may be fairly similar in principle, though they operate on a totally different time scale, as explained earlier.

Processor multiplexing algorithms may be classified according to the priority system they use and according to the hardware support they require.

4.1.   Priority Schemes

Consider *priorities* first. Some (rare) algorithms do not make any use of priorities: all abstract processors are treated as equal candidates to run. Most algorithms use fixed priorities: abstract processors are given some fixed priority for the duration of their existence. While waiting for an opportunity to run, they are sorted into ready lists corresponding to these priorities. Higher priority lists get preferential treatment. In large time-sharing systems, and in real-time systems, one may find algorithms using variable priorities. In such systems, the priority of an abstract processor evolves with time and is recalculated every time a new candidate must be selected to run.

4.2.   Hardware Support

From the point of view of hardware support, one distinguishes between *free algorithms, timed algorithms,* and *preemptive algorithms.*

   1.   Free algorithms assume that interrupts do not affect the selection of a candidate. An abstract processor may occasionally be interrupted, but is resumed as soon as the interrupt is logged by the processor management mechanism. As a result of an interrupt, the algorithm will never select an abstract processor other than the one that was interrupted. Aside from short intervals spent inside the processor management mechanism, an abstract processor runs until it has to wait for some event or completes its task.

   2.   With timed algorithms, only timer interrupts may affect the selection process. When a selection is necessary, preference is given to the abstract processor at the head of the highest priority ready queue that is not empty. The selected abstract processor runs for a certain *quantum* of time. In spite of potential intermediate I/O interrupts, which are logged by the processor management mechanism, the selected processor keeps running until the end of the quantum. After that time, signalled by a timer interrupt, the abstract processor is removed from the running state, appended at the back of the ready queue it came from, and another selection is made.

   3.   With preemptive algorithms, which require the use of priorities by definition, non-timer (i.e., I/O) interrupts do affect the selection process. An interrupt destined to a high-priority abstract processor may *preempt* a low-priority processor, i.e., the multiplexed (lower level) processor may be taken from the interrupted abstract processor and given to the abstract processor for which the interrupt is meant.

Following are brief descriptions of some of the most common dispatching/scheduling algorithms. For the sake of clarity, they are presented here as dispatching algorithms though they may also be used for scheduling. Some algorithms are found more often in one case than in the other, as pointed out in the description.

4.3.   Free Algorithms

a.   FCFS

Among free algorithms, the simplest example is called *first-come-first-served* (FCFS) or first-in-first-out (FIFO). It does not use any priorities. According to this algorithm, the set of ready virtual processors is implemented as one queue. Virtual processors are added at the end of the queue when they are ready and removed from the front when there is a physical processor available.

The main drawback of FCFS is that virtual processors running short jobs may have to wait in line behind processors running very long jobs.

b.   SJF

A classic free algorithm that uses fixed priorities is called *shortest-job-first* (SJF), shortest-job-next (SJN), or shortest-processing-time (SPT). As the name indicates, a SJF dispatcher associates with virtual processors priorities that decrease with their estimated processing time. This avoids the problem of FCFS and minimizes the average waiting time for all virtual processors.

However, SJF suffers from two problems. First, it requires estimates of future processing times, which may be hard to supply in certain cases. Second, it may lead to starvation in that some virtual processor with a very long estimated run-time may always be delayed due to the arrival in the ready list of higher priority jobs. SJF was often used for scheduling in early time-sharing systems, such as CTSS.

4.4.   Timed Algorithms

a.   RR

Among timed algorithms, the simplest example, which does not use priorities, is probably *round-robin* (RR) or processor-sharing (PS). With RR, every virtual processor is appended at the back of the ready list when it becomes ready. When it reaches the head of the list, it receives the physical processor. However, rather than running until it needs to wait or completes, the virtual processor is given a fixed quantum of time to run, whose end is signalled by a timer interrupt. Upon the interrupt, the virtual processor is recycled at the back of the ready list and the physical processor is given to the head of the list.

Contrary to FCFS, RR gives preferential treatment to virtual processors with short tasks: they complete after fewer time slices and thus after fewer cycles through the ready list. Because of its simplicity, RR is a classic algorithm found in many dispatchers: A priority algorithm is used for long-term scheduling, but, once scheduled, user processes compete on an equal basis given by RR.

4.5. Preemptive Algorithms

a. Deadline Scheduling

Among preemptive algorithms, the simplest one, found in many real-time and time-sharing dispatchers, uses priorities associated with the urgency of the tasks to be performed. In so-called *deadline scheduling* systems, the priority of a virtual processor may dynamically increase. Since any I/O interrupt results in some virtual processor's moving from the waiting state to the ready state, priorities may be reevaluated and are used after each interrupt to determine which virtual processor should be dispatched.

b. SRTF

Another classical algorithm is a more dynamic and preemptive version of SJF, called *shortest-run-time-first* (SRTF) or shortest-remaining-processing-time (SRPT). Like SJF, this algorithm requires estimates of processing time requirements for each virtual processor. However, these estimates serve to determine only starting priorities. Every time a virtual processor needs to wait or is interrupted, processing time elapsed so far is subtracted from the estimate. When the processor becomes ready again, it acquires a higher priority, reflecting the fact that it has less work remaining. With its higher priority, the processor may preempt some other one and be dispatched immediately after the interrupt.

c. MLQ

For the sake of completeness, it must be added that algorithms may use a combination of the above mechanisms. For instance, the *multilevel-queue* algorithm (MLQ) found in almost every modern time-sharing system combines timer interrupts and preemption.

In this scheme, the set of ready virtual processors is represented by multiple queues of different priorities. Virtual processors reaching the head of the first queue receive a fixed run-time quantum $Q0$. When their quantum is over, they are interrupted (time-out) and go to the tail of the second queue. Virtual processors in the second queue never receive physical processors as long as there are virtual processors in the first queue. When the first queue is empty, virtual processors of the second queue receive a fixed physical processor time quantum $Q1 > Q0$. When it is over they drop at the tail of the third queue, and so on.

The last queue is subject to a RR algorithm with a relatively large run-time quantum. However, if a virtual processor from queue i has not used up all its quantum $Q(i - 1)$ when an interrupt occurs that causes a virtual processor to be put in queue j ($j < i$), the virtual processor of queue i is preempted and the virtual processor in queue j gets the physical processor.

MLQ was first implemented in CTSS (Corbato *et al.*, 1962. Variations of it were used for dispatching in Multics, in IBM's VM and MVS, in DEC's TOPS-10, and in many others. Algorithms with similar effects are used for dispatching in THE (Dijkstra, 1968b), Unix, and DEC's VMS. In these systems, the priority of a processor decreases with the number of times it has been dispatched (in VMS) or with the ratio of the time it has been running to the elapsed real time. This effectively gives priority to I/O bound processors, while it treats all other processors in a round-robin fashion.

4.6. Comparison

One defines *virtual time* as time elapsed according to the clock of a virtual processor. Virtual time elapses thus only while the virtual processor is running. Plotting real time versus virtual time, the evolution of the same virtual processor under some of the above algorithms can be expressed by Fig. 27. One can see that FCFS penalizes virtual processors with short tasks and favors virtual processors with long tasks. RR favors short virtual processors and penalizes long ones. MLQ gives every virtual processor a response related to its length by behaving more like RR for short virtual processors and more like FCFS for long ones.

It should be kept in mind, however, that no algorithm can favor every type of virtual processor. Preference for one type is always at the expense of some other type. It has even been shown that some weighted sum of the waiting times averaged over all virtual processors is an invariant. We will not discuss this theoretical performance result in more detail here though.

Also, without giving any detail about its mathematical foundations, it is worth mentioning *Little's Law* here. In essence, this law shows that one should never load a system so that its ready lists are never empty as this would result in unacceptable response times, regardless of the scheduling and dispatching algorithms used. In other words, given the processing time requirements of a community of users, one should always choose a hardware system that offers (20–30%) more processing capacity than the requirements demand.

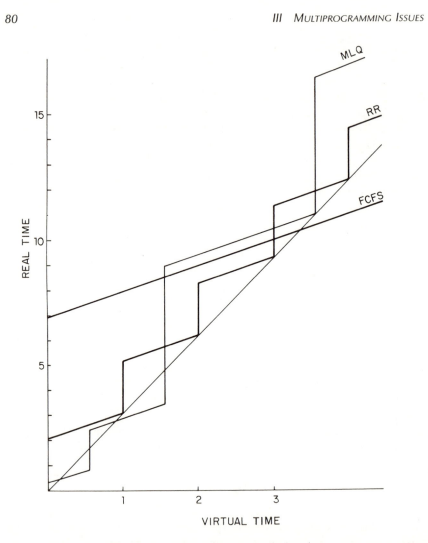

Fig. 27.   A comparison of dispatching algorithms.

A final word is in order about the relative efficiency of multiprogramming operations. As suggested earlier, scheduling is more expensive than dispatching because it usually requires access to peripheral storage. Even among different implementations of dispatching, one can observe timings varying between several microseconds (for real-time systems) to a few milliseconds (for time-sharing systems) depending on the complexity of the algorithm, the amount of state information to be saved/restored (e.g. additional protection registers), and the availability of hardware assistance (e.g. swapping between multiple register sets).

Suggested Reading and Classics

Saltzer, 1966, A classic on hardware/software support for multiprogramming.

Lampson, 1968. On the mechanisms for multiprogramming.

Brinch Hansen, 1971. Later review of the topic with discussion of short-term verus long-term scheduling.

Coffman, 1973. A discussion and performance evaluation of the most important scheduling algorithms.

Corbato, 1962. Multilevel queues in CTSS.

Bobrow, 1972. Scheduling in the Tenex system.

Whitfield, 1973. Scheduling in the Emas system.

Brinch Hansen, 1976; Redell, 1980. Examples of the use of multiprogramming in single-user computers.

Part 3

INPUT/OUTPUT MANAGEMENT

Chapter IV

Device Control

Part 2 described in detail the processor management mechanism of an operating system, i.e., the software necessary to multiprogram physical processors among virtual ones, to control the concurrency of these virtual processors, and to allow them to communicate. Processor management is the innermost mechanism of an operating system because it provides the necessary support for parallel programming, which is in turn essential to the management of any other type of resource by the operating system.

Using the virtual processor abstraction and the parallel programming primitives provided by processor management, the second type of resource managed by an operating system is peripherals, including both communication and storage devices, without any distinction for the moment.

The programs and data structures required to support processor management are all resident. Towards the end of Chapter III, we indicated that a higher level mechanism, called process management, using virtual memory instead of resident tables, was necessary to support large time-sharing systems. The division of a mechanism into two levels of different sophistication and functionality is not uncommon. The same phenomenon can be observed concerning I/O management. It is also divided into two levels, the lower of which, called *device control,* is resident and knows nothing about virtual memory, while the higher one, called *I/O control,* may use concepts of virtual memory.

At the device control level, there are clear implementation differences between storage and communication device software. However, there are no fundamental differences in principles: objectives as well as software structures are fairly similar and can be discussed together. By comparison with the topics of processor or memory management, where a general discussion of principles and mechanisms is feasible, device control does not lend itself well to a systematic study. There exist few general concepts, because devices vary so widely in their characteristics. Most of the control code for a device depends strictly on its operational characteristics, which vary themselves from one manufacturer to another. Only some engineering considerations of general interest will be discussed in this chapter.

By contrast, at the I/O control level, there are fundamental differences between the philosophy and the software structures used for communication devices and those used for storage devices. I/O control software, often referred to as *access method,* is very different for each type of device. File, disk, or storage access methods show no resemblence to network or communication access methods.

For no better reason than tradition, the topic of I/O control for communication devices, while certainly belonging in the operating system, is usually treated as a special application and as such discussed separately, in courses on communication architecture and network protocols. The interested reader is referred to such courses (e.g., Tanenbaum, 1981), and the topic will not be further developed in this book.

The topic of I/O control for storage devices has also been separated from the operating system and discussed in specialized courses for systems that make extensive use of storage devices, namely data base systems. For other systems, I/O control for storage devices is responsible for what is called file management. This topic is discussed in Chapter VII.

We now proceed with a more detailed definition of the functions encountered at each of the I/O management levels.

1.   I/O Control

Access methods directly interface with user programs. I/O statements in user programs are translated by language processors into procedure calls or interprocess messages targeted at the I/O control software. At the I/O control level, devices are typically referred to by name, while the hardware obviously refers to them by address. I/O control is also concerned with such high-level protection and accounting issues as the allocation of devices or portions thereof to user processes.

Access methods provide users with abstract or virtual devices, i.e., devices that only very remotely resemble real I/O devices. For instance, at this level writing to a printer or to a magnetic tape may look identical to the user program. Similarly, manipulating a disk or a diskette, aside from capacity considerations, may be transparent to the user.

In fact, it has been a trend in operating systems designed since 1970 (e.g., Unix) to make all I/O devices, whether storage or communication devices, look alike to a large extent and whenever possible. Clearly, disks exhibit a random access property that most communication devices cannot mimic. Applications making use of random disk access need corresponding support from I/O control.

However, many applications use disks as sequential devices, by simply read-ing/writing a character or a block of characters at a time from/to them. For such applications, I/O control makes disks look like communication lines, by provid-ing *I/O streams,* namely, abstract devices that can be read or written sequen-tially, a byte or a block at a time.

The interprocess communication concept of a *pipe,* first proposed in the Unix operating system (Ritchie and Thompson, 1974), and then offered under differ-ent names and somewhat different forms by later systems (e.g., in IBM's PC/DOS), even allows a user process to communicate with another user process as if it were performing an I/O operation on a stream communication or storage device.

Pipes, streams, and related concepts are extremely powerful in that they allow a program to do I/O from/to abstract devices that, for different invocations of the program, can be mapped to different real devices or processes. Prior to running a program, a user can tell the system what abstract, virtual, or logical devices he wants bound to what real device or process. This is referred to as *redirecting* the I/O of the program from/to different devices or processes.

A somewhat different but also powerful view of virtual devices is found in IBM's VM/SP system. The system provides each of its users with a virtual card reader, a virtual card punch, and a virtual printer. From the point of view of a user program, these virtual devices behave exactly like the corresponding real devices, although they are all realized by areas of disks. Each virtual device can be attached to a corresponding real device to cause real operation. However, as card I/O has become old-fashioned, virtual card readers and virtual card punches are used to totally different ends in today's VM/SP.

The system allows any user to cause messages or entire files to be deposited into the virtual reader of any other user, as a general purpose interprocess communication facility. Through the use of ad hoc network access software, the mechanism has been extended beyond single machines, thereby allowing users on remote machines to exchange information through virtual card readers. Stand-alone VM/SP systems can thus be connected into large networks, such as IBM's VNET, which joins close to 1000 machines supporting tens of thousands of users into a single global network.

2. Device Control

In contrast to I/O control, device control offers a much more concrete view of devices. Devices are addressed and not named. Every type of device has its own idiosyncrasies, so that primitives to operate on it can be very different for different devices. At the device control level, the appearance of storage devices is very different from that of communication devices.

While I/O control is primarily concerned with how I/O devices are allocated to, protected from, named by, and represented to user programs, device control is primarily concerned with the synchronization between user programs and I/O control software on one side and hardware devices themselves on the other side.

Another important function of device control is translating I/O requests issued by the I/O control mechanism into channel or I/O programs, namely, instructions and control structures that exactly fit the specifications of the particular device to be controlled.

As stated earlier, device control code and data must be resident. The reason for this is twofold. First, disk control code cannot be on disk, as it could not import itself. Second, even other device control software, such as terminal control code, should not be on disk. While such a design is conceivable in principle, it is practically inefficient. Every time the terminal sent a character to the processor, the processor would have to first fetch the terminal control code from disk before it could do anything about the new character. Thus there must be a minimum amount of code for each device in main memory at all times, for performance reasons if not by pure necessity.

3.   Device Sharing

A distinction exists between shared and private devices. Often, it is a matter of time grain. All devices perform one I/O operation at a time on behalf of some user process. Some devices remain attached to that user process for long periods of time, performing multiple operations in a row for the same process. They are called private devices. Other devices operate for a different user process typically every time they perform a different operation. These are ''sharable'' devices. Multiplexed interfaces to local or public networks are typical examples of shared communication devices. Subsequent data units flowing in and out of such devices typically come from and go to different user processes. Shared storage devices are usually of the random access type. This is the case of file system disks, to be discussed extensively in Part 5. Private devices are, for instance, terminals or tapes.

The distinction between private and shared devices is very important at the I/O control level. It influences the way these devices are allocated, the way they are addressed, the way data is presented to them, etc. At the device control level, the distinction between private and shared devices becomes less clear, since device control code is not concerned with device allocation and protection. Device control receives I/O requests that it knows have been prepared by I/O control and thus are acceptable regardless of who initiated them.

On the other hand, distinctions that are often hidden by I/O control are very clear at the device control level. The device controllers for a printer, a tape, and a diskette are very different from one another. The printer only supports output of data (though it can receive status codes), the tape can be rewound and dismounted, the disk can be accessed randomly, and some devices are character oriented while others are record oriented. These different devices furthermore present different interface characteristics from a synchronization point of view. This is studied next.

4.   Device Synchronization

Perhaps the most important aspect of device control from an operating system structure point of view is device synchronization, namely the coordination of the activity of a device with that of the processor. This synchronization problem is directly related to the type of hardware interface existing between the device and the processor.

4.1.   Programmed I/O

Programmed I/O interfaces date back to the early days of computing when we did not know of any better way to do I/O. With programmed I/O, only one I/O device operates at a time, and while it operates it draws all the attention of the processor. After issuing an input command, the device control software waits in a loop testing the input register from the device until the requested data arrive. After issuing an output command, the processor also waits in a loop testing the output register to the device until the device acknowledges having taken the data item out. This is a very primitive way to synchronize the processor with a device.

Such I/O is of course easy to program: The code for triggering the input or output operation and waiting for its completion can be implemented as a subroutine, which can be called from any user program. However, programmed I/O would be extremely inefficient in a time-sharing system, as it would mean that the whole system has to wait and do nothing while, for instance, some printer is putting out a character.

Yet programmed I/O is still used today in special cases, not involving time-sharing of course. One example is in monitoring and control operations. When a microprocessor is connected to a set of sensors and control devices, in an application such as regulating the temperature of a room by acting on the flow of heat through a heating device, it is programmed to do one and only one job all the time. Thus, it can read temperature sensors and set the position of the heat control at its leisure. In general, it does not have to wait before proceeding, and even if it did, it has all the time it needs to do so.

In general, programmed I/O is used when the processor is so inexpensive that it can be dedicated entirely to the task it is performing, even at the cost of waiting for I/O operations to complete. In such cases, it is cheaper to "waste" a whole

processor on the job than to try to be clever in the software to multiprogram
during I/O operations.

4.2.   Interrupt I/O

Aside from a few special cases such as those mentioned above, programmed I/O
cannot be tolerated. After the processor has issued an I/O instruction, it cannot
afford to wait for completion of the operation. Instead, the system must put the
issuing virtual processor in the wait state, and give the physical processor to
some other ready virtual processor. Completion of the pending I/O is signalled to
the waiting virtual processor at a later time by means of an interrupt. This is
called *interrupt I/O*.

Let us examine in detail how device control code may be synchronized with
user code in a typical system. The device control code may be implemented as a
virtual processor belonging to the system, as suggested in Fig. 28. This virtual
processor serves to synchronize user processes with the device. On one side it
communicates with user processes using one of the primitives seen in Chapter II.
It receives commands from user processes and returns data and/or status information to them when an I/O operation completes. On the other side, it issues I/O
instructions to the device and waits for *I/O interrupts* to come back when data
and/or device status is available.

For every request that it receives from I/O control, the device control virtual
processor issues one or more I/O instructions to the device. As soon as it has
issued an I/O operation, the device control virtual processor calls the processor
management mechanism to block itself. The physical processor is then given to
some other virtual processor.

At a later time, when the device has completed the I/O operation, i.e., provided the requested input character or taken the supplied output character, it
sends an I/O interrupt to the processor. The virtual processor running at that time
is interrupted, which causes its state to be dumped in some predefined location in
memory. Further interrupts are masked, and the processor management mechanism is entered. As explained in Chapter III, the processor management mechanism acquires the VPT lock, copies the state of the interrupted virtual processor
from the predefined area where it was dumped into the proper VPT entry, and
notifies the device control virtual processor that an interrupt has arrived for it.
This is done by moving it from the waiting to the ready state. Depending on the
dispatching algorithm used and on the relative priority of the device controller,
the dispatcher may or may not select the readied device controller to run immediately, or may often *call* its interrupt handler directly.

Thus, by implementing the device control as a special virtual processor belonging to the system, one can use the processor management mechanism to
multiprogram the physical processor(s) while I/O operations are being executed

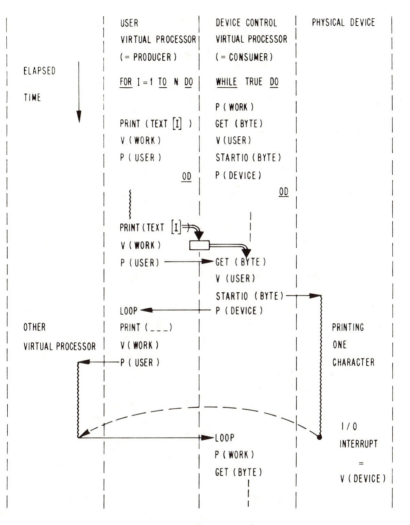

Fig. 28.   Device control as a virtual processor.

at their own pace. In effect, an interrupt from a device can then be regarded as a WAKEUP primitive coming from an external physical processor instead of an internal virtual processor.

The only, but essential, difference between a plain virtual processor and a device control virtual processor is a matter of privilege. In most computer systems, and certainly in all time-sharing systems, the execution of I/O instructions and the ability to handle I/O interrupts require adequate protection: a virtual processor running user code cannot be allowed to trigger I/O operations or manipulate interrupts directly, for fear that it might misuse a device. Virtual processors, as we defined them so far, are barred from using I/O instructions and manipulating interrupt masks, because these instructions require running in *privileged mode*.

To allow selected virtual processors acting as device controllers to use certain privileged I/O instructions, they are marked as system processors in the VPT. The processor management mechanism sets a bit in a register of the physical processor to force privileged mode when dispatching one of the device controllers.

An alternative solution to designing a device controller as a virtual processor is to design it as a monitor, as represented in Fig. 29. With this design, the device control code can be called as a subroutine inside any user process. Upon entering device control, the user process first secures the exclusive use of the monitor. The monitor directs the user process to issue the appropriate I/O commands. It then causes the user process to invoke a BLOCK or P primitive with the proper interrupt identifier as parameter. This puts the user process in the wait state until the expected interrupt signals completion of the I/O operation, whereupon the user process can be resumed.

With this design, the user process itself waits directly for the interrupt, instead of waiting for a device control virtual processor that handles the interrupt on its behalf. In many systems where multiprogramming requires a large number of instructions, the monitor approach to device control is more economical as it saves one multiprogramming operation.

With this design, the user process must be given the necessary I/O privileges when entering the monitor code. This implies that the call to the monitor cannot be a regular subroutine call. It must be a call that can be trapped by the processor management mechanism, giving it a chance to force switching into privileged mode while causing transfer to the monitor code. Privileged calls of this sort can be, and indeed are, implemented in many computers, where they are often called *supervisor calls* (SVCs).

In general, it has been shown (Lauer and Needham, 1979) that designing software modules as monitors or as virtual processors is equivalent. There is a duality between operating systems based on processes communicating with messages and those based on procedures communicating with calls. The choice between these structures depends primarily on the available hardware support and the personal taste of the programmer.

Interrupt I/O is the first handle on device synchronization. However, it is not sufficient. Interrupt I/O works fine as long as the devices exchange characters with the processor at a rate that first allows and second warrants multiprogramming. Indeed, while a single multiprogramming operation may take as little as $10-100$ μs on very special processors (e.g., processors with multiple register

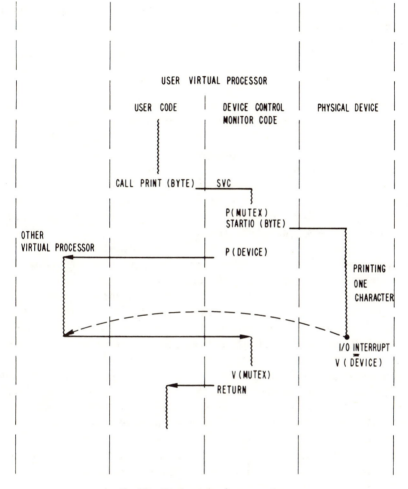

Fig. 29.   Device control as a monitor.

sets, avoiding the need to save state on every switch) or very optimized operating
systems (e.g., for real-time process control), more often than not a processor
switch takes a few (e.g., 1–10) milliseconds. Thus if a device approaches speeds
of 1K bits per second, or about 100 characters per second, multiprogramming on
every character becomes arguable if not impossible.

The problem becomes completely intractable with devices, such as disks and
tapes, that have long latency times but very high data transfer rates. In such
cases, the processor has the time to multiprogram between issuance of the re-

quest and start of data transfer, but once data start flowing, the processor might not even be able to follow in programmed mode with modern disk technology offering data rates in the megabytes per second.

4.3.   Cycle-steal I/O

The answer to the latter problem resides in the use of *cycle-steal,* or *channel I/O*. With long-latency but high-speed devices, one reverts to what amounts to a mix of programmed and interrupt I/O, albeit in a special sense: the processor operates in interrupt I/O mode, while a special purpose dedicated I/O processor operates in programmed I/O mode.

Specialized processors, called I/O processors, peripheral processors, channels, or *direct-memory-access* (DMA) controllers are dedicated to doing all the I/O. They operate in programmed I/O mode, doing essentially only data transfer at a very high speed with special hardware.

The main processor sends its I/O requests not directly to the devices, but to the dedicated I/O processors. While these processors carry out the data transfer, also worrying about latency times, etc., the main processor returns to other work. Of course I/O requests now do not bear on a character at a time, but on entire blocks at a time (e.g., screen images, printer lines, disk records, network messages). The main processor is interrupted by the I/O processors only when complete blocks have been transferred, which gives it time to do multiprogramming between interrupts.

Furthermore, while a data transfer take place, the main processor is interrupted, but in a very subtle way that does not cause it to lose time in multiprogramming. The memory bus of cycle-stealing systems is enhanced typically by a pair of lines allowing I/O processors to request permission from the main processor to steal memory cycles. In the main processor, some dedicated logic, not using regular registers, ALU, or control unit, grants the bus request and at the same time freezes the clock input to the main processor sequencing circuits.

The main processor in effect stops to a dead halt for as long as the I/O processor keeps the request line active, which may last for a whole block transfer. The I/O processor presents an internal architecture that is optimized for very high speed memory access, so that it can exploit contiguous memory cycles to sustain the very high data rates of even the faster devices.

Advanced I/O processors may even be enhanced by internal high-speed buffers to absorb any lag between data exchange with fast devices and acquisition of the bus from the main processor.

Since the whole purpose of interrupt I/O is to permit multiprogramming the processor while devices perform their I/O operations, it may seem counterproductive to dedicate entire special purpose processors to do only I/O in programmed mode. In reality, because these processors are special purpose ones, their cost can be relatively small compared to that of the main processor. Thus, it is in fact not unreasonable to do cycle-steal I/O as described above.

From a software point of view, cycle-steal I/O can be handled with virtual processor or monitor structures similar to those described earlier for interrupt I/O.

4.4.   Command-chained I/O

The most advanced I/O processors are even capable of *chained I/O*, queuing several I/O requests from the main processor. They do not interrupt until the last command in a so-called chain has been completed, unless an error occurs before the end of the chain.

Essentially, there is no end in sight to the sophistication of I/O processors. Technology is making integrated circuits so inexpensive and dense that the I/O processors of today are much more sophisticated than even the main processors of yesterday. One already sees today intelligent disk controllers that relieve the device control software from ordering I/O requests in a sequence that matches the topology of the disk and the movement of its arms. And telecommunication controllers are appearing that implement complete data link control protocols, including retransmission management in case of errors on the line.

5.   Device Buffering

Storage devices are always slaved to the processor, that is, the initiative to start a read or a write operation belongs to the processor. The operation follows to transmit a known amount of data to or from a known buffer.

The situation is not as easy with communication devices. Four factors complicate the management of input buffers:

1.   The processor does not have the initiative of input operations. Devices such as terminals or network interfaces do not send data to the processor upon the processor's request. Data are sent when some other, asynchronous agent (human user or computer) has something to send. Thus, device control must always anticipate input operations. This means it must always have a ready receive buffer and start a receive operation that may remain pending until satisfied. Alternatively, if device control does not anticipate receive operations, there must be external buffers in the I/O adapters to absorb data until device control sets up a receive buffer and issues a read operation.

2.   When data start arriving, they may arrive in unpredictable amounts. Thus, not only must device control anticipate receive operations, but it should also have enough buffers ready to receive any amount of data that could conceivably arrive, otherwise data will be lost.

3. The data that arrive are not data that had been stored out by this processor at an earlier time. Received data may be of an interactive or real-time nature, that is, the data may demand immediate action on the part of device control. For instance, the data may be a BREAK or ATTENTION character from a terminal, which should not be queued in some buffer until the relevant user process asks for it. The purpose of these characters is precisely to prompt immediate attention of a user process, typically following a user action that would cause the user process to embark onto undesired work if it could not be stopped.

4. Finally, in the particular case of shared communication devices such as network ports, the incoming data are addressed to a user process that cannot be identified until the data have been read in and the destination header can be inspected. Thus, the device control mechanism cannot, as in the case of storage or private devices, rely on the user process to supply receive buffers that it can use directly. Instead, it must use its own buffers and copy incoming information from there into user buffers only after figuring out which user buffer the incoming data belong in.

The problem of providing enough receive buffers usually is solved either by using *toggle buffers* or by using *circular buffers*. Using toggle buffers (or ping-pong buffers) means using two buffers at the same time. One is being filled by receive operations while the other is being processed by I/O control before being passed to the user process. Upon termination of a reception, the roles of the buffers are exchanged.

Should two buffers not be enough, more can be used in this game, which eventually leads to the concept of circular buffers. Circular buffers are functionally equivalent to many buffers linked in a circular list, though they are usually implemented by one large buffer that is used at the same time for reception and input processing, in a circular way. The I/O processor or the device always fills the buffer from beginning to end and then starts over again. At the same time, I/O control and the user processes consume the data in the same fashion. The device writing into the buffer and the user reading from the buffer chase one another around the buffer in a classical producer–consumer problem.

Synchronization is implemented by two pointers, one indicating where the device must write the next character, the other indicating where the user is reading the buffer. When the user pointer catches up with the device pointer, the user process is put to sleep for lack of any work to do. If the device pointer catches up with the user pointer, which is very undesirable, there is character overflow and data will be overwritten or more likely lost, depending on the policy adopted in such a case.

The problem of special characters such as BREAK and ATTENTION arriving in an input buffer is not as simple as it sounds. While it is a simple matter for the device control mechanism to check what character arrived and to inform the receiving user process immediately, this is not sufficient. Two complicating factors must be considered. First, the user process may not yet have received from the buffer some information that arrived before the special character. Second, some new information may immediately follow the special character.

Thus, the simplistic approach of telling the user process that a special character arrived and then discarding the content of the buffer is inadequate. It would get rid of the information preceding the special character, which may be desirable; but it would also discard following information, which would be wrong. The special character must be signalled to the user process immediately, but it must be left in the buffer. The user process can then read the buffer up to the special character and discard the preceding information. Normal processing resumes after the special character.

6.   Device Scheduling

6.1.   Random Access Device Scheduling

Another problem that device control software has to deal with in the case of random access storage devices, such as disks or drums, is their scheduling, namely the determination of the order in which I/O requests triggered by user software will be performed by the device.

For communication devices as well as strictly sequential storage devices, such as tapes, there is no scheduling problem. Input and output operations are not targeted to an address on the device. Thus no operation requires such a thing as moving an arm to the right cylinder or track.

For random access storage devices, every I/O operation may potentially require moving the read/write head to the right location on the device prior to doing the actual data transfer. In the case of disks, one speaks of *seeking* and *latency*. Seeking is the operation that brings the device head over the proper cylinder or track. Latency is the phenomenon whereby data transfer cannot proceed until the disk rotation has brought the proper sector under the device head.

In all disk assemblies, latency time is longer than the actual data transfer time, and seek time is even much longer than latency time. Thus for the device control software to honor I/O requests in the (close to random) order in which users generate them could be highly inefficient, in that most data transfers would be penalized by long seek and latency time. In order to minimize I/O time and to optimize disk utilization, the device control software must minimize seek and latency times. This implies that I/O requests must be sorted according to the disk addresses they are targeted at instead of being performed on a FCFS basis.

The algorithms used by disk control software to sort I/O requests into lists matching seek and latency order are fairly similar for both types of operations. We will discuss them here for the case of seek operations. In fact, in order to limit software complexity and overhead, many operating systems do not bother to try to minimize latency times for two reasons. First, seek times are much more important than latency times. Second, latency times are often so short that whatever time could be gained by ordering I/O requests for minimal latency is lost in computing the optimal order itself.

a.   The SSFT Algorithm

A first algorithm that has been proposed to minimize seek time is called *shortest-seek-time-first* (SSTF). As the name indicates, every time a data transfer is completed, the device controller selects for the next operation that I/O request which requires the smallest lateral displacement of the disk head.

This algorithm is by definition optimal as far as seek times are concerned. However, it presents the problem that I/O requests targeted at the middle tracks or cylinders of the disk obtain much better service times than those targeted at the innermost and outermost disk areas. Indeed, in the presence of I/O requests targeted at disk addresses quasi-randomly distributed between the edge tracks, the farther a track is from the middle track, the longer the average seek time to it will be. Thus some edge I/O request might be held in the device control queue for unacceptably long times. Overall disk seek times are minimized, but this happens at the expense of the service time of selected I/O requests.

b.   The SCAN Algorithm

In order to improve the situation, a second algorithm is often used, which offers better service to the outer tracks. The algorithm is called *SCAN,* because it causes a back and forth scanning of the disk tracks.

I/O requests are ordered as they arrive so as to minimize seek times, as in the SSTF system, but the ordering process takes into account the current scanning direction of the disk head. In other words, all pending requests are processed by increasing or decreasing order of track number. While they are processed in increasing order, any new request addressed to a track that has already been scanned is put in the queue for the next decreasing scan, even if it is immediately behind the current head position. As a result, total seek time is not optimal but still very good, while edge tracks get better service times, though still not as good as middle tracks do.

c.   The C-SCAN Algorithm

The *circular-scan* (C-SCAN) algorithm offers absolutely fair service to all tracks at the expense of overall performance, which may be somewhat less than optimal. With this algorithm, the disk surface is also scanned by the disk head. However, instead of alternating direction as in the plain SCAN algorithm, scanning is cyclic, always increasing or always decreasing, with an idle edge-to-edge seek between consecutive scans.

6.2. Shared-access Device Scheduling

The topic of device scheduling would not be complete without at least a brief mention of a scheduling problem proper to large computer systems. While it is not appropriate to give a complete treatment of this very complex topic in the context of an introductory book on operating systems, one cannot ignore its existence and its impact on the operating system structure.

In many micro- and minicomputers, there are relatively few attached I/O devices, so that the usual technique is to attach each device, through its dedicated I/O processor or controller, to the main memory bus. Thus, as soon as a device control virtual processor has built the set of I/O instructions implementing a requested I/O program, the first instruction can be issued to the device.

However, in large systems, carrying sometimes hundreds of telephone lines and dozens of tape drives and disk spindles, it would be physically impossible to bring one I/O processor per device right to the rack where the central processor and memory are. There would be so many wires fanning out of the rack that it would look like a huge spider web and be very awkward to access for maintenance. On the other hand, it is impossible to stretch the main memory bus outside the rack, as this bus is not designed as a local network and operates too fast for communicating over distances beyond a few meters.

The only solution is to build multiplexed I/O processors that carry an extended, slower, and different type of bus outside the main processor rack, over longer distances. Such a bus is often called an *I/O channel* itself. Devices are then attached to the processor remotely, over the channel. In fact, there often is even a second level of remote multiplexing. The channel is attached itself to so-called device *control units,* and these in turn attach to devices, where several devices of the same type are often attached to one shared control unit.

This poses a new problem to the operating system. Now, it is not sufficient to build an I/O program before talking to a device, it is also necessary to check with a new piece of code, a program called the *I/O scheduler,* to determine if the shared channel and control units are free and can be given the I/O program to execute. This adds one step in the mechanism for starting a device. There must be one I/O scheduler program per channel to keep track of the busy/free status of all shared units between the main processor and the devices.

The I/O scheduler is inserted as a monitor or a virtual processor between the monitors/virtual processors controlling devices and the corresponding channel hardware. This implies that it receives I/O programs for the devices from the device control virtual processors on one side and interrupts for the virtual processors from the devices, over the channel, on the other side. Since all of these mechanisms must be resident, the various buffer queues that they need to pass signals back and forth must be very carefully dimensioned at system generation so there always will be enough space during normal operation. Potential bottlenecks must be identified, and synchronization mechanisms must be foreseen where necessary, so that if congestion builds up in the low levels of the I/O system, it will propagate backwards to the user processes that caused it and eventually force them to wait for lack of space in the system I/O request queues.

Even this solution is sometimes insufficient. Once an I/O channel is busy, all devices attached to it, except the one currently active, must wait. In certain cases, this cannot be tolerated. Thus, to improve accessibility to devices, they are attached to multiple I/O channels. If one channel is busy, the devices and the main processor can still hope to communicate over another path.

With such a design, the individual device control virtual processors not only must all pass through a common agent, namely the I/O scheduler, but there cannot be one I/O scheduler per I/O channel, as in the above design. There must be one for the whole system. Such an I/O scheduler implements a very complex routing function that depends on the topology of the I/O network and must, for every request received from any device control virtual processor, analyze the optimum routing and scheduling possibilities to carry as many I/O operations in parallel as possible.

Suggested Reading and Classics

On different views of device drivers:

> Richards, 1979. Drivers seen as degenerate processes in Tripos.
> Ravn, 1980. Drivers seen as monitors.

On I/O architecture:

> Organick, 1972, Chapter 8; Ossanna, 1965. I/O software architecture in Multics.
> Ritchie, 1974. Virtual I/O in Unix.
> Buzen, 1975. Hardware architecture and impact on the operating system.

On I/O scheduling:

> Coffman, 1973. Contains in-depth study of theory.
> Smith, 1981. An extensive bibliography.
> Denning, 1967
> Teorey, 1972a
> Teorey, 1972b
> Wilhelm, 1977

Part 4

MEMORY MANAGEMENT

Main Memory Management

1. Address Interpretation

In this first section on storage management, we discuss the topic of address interpretation in a *one-level memory* system. As we still know nothing about multilevel storage management, the one-level (main) memory considered in this section is assumed to be always big enough to contain all the desired information.

Address interpretation deals with the translation of the addresses used by object programs (*logical addresses*) into addresses understood by the hardware (*physical addresses*) to denote locations of memory. Logical addresses are those left in an object program by the compiler or assembler at translation time, while physical addresses are those that the main memory hardware of the system can interpret. Similarly, the logical address space is the conceptual address space into which a language translator maps the object program it generates, while the physical address space is the actual address space into which the object program will execute. Although these two types of address spaces may be identical in primitive systems, more often than not they are different in modern systems. In such a case, a set of mechanisms known as the address interpretation mechanisms are necessary to map logical addresses into physical ones.

1.1. Absolute Addressing

In very early computer systems as well as in the simple microprocessors of the past decade, logical addresses were identical to physical addresses. Compilers and assemblers were coded to generate object programs such that the references to memory that they contained were directly interpretable by the hardware of the main memory. This is called *absolute addressing* (Fig. 30).

The key disadvantage of absolute addressing is that a program, once trans-

● LOGICAL ADDRESS ≡ PHYSICAL ADDRESS

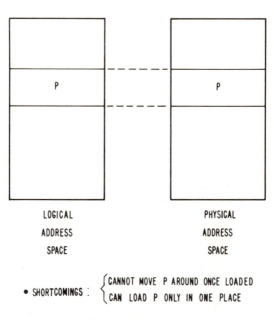

● SHORTCOMINGS : { CANNOT MOVE P AROUND ONCE LOADED
                   { CAN LOAD P ONLY IN ONE PLACE

Fig. 30. Absolute addressing.

lated, can be loaded into only one area of the physical memory, since logical addresses (internal references) that are built into it are directly bound to physical addresses. Furthermore, once loaded the program cannot be moved to another area of memory. Thus, every deleted program leaves a *hole* in memory, which can be reused only by a program designed to use the same absolute addresses. As more programs are deleted, many non-contiguous holes may appear. It is impossible to let these holes "bubble" to either end of memory since programs remaining in memory cannot be moved.

1.2.   Static Relocation

A better address interpretation technique is called *static relocation*. When static relocation is used, language translators generate *relocatable code* instead of *absolute code*. Relocatable code is generated by assuming that every object program executes in a logical address space starting at address 0. Every logical address in the object code is either flagged by a special bit or recorded in a relocation table appended to the object code. The relocatable object code can be punched out or stored in peripheral storage. Every time a user needs it, he can invoke a relocating loader. This program will allocate space for the relocatable code in memory, load that code into the space and search all flagged logical addresses. Every such address is then translated into a physical address by adding to it the offset of the base of the program (Fig. 31). The loader finally transfers control to the program.

With static relocation, a program can be translated once and thereafter relocated and loaded in any area of the memory. However, static relocation, i.e., the search for all flagged logical addresses, is still expensive and cumbersome. Furthermore, the mobility of relocated code in memory is still null once the program is loaded.

1.3.   Dynamic Relocation

To remedy this problem, the concept of *dynamic relocation* has been proposed. This concept has been extensively used in the IBM 360 OS/MFT and OS/MVT operating systems. It was also used in the CDC 6000 SCOPE operating system and in the Univac 1108.

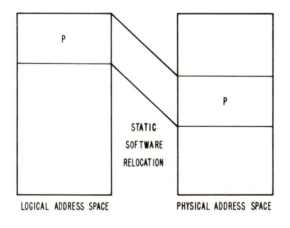

Fig. 31.   Static relocation.

The idea is to have relocation done automatically in hardware. As part of the state description of each user process, there is one descriptor register, called the *base-and-bound* or *base-and-limit* descriptor, which defines the physical addresses of the base and the bound of the area addressable by that user process. When a user process receives a processor to run on, the value of the user base-and-bound descriptor is loaded into a privileged processor register, the base-and-bound register (BBR). In correlation with this hardware feature, compilers generate relocatable code, as explained in the previous paragraph. During execution of a user program, all logical addresses are then interpreted relative to the base and within the bound (as a protection measure) of the address space of the user (Fig. 32).

Thus, it is no longer necessary to relocate code statically by using a relocating loader. Instead, a plain *absolute loader* may be used, and relocation is done dynamically and automatically by hardware. It is then possible to move programs in memory. If a user program terminates and is purged out of the memory, the remaining user programs can be *recompacted* to fill the hole: all it takes is to

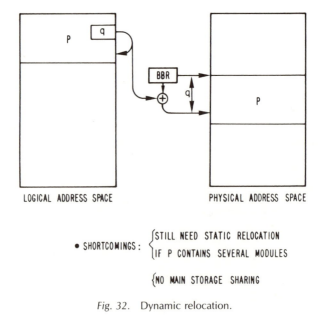

- COMPILER GENERATES RELOCATABLE CODE
  RELOCATION IS DONE DYNAMICALLY IN HARDWARE

LOGICAL ADDRESS SPACE   PHYSICAL ADDRESS SPACE

- SHORTCOMINGS: {STILL NEED STATIC RELOCATION
                IF P CONTAINS SEVERAL MODULES

  {NO MAIN STORAGE SHARING

Fig. 32. Dynamic relocation.

readjust the base-and-bound descriptor of each user affected by the move. Internal program references need not be changed.

Dynamic relocation represents an essential step forward in system architecture. It is the minimal requirement to accommodate multiple user processes in the memory at the same time. Without dynamic relocation, all programs address memory with absolute addresses. Thus, by just making up any address it wants, a user process could spy on or damage the code/data of other user processes, for lack of any protection. To avoid such accidents on machines that do not offer dynamic relocation, the only solution is to load only one process at a time in memory, which is very inefficient. Thus dynamic relocation is essential to achieve efficient multiprogramming.

While dynamic relocation offers a solution much better than anything seen so far, it still has limitations. First, the relocation by hardware works fine only as long as each user uses only one program. The moment the first program needs a second, separately compiled program (e.g., a subroutine), that second program must be relocated by software, since the relative address 0 of the user's address space is already occupied by the first program. Second, by giving users their own private address spaces, the mechanism completely isolates users and makes impossible the sharing of copies of common data or programs in memory.

1.4. Segmentation

The purpose of *segmentation* is to allow users both to share programs and data in memory, thereby saving space, and to avoid all relocation by software even when several independently compiled program modules are used. Segmentation consists of using the BBR concept at the program level instead of the user level. Of course, there cannot be one hardware BBR per program. Thus, the concept of a register is implemented strictly in software, i.e., in memory. Every program module or data area is denoted by its own base-and-bound addresses. Every such address pair defines what is called a segment. Figure 33 represents a segmented memory.

Every segment is addressed by a numerical *unique identifier,* further noted *uid.* A uid is unique over all segments and over all time. Every new segment receives a new uid. When the segment is deleted, the uid is also deleted for ever. (For a figure, 32-bit uids are necessary to allow creation of a segment every second for 100 years, or every 100 ms for 10 years.) The set of uids constitutes a universal address space that allows sharing of segments in main memory, since any uid can be used, in principle, by any user.

A corner of main memory is set aside that, for every existing segment, gives the base-and-bound values corresponding to its uid. This corner of main memory is organized as a hash table for uids. We will call it the *System Segment Table* (SST).

• PUSH BBR CONCEPT INTO MEMORY

USE IT AT MODULE LEVEL ⟶ ONE UID PER SEGMENT

PHYSICAL MEMORY

• SEGMENTATION AVOIDS RELOCATION

Fig. 33.　Segmentation.

Object code references memory by segment uid and word offset. In order to access main memory at some address given by an object program, the hardware first looks up the uid in the SST and then adds the offset to the base value found in the SST.

This means accessing memory twice for every effective memory reference. To speed up this double reference to memory, a small but fast associative memory, further referred to here as the *Segment Associative Memory* (SAM), is used as a cache memory to hold the SST entries for segments currently in use. On every memory reference, the SAM is searched to see whether the desired uid is in it. If the uid is not found, it is fetched in the SST and replaces in the SAM the uid of a segment no longer in use. Chapter VI will make it clear that cache memory is just one example of a multilevel memory. For more details on the hardware operation of caches, the reader is referred to (Conti, 1969).

The SAM plays the role of the BBRs in the previous scheme. Instead of being loaded and unloaded by explicit programming, the SAM is loaded implicitly by the hardware or by a microprogram, which keeps track of the usage of every SST entry and keeps the most heavily used ones in the SAM.

In conclusion, a segmented memory appears to the users as a collection of segments, each of which constitutes in effect one linearly addressable memory (Fig. 34). Every separately compiled program or data module resides in its own segment, avoiding the need for software relocation. The segmented memory is implemented with one large linearly addressed memory and one small associative memory. The management of the SST is the role of the segment management mechanism. Just as the processor management mechanism can be viewed as a software extension to hardware processors, so the segment management mechanism can be viewed as a software extension to the plain main memory.

In addition to all the above advantages, segmentation, just like dynamic relocation, allows an easy recompaction of memory: in order to coalesce holes left by deleted segments, one may just move segments as desired and update the SST entry for any moved segment.

Notice that the above descriptions of the management and the use of the SST and the SAM are provided only to give a conceptual idea of the operation of a segmented memory. More explanations are not necessary for now. However,

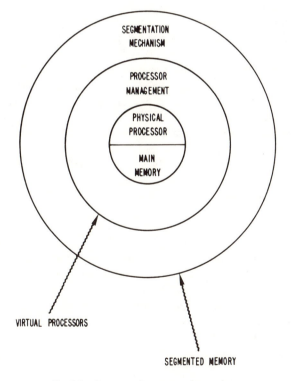

Fig. 34. Segmented memory abstraction.

more details about theoretical foundations and feasible realizations of these mechanisms are provided later. An existing system that comes very close to realizing our conceptual model of segmentation is Multics (Bensoussan *et al.*, 1972). Many systems support a somewhat different model of segmentation, where segments are not addressed by uid but by reusable numbers of which there is only a limited supply. Such is the case of IBM's 370 systems and Burroughs's 5500, 6500, and 7600 machines, for instance. The significance of having a limited supply of segments will be discussed in Chapter VII and is unimportant for now.

2.   Space Allocation

2.1.   Contiguous Allocation

We have studied four different ways to interpret addresses. From now on and throughout our study of the other mechanisms of operating systems, we will assume the most sophisticated addressing mechanism, i.e., segmentation, unless explicitly stated otherwise.

We now turn our attention to the study of a first technique for allocating memory space to user programs: *contiguous allocation* (Fig. 35). The technique can be used in systems offering a segmented main memory, such as the Burroughs 5500 or 6500 machines. It is also applicable to systems with absolute or dynamically relocated addresses, such as Unix. Contiguous allocation can also be used for disk storage allocation. We discuss it here in the context of a segmented memory.

Space management with contiguous segments is conceptually simple but practically difficult and time-consuming to implement. Conceptual simplicity results from the fact that space for each newly created segment is allocated, as the name indicates, in one contiguous area of memory. While simple, this technique presents some interesting challenges to the software designer.

a.   Recompaction

One problem is that of *recompaction*. When users delete segments, they foster holes in the memory. As much as possible these holes are reused to create new segments. However, more often than not, new segments do not have exactly the same size as deleted segments. The creation of a new segment in a hole generates a smaller hole. Thus, as time elapses, the average size of holes decreases. After many segment creations and deletions, many small holes may appear in the memory, the sum of which is sufficient to hold new segments, but none of which is large enough to be useful. This is called *external fragmentation*.

To remedy this situation, the system must eventually do recompaction, i.e., move remaining segments towards either end of the memory to let all holes

- CONCEPTUAL SIMPLICITY

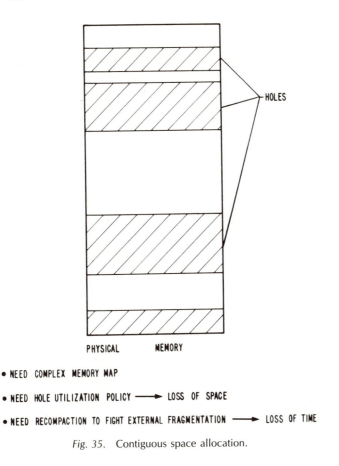

Fig. 35. Contiguous space allocation.

- NEED COMPLEX MEMORY MAP
- NEED HOLE UTILIZATION POLICY ⟶ LOSS OF SPACE
- NEED RECOMPACTION TO FIGHT EXTERNAL FRAGMENTATION ⟶ LOSS OF TIME

"bubble" to the other end and coalesce into one big hole. Recompaction is a complex and expensive operation. Indeed, during recompaction, no user can execute, as the SST may be temporarily inconsistent and the processor is busy moving segments around. Moreover, due to the continuous creation and deletion of segments, one cannot avoid the existence of holes that cannot be reused until the next recompaction. Thus, on the average, over the operational lifetime of the system, a fraction of memory is wasted in holes.

b. Hole Utilization Policy

In order to minimize the need for recompaction, one should reuse holes due to deleted segments as much as possible to create new segments. However, this poses several problems. The first problem is the search of the memory for a suitable-size hole. Assume that a memory map is maintained simply as a linked list of holes and segments, each pointing to its two immediate neighbors.

One technique for searching for a suitable-size hole to create a new segment is called *FIRST-FIT*. It is used, for instance, in Unix. The memory map is searched sequentially from either end for the first hole large enough to hold the new segment to be created. Another technique, called *BEST-FIT*, assumes that the memory is searched completely for the smallest hole large enough to hold the new segment. Yet another technique, called *NEXT-FIT*, assumes that memory is searched sequentially, as in FIRST-FIT, but the search picks up every time where it left off the previous time.

Of these techniques, FIRST-FIT and NEXT-FIT make the search for a suitable hole shorter than BEST-FIT, which must scan the entire memory map at least once before making its decision. On the other hand, BEST-FIT, by creating minimal-size holes, minimizes fragmentation and therefore minimizes the need for recompaction. It has been shown, however (Bays, 1977), that overall performance of FIRST-FIT may beat that of BEST-FIT in many cases, because FIRST-FIT, by always searching memory from one end, tends to preserve larger holes at the other end.

c.   Memory Map Organization

The above hole reuse policies assumed that the memory map was a simple linked list. By resorting to more sophisticated memory map structures, one can improve hole search time. Since nothing is free, this improvement in search time must of course be paid for in increased memory map maintenance time. The memory may be divided into any number of segments and holes of all sizes. Keeping track of such information in a readily usable form is more expensive.

d.   Hole Coalescence

To further minimize the need for recompaction, one can coalesce holes together when two adjacent segments are deleted. So-called *buddy systems* combine the use of a sophisticated memory map to minimize hole search time with the coalescence of holes to minimize the frequency of recompaction.

A typical buddy system is as follows (Fig. 36). The memory contains a number of words equal to a power of 2. Space is allocated to a segment by recursively dividing the smallest hole large enough to hold the segment into two holes of half its size, until a hole is reached that could not hold the segment if further divided. That entire hole is allocated to the segment. The waste of space resulting at the end of most segments is called *internal fragmentation*.

Given this allocation technique, the length in words of all holes and allocated segments can be expressed as a power of 2. The first word of each hole or

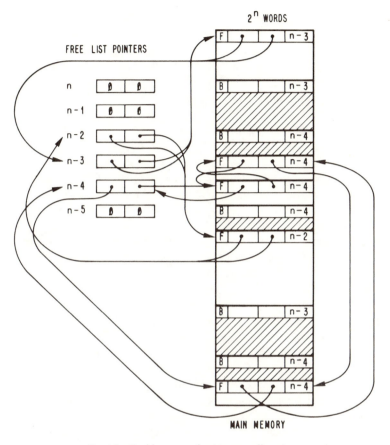

Fig. 36.   Buddy system for memory allocation.

segment specifies whether it belongs to a hole or a segment and contains the
binary logarithm of its present length. For each power of 2, the system maintains
a linked list of holes of corresponding length, thereby making the search for a
suitable hole shorter. Furthermore, given any newly generated hole, it is possible
to determine the base address of its "buddy", i.e., the adjacent space of equal
size, that must have resulted from an earlier halving operation. If this buddy is a
hole of equal size, the two buddies are merged again to form a larger hole.

2.2.   Block Allocation of Space

Block allocation of space is somewhat more complex than contiguous allocation
from a conceptual point of view and requires more expensive addressing hard-

ware, but it avoids the problem of external fragmentation and the loss of time due to recompaction. It also simplifies the maintenance and look-up of the memory map.

Although block allocation can exist without the concept of segmentation, such as in the XDS-940 and Tenex (PDP-10) systems, it is presented here in the context of a system supporting segmentation, such as found in Honeywell's Multics or IBM's S/370 systems.

Both real memory and segments are divided into blocks of a fixed number of words *K*. Segments are viewed as collections of fixed-size blocks called *pages*. The last page of a segment may be partly empty if the segment does not require an integer number of blocks. This is again called internal fragmentation. Memory space is allocated in entire blocks. The pages of a segment need not be mapped into contiguous blocks of the memory. The problems associated with contiguous allocation can be eliminated.

The *memory map* is simply an array of bits, where each bit corresponds to one block of memory and indicates whether or not that block is free. Shrinking or deleting a segment only requires marking a few blocks as free. Growing or creating a segment only requires allocating a few free blocks from the memory map. Recompaction is totally unnecessary, as should be obvious.

Of course, the problems of contiguous allocation have been avoided at a certain cost. There are now implementation problems: How can one address a segment divided into pages that may be scattered through memory? Furthermore, there is no longer wasted time due to recompaction, but more space is consumed by the implementation, as explained below.

Associated with every segment is a data structure called a *Page Table* (PT) which indicates where all the pages of a segment are. The PTs of all the segments in the system are collected in a table called the *System Page Table* (SPT). Every SST entry, rather than giving the address of the base of the segment, as it would with contiguous allocation, gives the base of the PT of the segment, as represented in Fig. 37.

In order to interpret a reference to (uid *S,* offset *W*), the hardware proceeds as follows. It first fetches the SST entry corresponding to S to retrieve the base of the PT. It then computes the number *P* of the page being referenced, which is equal to the integer part of *W*/*K*. In practice, *K* is an integer power *k* of 2, so that *P* is obtained by dropping the last *k* bits of *W*. The hardware then uses *P* to retrieve from the PT a pointer to the base *B* of the desired page, and finally picks the desired word by computing its absolute address *A*:

$$A = B + W(\bmod K)$$
$$= B + W - PK$$
$$= B + Q$$

• SIMPLE MEMORY MAP

• PAGING AVOIDS RECOMPACTION

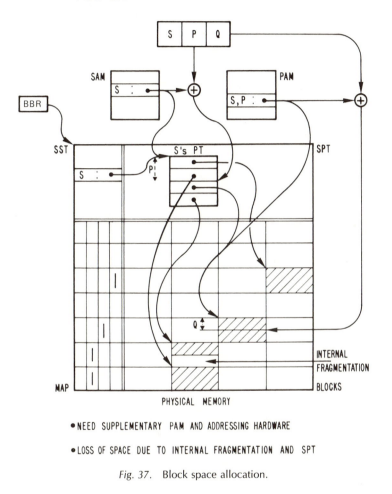

Fig. 37.   Block space allocation.

• NEED SUPPLEMENTARY PAM AND ADDRESSING HARDWARE

• LOSS OF SPACE DUE TO INTERNAL FRAGMENTATION AND SPT

where Q is the integer represented by the last k bits of W. In all, one reference to the segmented, paged memory requires three references to the real memory: one to the SST, one to the PT, and one to the desired word. Of course, we have said that a fast SAM can be used to hold SST entries. Similarly, a fast *Page Associative Memory* (PAM) can be used to hold currently used PT entries.

The implementation of block allocation buys a gain in time at the expense of a cost in extra hardware and space. The effective size of main memory is reduced by the space consumed by the SPT.

Suggested Reading and Classics

Two classics that introduced the concept of segmentation:

Dennis, 1965
Dennis, 1966

Two classics on the Multics memory system, including segment addressing:

Daley and Dennis, 1968
Bensoussan *et al.*, 1972

On memory allocation algorithms:

Knowlton, 1965.   The original paper on buddy systems.
Bays, 1977.   On NEXT-, FIRST-, and BEST-FIT.
Knuth, 1969.   Volume 1 contains an extensive survey of memory allocation policies.

On memory fragmentation:

Shore, 1975.   External fragmentation with FIRST- and BEST-FIT.
Randell, 1969.   Classic on both types of fragmentation.

Chapter VI

Multilevel Memory Management

Having covered the subject of addressing and allocation of space in a one-level memory system, we turn to the study of *multilevel memory management*. The objective of a multilevel memory management system is to organize the allocation of space at all levels of the memory system and to manage the transfer of information between these levels as appropriate.

A typical system may offer a limited amount of central memory with a vast amount of peripheral storage. Throughout the rest of this chapter, we will be talking about such a two-level storage system (e.g., main memory and disk). This is sufficient to explain all multilevel memory management principles.

Note however, that a large time-sharing system may have five or more storage levels: a very fast (<10 ns) and very small (<100 KB) bipolar cache memory; a fast (100 ns), small (1–10 MB) main memory; a slow (2–4μs) and large (>10 MB) extended memory; a comparatively very slow (50 ms access time) but huge (100–1000 MB) on-line disk capacity; and an essentially unbounded number of removable disk packs and tapes.

1. Explicit Swapping of Contiguous Segments

We first consider the problem of multilevel storage management in a system supporting contiguous allocation of space in both primary and secondary storage. Storage management with contiguous storage allocation means copying segments in and out of primary memory as they are needed. This is called *swapping* or rolling segments. Segments usually are swapped in and out explicitly. Explicit swapping means that when the process of a user is about to start executing a program, it must direct the system to load all the segments composing the program prior to execution. In some systems, notably some Burroughs operating systems, swapping can be done on demand, meaning that segments are swapped in and out automatically by the system when it detects that they are needed. The mechanism for detecting that a segment is needed is analogous to the demand mechanism used for paging, described in Section 2.

Swapping is the oldest and the simplest multilevel storage management scheme. It is still used today in many personal computers of the first generation that support only absolute addressing. It has been used and is still used extensively in most systems with a BBR architecture.

Contiguous allocation with swapping performs acceptably well for batch systems but is not recommended for time-sharing systems. In a batch system, a program segment is swapped in together with all its associated data segments when the associated process is ready for execution. Then the program remains in memory until it completes or until it must be swapped out because it has used up some quantum of processor time and the process is unloaded. This may represent minutes or even hours in a batch system.

By contrast, in a time-sharing system, a procedure segment is swapped in when a user types in a command invoking it. Then, the procedure executes not for minutes but for seconds or often a fraction of a second before it has to wait for the user to interact with it. During such waiting, the procedure must be swapped out to make room for the segments of other users. This movement to primary memory and back out corresponds to the allocation and subsequent deletion of a segment in primary memory. A high rate of allocation and deletion of segments in time-sharing systems implies a fast rate of creation of holes in primary memory and thus a frequent need to recompact, which would be expensive. In summary, time-sharing requires swapping entire segments in and out too often, which increases the need to recompact and makes contiguous allocation an unattractive scheme.

2.   Demand Paging of Blocked Segments

To avoid the problem of recompaction altogether, most time-sharing systems use block allocation of space at all memory levels. In addition, the movement of information between memory levels is performed on a block basis rather than on a segment basis. Finally, this movement is carried out by the system automatically. It does not require explicit actions from the user programs. This multilevel memory management technique is called *demand paging*. It is the foundation of *virtual memory*.

It was first used in the Atlas system at Manchester University (Fotheringham, 1961; Kilburn *et al.*, 1962). It was also used very early in the XDS-940 experimental system. Today it is used in most time-sharing operating systems. Some systems that were originally designed without demand paging have even been upgraded to incorporate it. Such is the case, for instance, of IBM's MVS and of Unix.

2.1. Advantages

There are several reasons why it is better to let the memory management mechanism manage storage automatically than to count on user programs to tell the system when to move what information between which memory levels.

1. Leaving memory management to user programs forces programmers to learn how the various levels of memory work and how they are best managed, which is a non-trivial task.

2. Memory management is not the objective of any user program. If programmers have to worry about it, their programs get more complex, because they must explicitly call specific operating system primitives. Also, such programs (or at least the run-time language support they depend on) are less easy to port from one system to another, since they include calls to the primitives of the specific operating system they were designed for.

3. Every time a user program or the memory configuration it runs on is modified, the program has to be reoptimized with respect to memory management. This may be costly, particularly if the person who modifies the program is not the original programmer and does not know how the program managed memory originally.

4. While a good programmer can probably optimize memory management for his program better than any operating system can, the global result of all programmers optimizing their own programs in a large shared system may be worse than what an operating system can do because of the diversity and potential conflicts among the optimization methods used by individual users.

5. Even if the operating system performs memory management for the users, this does not prevent programmers from optimizing their programs if they insist, by organizing them in ways that suit the memory management algorithms implemented by the operating system.

6. Finally, in a typical time-sharing system, no matter how memory management is implemented, most information ends up having to move into memory when a user interaction requires it and migrate back to secondary storage when the interaction is over. Neither an operating system nor users can improve memory management much in view of such a clear-cut scheme. Thus, one is well advised to relieve the users from the burden of managing memory and let the operating system do it.

2.2. Implementation

The following description of a demand paging mechanism is given in the context of a system offering a segmented memory, such as Multics (Bensoussan *et al.*, 1972) or VM/SP. However, demand paging in no way requires segmentation.

Many systems [e.g., Atlas (Kilburn *et al.*, 1962), Tenex (Bobrow *et al.*, 1972), and DEC's TOPS-10] support paging with a BBR architecture instead of segmentation.

Demand paging assumes that space is allocated in blocks both in primary memory and secondary storage. The migration of information between the memory levels is achieved by copying individual pages of segments between primary memory and secondary storage. A detailed description of a possible paging implementation follows.

As explained in Chapter V, every word of the PT of a segment contains the address of the corresponding page. With demand paging, this address can be a main memory address or a disk address. A one-bit flag differentiates the two (see Fig. 38). If a user references a page that is not in primary memory, the one-bit flag triggers a processor exception called a *page fault*. The virtual processor that caused the fault is interrupted. The processor management mechanism saves the state of the interrupted virtual processor, as it always does in case of interruptions. In addition, it puts the faulting processor in the waiting state, since it cannot proceed until the missing page is imported from secondary storage.*

Let us now consider what happens after the page fault. As in the case of device control, two possible and dual implementations are possible. One can envision a system encouraging a monitor-based implementation or a system encouraging a virtual-processor-based implementation. Let us consider the latter one. The former is left to the reader as an exercise.

Once the faulting processor is interrupted, a system virtual processor, implementing the memory management mechanism and thus responsible for paging, is immediately waked up by the processor management mechanism. Upon waking up the paging processor, the processor management mechanism passes to it in some register an argument identifying the faulting processor. The paging processor then receives control, analyzes the state of the faulting processor to determine which page is missing, logs the identity of the faulting processor together with the identity of the page it is waiting for in some internal table, finds a free block of main memory in the memory map, and sends an I/O request to the disk control virtual processor to fetch the missing page from secondary storage.

The paging processor may decide to eject a few pages from memory if free main memory blocks are about to be exhausted, which may require starting some additional output operation. The paging processor also sets a lock bit in the PT entry of the missing page, as a memo to itself that the page is about to be

---

*Notice that a page fault, unlike a classic interrupt, occurs in the middle of an instruction and not between instructions. Thus, machines implementing demand paging must maintain in the state of each virtual processor enough information to be able to determine what caused the page fault (e.g., the instruction fetch itself, the first operand, the second, the result, which byte), and they must allow restarting virtual processors in the middle of the instruction after the page fault is resolved.

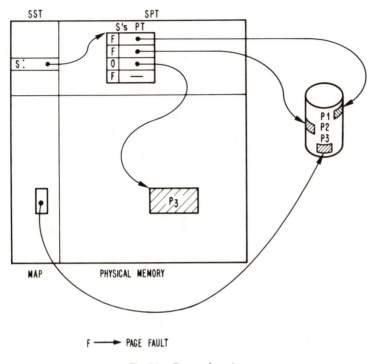

F ────► PAGE FAULT

Fig. 38. Demand paging.

imported. Indeed, while the disk I/O operation is taking place, some other virtual processor might also step on the same page and cause another page fault. This second fault on the same page should not cause the paging mechanism to trigger a second I/O operation, however.

Then the paging processor goes back to sleep, waiting for the next event of interest to it: another page fault, or a message from the disk control processor signalling completion of some page fetch or page eject requested earlier. The physical processor is given to a virtual processor (other than the one waiting for its page to arrive) that is ready to run.

From the above discussion, one can see that a page fault in effect is a hardware event carrying two meanings:

1.   It informs the processor management mechanism to immediately stop the faulting processor, as if it had been interrupted.

2.   In addition, it is interpreted by the processor management mechanism as a peculiar sequence of WAKEUP(paging processor) followed by BLOCK, executed by the faulting processor. As a result, the paging processor is set in the ready state and the faulting processor is set in the blocked state. Aside from being

triggered in hardware, this peculiar brand of signalling primitive carries two
elements of semantics not included in plain WAKEUP/BLOCK primitives:

a. The primitive implies immediate processor switching from the sender
    to the receiver.
b. The operation is associated with a message transfer, as in our earlier
    example of the producer–consumer problem. However, this message is
    not stored in an explicit buffer as in the example. Instead, it is passed
    directly in an agreed upon register, which is feasible in this particular
    case because the message is handled in real time (no queuing) and is
    known to be very short: it may be just an index into the VPT identifying
    the faulting processor.

At some later time, when the missing page has been read into main memory,
an I/O interrupt occurs. Whatever virtual processor is running currently is put in
the ready state. The processor management mechanism wakes up the disk control
processor, which in turn wakes up the paging processor. Upon analysis of the
event and consultation of its internal tables, the paging processor updates the PT
entry corresponding to the missing page to reflect arrival of the page in main
memory, retrieves the identity of the faulting processor (there can be more than
one) that was waiting for this page, sends it a WAKEUP signal, and returns itself
to sleep. The faulting processor is then ready again and will resume execution at
some later time when a physical processor becomes available.

Paging is much more effective than swapping for time-sharing systems not
only because it avoids the recompaction problem. It also allows keeping more
useful information in primary memory at the same time, and it minimizes the
amount of disk to memory traffic.

With contiguous allocation, entire segments must reside in primary memory.
The sum of the segments used by 2 or 3 user processes may be enough to fill the
whole primary memory. Thus, only 2 or 3 user processes at a time may be loaded
and ready to execute, the rest having to wait, for lack of space. However, on a
typical time-sharing interaction, a user process needs only a few pages of the
segments it uses. By holding only these pages rather than entire segments in
primary memory, it may be possible to accommodate the most needed information of 10–20 users in primary memory, instead of only 2 or 3. Also, moving
pages rather than entire segments greatly limits disk traffic.

3.   Virtual Memory

3.1.   Principles

The main issue with demand paging is that during normal operation, primary
memory is filled with pages. To bring a new page in, it is often necessary to

remove some other page. The question is, What other page should be removed? Or to put the problem more fundamentally, If the system is supposed to manage storage for the users automatically, can it predict what information is needed in primary memory and tell what information may migrate back to secondary storage? This is a fundamental question. If it could not be answered and the system would eject from primary memory any random page, there would be a fair probability that that precise page would be needed again soon thereafter and would have to be refetched. If so, the overall access-time of the multilevel storage system would be closer to the access-time of secondary storage than to that of primary memory, on the average.

Fortunately, the system can predict to a certain extent and with a varying accuracy what pages should be kept in memory and what pages can be ejected. The reason behind this resides in the so-called *principle of locality*, which is the basic foundation for the whole concept of virtual memory. Virtual memory, which consists of paging information on demand between a small amount of fast memory and a vast amount of slow memory, is a valuable idea because of the principle of locality: *At any instant during the execution of a program or group of programs, all the references to memory that are possible are not equally probable.*

In other words, given a program at some stage of its execution, one can more or less predict what it will reference next. This principle is illustrated in practice by many facts. A program executing instruction I and operating on data stored at address D is very likely to next execute instruction $I + 1$ (the following one) or $I + K$ (jump K instructions ahead, with K small), or $I - K$ (loop), and to operate on data in the vicinity of D (because the working data of a program are usually aggregated, e.g., arrays and structures, and collected in a local working area, e.g., push-down stack). Compared to the total number of instructions executed and data processed, the probability of jumping to a faraway subroutine and referencing unrelated data is relatively low.

This locality of program reference is the fundamental principle that is exploited to implement virtual memory. The principle of locality may be rephrased informally by stating that, in general, a very small fraction of the information kept in a system is the target of most of the references. Therefore, the system wins *if* it can arrange to store the heavily referenced fraction of the information in an expensive but relatively small, fast memory and the remaining bulk of the data in a less expensive, but large, and slow memory.

Indeed, assuming that the system finds what it needs in primary memory 99% of the time and that primary memory represents 1% of the total memory, the average overall access time of the combined memory system will be

$$t = 0.99 \, t_1 + 0.01 \, t_2$$

which for typical integrated memory ($t_1 = 100$ ns) and disk ($t_2 = 50$ ms) would be about 500 μs, or two orders of magnitude better than the slow memory composing 99% of the system. In addition, the price per bit paid for such performance is

$$c = 0.01 \; c_1 + 0.99 \; c_2$$

or only about one order of magnitude more than the disk cost per bit, typically. The access time can be plotted versus the cost per bit as in Fig. 39.

The whole problem, of course, consists of keeping in primary memory at all times the most needed information, i.e., properly guessing what pages are less needed and can be removed from main memory when space is needed. This is not a trivial task because the set of pages that are most needed varies with time, as users come and go and execute various programs. How the system can make correct predictions is the topic of the remainder of this chapter.

Before we start discussing various ways to make the guess, we need a few useful definitions that will thereafter help us describe and compare the algorithms we encounter.

The *reference string* of a computation (a user process or a set of user processes) is a string giving a list of the pages that that computation references in the order in which it references them.

The *resident set* of a computation is the set of all pages that are kept for that computation in the primary memory. Its size will be noted W.

The *swapping curve* of a given memory management algorithm operating on a given reference string is the expression of the page fault rate as a function of the size W of the resident set of the corresponding computation (Fig. 40).

The *success function* or *life function* of a page removal algorithm on a given reference string gives the ratio of references satisfied by primary memory to all

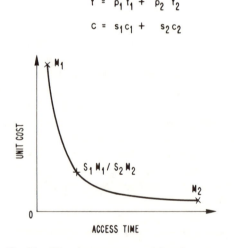

Fig. 39.   Virtual memory cost and performance.

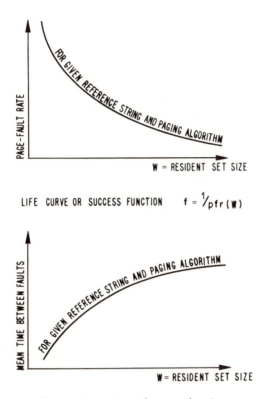

SWAPPING CURVE OR PAGE-FAULT FUNCTION

LIFE CURVE OR SUCCESS FUNCTION $f = \frac{1}{pfr(W)}$

Fig. 40. Swapping and success functions.

references as a function of the size of the resident set W of the computation. Thus, it is the inverse of the swapping function. Saltzer has pointed out that the success function is homomorphic to the mirror image of the cost/access-time function of a memory system for the same page removal algorithm and the same reference string. Indeed, the resident set size axis of the former function can be mapped onto the cost axis of the latter function, while the page lifetime axis of the former can be mapped onto the access-time axis of the latter.

With these concepts in mind, we can attack the study of *paging algorithms*, i.e., algorithms for selecting a page to be removed from primary memory when a block is needed to move in another page.

3.2. Fixed Space Algorithms

Paging algorithms can be divided into two categories. The first category, *fixed space algorithms*, will be studied first. Algorithms in this category owe their name to the fact that they manage a paging area in primary memory whose size is fixed in the course of time.

a. The FIFO Algorithm

A first algorithm for trying to predict which page will not be used in the near future and may be removed from primary memory is the *first-in-first-out* (FIFO) algorithm. According to this algorithm, the one page which is always selected for removal next (first out) is the page that was the first in, i.e., the page that has been in primary memory for the longest time. In other words, the algorithm treats primary memory as a big pipeline or queue of pages, pushing pages in at one end and dropping them down at the other.

This algorithm stems from the assumption that as time passes, the execution site and the data area used by a computation evolve along a "linear" reference string, i.e., a reference string where the page used at time t is never reused within a reference substring of length comparable to the resident set size. While this algorithm may seem attractive and natural, it presents one defect exhibited in the following example, where $M1$ and $M2$ denote primary and secondary memory.

Assume that $M2$ contains five pages a, b, c, d, and e, and the reference string of a computation is

$$R = \langle d, c, b, a, d, c, e, d, c, b, a, e \rangle$$

Figure 41 shows the results of simulating the behavior of the FIFO algorithm on reference string R with primary memories of sizes 3 and 4, respectively. We notice that increasing the size of $M1$ has decreased the value of the success function, a very undesirable effect.

What has happened? The first substring, $\langle d, c, b, a \rangle$, loads the queue. The second substring, $\langle d, c \rangle$, has no effect in the case $W = 4$ because d and c are already in $W1$. However, in the case $W = 3$, the second substring causes the queue to be reordered with c and d at its end rather than at its beginning. Then, the third substring, $\langle e \rangle$, brings e into $M1$ in both cases. Now, the fourth substring, a repetition of $\langle d, c, b, a \rangle$, causes a complete cycle in $W = 4$ because it occurs in the order of the queue and systematically kicks out the page that is needed next. Yet, for $W = 3$, this is not the case because the earlier $\langle d, c \rangle$ substring reordered the queue. As a result, when the last substring, $\langle e \rangle$, occurs, it does not cause anything for $W = 3$ but generates a page fault for $W = 4$.

The FIFO pattern of the algorithm and the non-FIFO pattern of R have conspired so that, just before the last reference to e, $W = 3$ contains something (e) that $W = 4$ does not contain. In clear language, the *FIFO anomaly* results from the fact that the FIFO predictor assumes linear reference strings, while the reference string of the example has a loop.

•PAGES ORDERED BY ARRIVAL TIME

•PRIMARY MEMORY = PIPE − LINE

ANOMALY :

```
|W| = 3 : R =    d   c   b   a   d   c   e   d   c   b   a   e

         Q =     d   c   b   a   d   c   e   e   e   b   a   a

                 d   c   b   a   d   c   c   c   e   b   b

                 d   c   b   a   d   d   d   c   e   e

   9  pf :       *   *   *   *   *   *   *           *   *
                                 └───────┘
                                  REORDER

|W| = 4   R =    d   c   b   a   d   c   e   d   c   b   a   e

          Q =    d   c   b   a   a   a   e   d   c   b   a   e

                 d   c   b   b   b   a   e   d   c   b   a

                 d   c   c   c   b   a   e   d   c   b

                 d   d   d   c   b   a   e   d   c

  10  pf :       *   *   *   *           *   *   *   *   *   *
                                         └───────┘
        SUCCESS FUNCTION                 AVALANCHE
```

Fig. 41.   The FIFO algorithm anomaly.

b.   Stack Algorithms

A general class of algorithms, called *stack algorithms,* comprises all algorithms that yield monotonically non-decreasing success functions by precisely avoiding the pitfall of the above example.

A stack algorithm (Fig. 42) is such that the content of a memory of size W is always a subset of what the content of a memory larger than W would be with the same algorithm. Thus, if one constructs by simulation the set of pages that would

— PROPERTIES: • MONOTONICALLY NON – DECREASING SUCCESS FUNCTION

• CONTENT $(|W| = i) \subset$ CONTENT $(|W|=j)$ $(i < j)$

• TOTAL ORDERING OF PAGES INDEPENDENT OF MEMORY SIZE

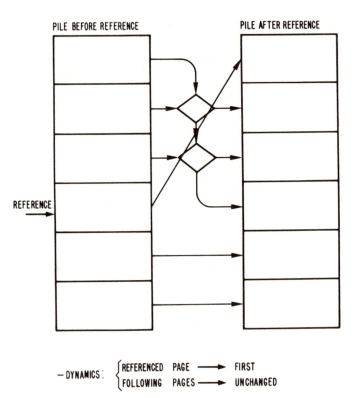

— DYNAMICS: $\begin{cases} \text{REFERENCED PAGE} \longrightarrow \text{FIRST} \\ \text{FOLLOWING PAGES} \longrightarrow \text{UNCHANGED} \end{cases}$

Fig. 42. The stack algorithm family. (Adapted from "Topics in the Engineering of Computer Systems," by J. H. Saltzer. Used with permission.)

be in $M1$ at a given time and for a given reference string, for all possible sizes of $M1$, one notices that the set corresponding to a size $W = i$ is a subset of the set corresponding to a size $W = i + 1$, for all i. Each set contains all the pages of the smaller set plus one new page. Hence, at every step along a given reference string, there exists a total ordering of pages that is independent of the size of $M1$ and shows what the content of $M1$ would be for each size. This total ordering represents a stack of pages, which justifies the name of the class of algorithms.

In contrast with the FIFO algorithm, the list of pages in $M1$ is not a queue at the end of which recently imported pages are appended. Instead, the list of a stack algorithm represents a total ordering that may change drastically between two references, as represented in Fig. 42.

When a page p is referenced, it must become the top of the list to guarantee the stack property. Indeed, since the stack is the same for any size of $M1$, it applies to $W = 1$ in particular. Since page p is obviously in $M1$ after the reference to it, it must be the top of the stack, which represents the content for $W = 1$. Pages that used to be above p are subject to a reordering dictated by the decision boxes represented in the figure. What those decision boxes do depends on the particular algorithm in the stack family. If p was not in $M1$, it is read in and the page that drops out of the lowest decision box is moved out. If p was already in $M1$, the list is simply reordered but no paging is necessary. Thus, the pages below p are never reordered, because reordering them would imply that artificial and useless page fetches would have to occur for larger memory sizes!

c.   The OPT Algorithm

A first stack algorithm is the *OPTimal or MINimal* paging algorithm. Every OPT decision box selects the page to be used sooner for insertion in the list and drops the other page into the next decision box. Of course the OPT algorithm is totally impractical, as it would require that the system look into the future to decide which page will be needed sooner and eject the page that will be needed later. However, it is useful to consider the OPT algorithm because it represents a theoretical upper bound on the success of any paging algorithm. By comparing the success function of a real algorithm on a reference string to the success function of a simulation of OPT on the same string, one can see how good the real algorithm is.

d.   The LRU Algorithm

The simplest and most popular stack algorithm is the *least recently used* (LRU) algorithm. The LRU algorithm selects for removal the page that has been used least recently. This imposes a total ordering of pages that is independent of W. The LRU operation is drawn in Fig. 43. The LRU algorithm assumes that the page that is least likely to be needed next is the one that was used the longest time ago. Of course, this may not be the case on occasion, so the algorithm may occasionally be a bad estimator of program locality. However, if it makes a bad decision, at least it makes it consistently for any memory size, unlike the FIFO algorithm. Thus, if computer center managers buy more primary memory, they may not observe a better performance, but they will not observe a worse performance either.

Notice that if the reference string is strictly sequential, i.e., fits the assumption of the FIFO algorithm, the performance of the LRU is identical to that of the

BEFORE   AFTER

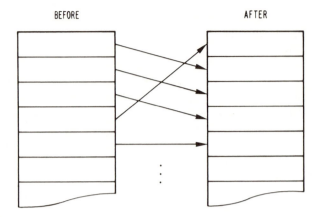

Fig. 43.   The LRU algorithm. (Adapted from "Topics in the Engineering of Computer Systems," by J. H. Saltzer. Used with permission.)

FIFO, because saying FIFO is the same as saying LRU in this case. Also notice that the performance of LRU is the same as the performance of OPT on the inverse reference string, because LRU ejects that page which was used the longest time ago, while OPT ejects that page which will be used the latest in the future—which means the same thing for inverse reference strings.

3.3.   Variable Space Algorithms

As is clear from the definition of the swapping and success functions, the size of the resident set W plays a dominant role in the determination of the performance of an algorithm on a given reference string.

If we consider the set of all running programs as the computation generating the reference string, the size of the resident set for that compound string is the size of the whole area reserved for paging in the primary memory. For a given system, this size is fixed and therefore determines for a given page removal algorithm the performance which will be observed for a given mix of programs.

One may of course envision systems where the paging area itself is divided among all the running processes in a predefined fashion so that a process executes alone in its partition of the memory and never competes with others for primary memory frames. Any of the algorithms seen so far could operate in such an environment. However, they do not provide a solution to the problem of determining how big a partition should be reserved for each running process. Not all processes need the same amount of memory. If a process running a 100-KB program and a process running a 1-MB program are each given a 50-KB partition of the paging area, the latter process will very likely generate many more page faults than the former.

Thus comes the problem of deciding how to partition memory. This problem is compounded by the fact that it may be, and in general is, better to vary the size of the partitions with time to adapt it to the changing requirements of programs and program phases. This idea is at the origin of the concept of *variable space algorithms* for page replacement.

In such algorithms, rather than fixing a space window W equal to the size of the resident set of program, one fixes a virtual time window, which we can still call W, that will in one way or another impose a limit on the lifetime of a page in primary memory. A discussion of a few variable space algorithms follows.

a.   The PFF Algorithm

One algorithm that has been proposed is the *page fault frequency* (PFF) algorithm. In the PFF algorithm, the parameter W is chosen to be the desired time between two page faults. Every time a page fault occurs, the time since the last page fault caused by the same computation is compared to W. If this time is superior to W, it is an indication that the resident set of the computation under concern is too large, and that it could afford to run in a smaller partition, and all pages that have not been used since the last page fault are ejected from the main memory. If, on the other hand, the measured inter-page-fault time is inferior to the target W, the resident set of the computation is too small and should be allowed to grow at the expense of the free page pool that results from the shrinkage of the resident set of other computations.

While this algorithm is clearly easy to implement, it presents the same sort of anomaly as the FIFO algorithm seen earlier, and for the same reason: It may happen that by increasing the window W, i.e., by allowing the process to load a larger resident set, one actually observes a higher page fault rate. Indeed, by increasing W, one allows the process to load all the pages it needs to proceed without page faults for a long time. However, if the process then references only a small subset of its resident pages, when the next page fault occurs, all unused pages will be brutally ejected, although they might be needed just next. In other words, in the absence of page faults for a long time, the PFF algorithm effectively stops tracking the locality of the process with accuracy.

PFF exhibits a curious flavor of negative feedback on its own decision making: since it estimates locality at page fault time, by letting W grow one lets the page fault rate drop, intuitively, in a first stage. This degrades the accuracy of the estimator and may cause it to make bad decisions and fall back into a high paging phase in a second stage.

b.   The WS Algorithm

The right question to ask is whether the same inclusion property found in fixed space stack algorithms can be formulated for variable space algorithms. In other words, is it possible to find algorithms where an increase of the parameter W is certain not to lead to a decrease of the success function of the algorithm for any reference string.

It turns out that there are such algorithms. One of them is called the *working set* (WS) algorithm. The working set of a process is the set of pages referenced by that process within the last W seconds during which that process has been running (virtual seconds). The WS algorithm forces at all times the working set of the process to be equal to its resident set. Hence, a page fault will occur if and only if the referenced page has not been referenced for the last W seconds, otherwise the page would still be in primary memory. Thus, an increase in W will result in an inclusive increase of the working set, implying an inclusive increase of the resident set and in turn an increase in the average page life. This is the inclusion property.

The difference between the PFF algorithm and the WS algorithm is that PFF ejects from memory, at page fault time, all pages that have not been used since the last page fault, even though they might be needed next, whereas the WS algorithm ejects from memory, *as time passes,* pages that have been there for longer than the parameter W. Thus the locality tracking ability of the WS is superior and guarantees the inclusion property.

c.   The VMIN Algorithm

Just as there is an optimal though fictitious paging algorithm in the fixed space domain, there is one in the variable space domain. It is called VMIN, for variable space minimal paging. It also bases its decisions upon a look ahead into the future, but uses a fixed time window as opposed to a fixed space window.

d.   The GWS Algorithm

Both the WS algorithm and the stack algorithms appear to be restricted forms of a more general algorithm called the *generalized working set* (GWS), which assumes demand swapping of entire segments. Where the stack algorithms fix a spatial window and WS fixes a temporal window, GWS defines the window W to be the space–time product cost paid for retaining a variable size segment since it was last referenced. The algorithm continuously maintains a pool of free space by ejecting those segments with a *retention cost* higher than the chosen threshold parameter W. The algorithm of course verifies a generalized inclusion property in the space–time domain.

Before proceeding with our discussion of virtual memory, it may be worth pointing out here that the concept of locality should be taken with some care. While it is obvious that locality *drifts* slowly as programs move along their instruction stream, it is also true that all programs go through phase transitions (e.g., from compilation to execution, or from merging to sorting, etc.) during which the locality drift becomes overwhelming. It has been measured that typical programs spend no more than 5% of their time between phases, but that the page fault rate can be 100 times higher then than during phases. Thus a large number of page faults happen during phase transitions, making it impossible for any algorithm to cope. They all perform "as badly" during phase transitions.

3.4. Paging Implementations

Another word of care concerns the implementation of paging algorithms. As any alert computer science student should have realized, the housekeeping of a data structure like a LRU stack is a mildly sophisticated programming task. No system programmer in his right mind would ever dream of including a subroutine in his operating system that would run after every user memory reference to update the paging stack! All the foregoing discussion is theoretically instructive but sheds no light on possible realizations in practice.

a. CLOCK–FINUFO

Consider the case of the LRU algorithm first. On many machines, the algorithm is used not only to manage the paging of information between main and peripheral memory, but also to manage cache memories and segment and page associative memories. Indeed, the migration of pages between cache and main memory and the migration of table entries between associative and main memory represent cases of two-level memory management systems, just like virtual memory as we have discussed it so far.

In these cases, LRU can be implemented accurately in hardware because the cost of the hardware for the few entries to be managed in such high-speed, small-size memories is acceptable. Different implementations realizing LRU more or less exactly are conceivable (Conti, 1969). However, when LRU is used for the actual paging between primary and secondary memory, its implementation requires a substantial departure from the theoretical LRU estimator.

In one implementation, known as CLOCK or FINUFO (first in, not used, first out), hardware is designed so that bits of primary memory (located in a separate table or in every entry of the SPT, for example) are set aside to keep track of page usage (Fig. 44). Every time a page is touched, i.e., when its SPT entry is loaded in the PAM, the hardware turns on the *usage bit* corresponding to that page. This bit serves as a crude estimator of page usage.

Least recentness of usage is also crudely estimated in the following way. First, it is not estimated after each memory reference. It is estimated by software only after a page fault, when software is involved anyway to bring in the missing page. Second, the estimation is very approximate, in that any page that has its

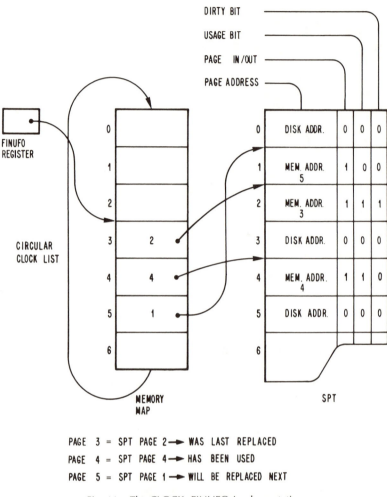

PAGE 3 = SPT PAGE 2 → WAS LAST REPLACED
PAGE 4 = SPT PAGE 4 → HAS BEEN USED
PAGE 5 = SPT PAGE 1 → WILL BE REPLACED NEXT

Fig. 44.   The CLOCK–FINUFO implementation.

usage bit off at the time the software is invoked is as likely a candidate for ejection as any other. It could have been unused for seconds or minutes; the usage bit does not give this information.

In practice, all usage bits are organized in a circular list. Every time the software looks for a page to throw out, it selects the first page it finds in the list, with the usage bit off, starting the search where it left off on the previous page fault. The circular list can be materialized, for instance, by the entries of the main memory map. These entries, described so far as containing a single busy/free bit, can be expanded to a word containing an index into the SPT. When a memory block is busy, the corresponding memory map entry denotes the SPT entry of the page currently occupying the memory block. By circularly scanning the memory map, the CLOCK algorithm can thus reach the usage bits kept in the SPT.

However rough this type of estimation may seem, there is overwhelming practical evidence that it works satisfactorily, as most virtual memory systems use such an LRU approximation and many achieve hit ratios of 99%, witnessing the quality of the estimator.

b. WS

A second example is the case of WS, for which Denning (Denning, 1980) suggested an accurate implementation. With every page frame in primary memory, one associates a hardware counter connected to a clock circuit. Every time the clock ticks, all counters are incremented. Every time a page is referenced, its associated counter is reset to zero. Thus, the counter of a page is a true measure of the lifetime of the page in primary memory. As soon as a counter overflows, it stops counting and indicates that the page has exhausted its time window and should be removed from memory. This is shown in Fig. 45. The window is equal to 2^kT, where k is the number of bits in the counters and T is the clock cycle. This cycle can be adjusted by program to vary the window.

A further tip about implementation of page removal algorithms is that pages are in fact not actually removed unless they were modified, because secondary storage is assumed to contain a copy of all pages at all times. Detecting whether a page was modified while in primary memory can easily be done with one bit in the SPT entry of every page, or in a separate table, as for usage bits. This so-called *dirty bit* is maintained by the hardware. Every time a page is written into, the bit is turned on. Secondary storage usually contains a copy of all pages for two reasons. First, this enhances the robustness of the system. If a crash leaves primary memory in an inconsistent state, the users of the system may at least fall back on secondary storage to retrieve the last known consistent image of their information. Second, it saves time at page ''removal''.

c. Ad Hoc Implementations

In many systems, one finds implementations that do not try to realize or even to approach a specific theoretical algorithm but realize some practical algorithm instead.

Such is the case, for instance, in the Atlas system (Kilburn *et al.*, 1962). In Atlas, a hardware-maintained usage bit, such as the one described above, is associated with every page of the memory. After every 1000 processor instructions, all usage bits are read, saved in memory, and reset. The past history of

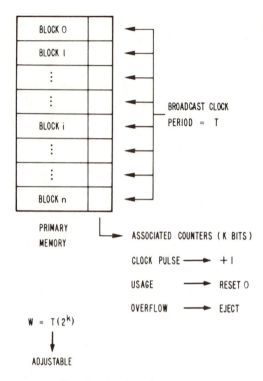

Fig. 45. A WS implementation.

each usage bit is thus saved for some time and can be inspected. For each page, the page removal algorithm computes the time t_1 (in increments of 1000 instructions) since the page was last used, and the time t_2 between that last use and the previous use. It then ejects any page for which $t_1 > t_2$. This represents an attempt at detecting circular reference strings. With a circular reference string, a page will be referenced at regular intervals. Thus if the latest time interval without reference (t_1) becomes larger than the previous interval (t_2), this is an indication that the page has migrated from the locality of the current working set. If no such page can be found, the page with the largest t_1 is ejected, which approximates LRU.

Another example of an ad hoc implementation is given by DEC's VMS system. VMS operates with a variable space algorithm. The size of the resident set of a process is allowed to grow until the process page fault rate drops below a certain threshold, as with the PFF algorithm. However, when the page fault rate drops below that threshold, the selection of pages to be removed is FIFO, with a slight modification to try to avoid the FIFO anomaly. When a page is selected for removal, it is not immediately ejected. Instead, it is only logically removed, i.e., queued for ejection if it was modified, or simply recycled to the free pool if it was not modified. In either case, it is marked as "just removed". Then, if the process references it again soon after it is logically removed, it is retrieved from the pool where it was logically removed, and it is reactivated, without causing a page fault.

4.   Engineering Issues

4.1.   Interference with Processor Management

In Parts 2 and 3, we discussed processor and communication management, and in this part, memory management. While the discussions kept the subjects completely separate from one another, the reality is that memory management interacts in several subtle and important ways with the other two mechanisms, as explained below.

a.   Multiprogramming Level and Optimum Scheduling

First, consider the level of multiprogramming. If the level is too high, the competition between users for space in primary memory can be fierce.

Suppose that a virtual processor P has a working set of 10 pages that it references very frequently in the course of some computation. Assume that half of these pages are in primary memory. When it references a sixth page, it will take a page fault. Thus, it must wait for the desired page to arrive in primary memory to proceed. If the level of multiprogramming is too high, many other virtual processors might execute while P is waiting and will all cause more page faults, requiring more page ejections. Thus, by the time P is ready to execute again, none of its initial 5 pages may be there any more. As a result, P would almost immediately take another page fault, thereby kicking out a page of some other user. In such a situation, the system would waste a great percentage of time doing paging, a phenomenon called *thrashing*. To remedy this situation, the level of multiprogramming must be limited to reserve a decent resident set to each virtual processor. Alternately, the system may preallocate a paging area to each virtual processor and maintain a separate page pool for each virtual processor. However, this has some effects on accounting for shared pages.

On the other hand, if the level of multiprogramming is too low, a virtual processor P may be allowed to run for so long that it fills up all primary memory pages with its own working set. As soon as another virtual processor arrives, it causes a flurry of page faults to try to bring in its working set. Now that virtual processor would have to wait for the pages to come in. But if the level of multiprogramming is too low, only P would be ready to run in the mean time.

Thus, it may immediately reclaim the few pages that the other processor took from him and consistently prevent it from building up a reasonable resident set, a phenomenon called *capture*.

Now, the question is, What is a good multiprogramming level that is neither too low nor too high? In fact, one can even ask if there exists an optimum among all possible levels, which would maximize the *throughput* of the system.

It has been shown and intuition suggests that the average throughput of the system (say in jobs or transactions per unit of time) multiplied by the average space–time product of the jobs or transactions (i.e., the average number of pages required times the average life of these pages in primary memory) is equal to the size of the primary memory paging pool, which is a constant for any system. Thus, in order to maximize the throughput of the system, one should minimize the average space–time product of programs. This allows rephrasing the earlier question as, What multiprogramming level will minimize the space–time product of the programs.

With fixed space paging algorithms, treating the whole memory as a big paging pool, one has no influence on the resident set of individual processes. The only space parameter at hand is the total pool size, and it is fixed. Thus, one can only hope to influence the rate at which a job is processed. One cannot vary the resident set it will receive.

It has been suggested that a good multiprogramming level is such that the average interpage-fault time is equal to the average disk access time. This means that the processor(s) will never have to sit idle, because when it encounters a page fault, some other page fault will just have been resolved, thereby readying another process. It also means that the disk bandwidth will be fully utilized, since a page fault will occur on the average at the same time that the disks have completed a previous page fetch.

Any higher multiprogramming level would start causing thrashing, thereby degrading system throughput. Any lower multiprogramming level would mean that the paging mechanism is not fully utilized, or in other words that the system is captured by only a few users while others are unnecessarily waiting. Thus, the time that the pages of the privileged processes live in primary memory is longer than necessary, which increases their space–time product and decreases system performance.

While the above suggestion is fundamentally correct, it does not take into account the page fault handling time by the processor. Moreover, it does not really offer direct control of the multiprogramming level. The control comes from a rather sophisticated feedback loop involving the paging activity.

With a variable space paging algorithm, however, the situation is simpler. Indeed, the WS policy is precisely driven by the space–time product of running processes. Thus using a WS policy directly offers the desired handle on the choice of the multiprogramming level. The scheduling algorithm can load processes as memory is made available for them by the WS mechanism. In other words, the multiprogramming level is directly slaved to the WS policy. The key problem consists, of course, of picking the right window W for the WS to minimize the space–time product of all programs. Picking a good value for W depends on the pool size and the job mix. Denning (Denning, 1980) has shown by empirical studies backed by simulations that, in a typical system, it is possible to calculate one value W for all programs such that each program will execute within a few percent (10%) of its optimum space–time, thereby causing the overall throughput of the system to be within some 10% of the optimum achievable.

b.   Cache Usage in Multiprocessor Systems

Another interaction between memory and processor management deals with multiprocessor systems with cache memories. Cache memories buffer information between processors and what is traditionally called primary memory. Usually, caches come attached to processors rather than to memory banks, which raises a problem with multiprocessor systems. What happens if two processors have a copy of the same information in their cache and one modifies its copy? For consistency, the other copy should also be modified. The problem is solved in two different ways in practice. According to one solution, data that are declared writable are never put in the cache, so that the problem of updating multiple copies is eliminated. According to the other solution, when a processor modifies its copy of some information, a "write-through" mechanism is used to update the primary memory copy as well, and an interrupt is sent to all other processors telling them to clear their cache. This causes them to refetch the updated information from primary memory.

c.   Interrupts and Memory Management

A third interaction with processor management concerns the masking of interrupts. It is advisable, when entering the memory management mechanism, to mask interrupts, the reason being not a matter a mere consistency as in the processor management case, but rather a matter of protection and performance. If a virtual processor could be interrupted while in the memory management code, it could lose the physical processor after it has locked several memory management tables (e.g., SPT, SST) to protect itself from interference over these tables from other processors. Consequently, other virtual processors may try in vain to enter the memory management mechanism, since it is locked and the processor that is supposed to unlock it has just been interrupted.

d.   Residency Considerations

A fourth interaction with processor management concerns the justification for making the processor management resident in primary memory. The memory management mechanism quite obviously must be resident, because it could not import any page or segment otherwise. But, as explained at the very beginning of this chapter, upon a page fault or a segment load request, the memory management mechanism that is invoked must give the physical processor to another virtual processor while the virtual processor that just caused the page fault or requested a segment load is waiting for the secondary storage access to complete. This requires invoking the processor management mechanism. Thus, the processor management mechanism itself must be resident, otherwise multiprogramming to wait for page faults to be resolved would recursively cause page faults on the multiprogramming primitive itself.

4.2.   Interference with I/O Management

a.   I/O Buffer Locking

An important interaction between memory management and communication management concerns the handling by memory management of memory areas used as I/O buffers.

When a paging I/O operation is started, the paging mechanism locks the corresponding PT word as a reminder to itself that this page is currently undergoing I/O. Thus, no other I/O operation should be started on it until the previous one is completed. In particular, this allows the paging mechanism to guarantee that a page it has just requested to import will not be selected for removal before it has had a chance to be used.

However, when an I/O operation other than paging is started, e.g., an I/O operation on a communication device, the paging mechanism is not *de facto* informed about it. Thus, when the I/O mechanism is starting an I/O operation into or out of some segment, it must inform the paging mechanism to import and lock the affected pages. If it did not, an I/O device might find itself in the very awkward situation where the buffer area it needs to access is not in main memory. Because of device timing considerations, this is unacceptable in most cases and complicated anyway. The I/O device usually cannot wait for the buffer area to be imported to complete the I/O operation.

b.   I/O Address Interpretation

In practice, since it is always desirable and often absolutely necessary that pages involved in I/O operations be locked in main memory, providing I/O processors, channels, etc., with virtual address translation hardware (i.e., SAM and PAM) becomes questionable. Indeed such hardware adds cost and is not really necessary, since it is known in advance that no segment or page faults will be generated by I/O processors. Thus, one often finds that I/O processors use absolute addresses. This of course requires that the I/O mechanism translate the virtual addresses it receives from users into absolute addresses that can be passed to the dedicated processors.

4.3.   System Page Table Management

Now is the time to discuss a problem that was not mentioned explicitly so far in order not to confuse the reader. In any realistic system, there are so many segments that it is impossible to keep all their PTs in primary memory at once. This introduces the distinction between an *active segment,* whose PT is in primary memory, and a *passive segment,* whose PT is in secondary storage.

Migration of PTs from primary to secondary storage is usually on a LRU basis, while migration in the opposite direction can be on a demand basis, using segment faults. A user process causes a segment fault when it produces the uid of a segment that the SST says is passive. This is indicated in the SST by an appropriate flag. As a result of a segment fault, the desired segment is activated, i.e., its PT is fetched from the secondary storage address listed in the SST and brought into primary memory, which brings up the issue of the management of PTs. Where are they stored in secondary storage? How are they moved to primary memory?

There can be many answers to these questions. A frequent approach consists of partitioning secondary storage in a way similar to primary memory. Every secondary storage device (usually a disk) is divided into a page area and a map area often called a *volume table of contents* (VTOC). [In Unix (Ritchie and Thompson, 1974), it is called an i-list.] Every segment resides entirely on one secondary storage device. Thus, if a secondary storage device fails, crashes, is damaged, or is disconnected, all the segments on it become completely inaccessible but the other segments remain totally unaffected. While a segment is passive, thus residing on disk, its PT is often called a *file map* and resides in the VTOC, and all its pages are stored in the paging area. (In Unix, the i-list of a disk contains one i-node per segment. The i-node contains several segment attributes besides the file map.)

In addition to containing file maps for all the segments on its disk, the VTOC also contains a *disk map* indicating the free/busy status of every block in the paging area of the disk. As the need arises, the system may read selected disk maps into memory. Disk maps are written out at periodic intervals to update their original version in VTOCs.

In summary, primary memory is divided into two areas: (1) the resident area, where space is allocated when the system is brought up for the processor man-

agement, device control, and memory management mechanisms, the VPT, any
I/O device control table, the main memory map, disk maps, the SST, and the
SPT; and (2) the paging area, for pages of segments of all other mechanisms of
the operating system itself and user programs. The same division can be observed for disks between the VTOC, containing the disk map and file maps, and
the paging area, containing segment pages.

4.4.   Faults and Interrupts Definitions

In Parts 2 and 3, we encountered one kind of event: time-out, preemption, and
I/O interrupts. In this chapter on memory management, we have encountered a
second kind of event: segment and page faults. The difference between interrupts
and faults is worth a short digression here.

Interrupts are by definition asynchronous to the execution of a process, while
faults are synchronous to the activity of a process. In other words, interrupts
occur at points that cannot be predicted. This is because they are generated by
other processes, other processors, users, or clocks to signal asynchronous events.
Faults occur at points of execution that can be predicted precisely, because they
occur when a process references a new segment or a new page.

Interrupts are just a means to signal asynchronous events between processors
or processes. As a result of an interrupt, the state of an interrupted virtual
processor is saved, the processor management mechanism is invoked, and most
of the time the physical processor is given to another virtual processor.

By comparison, faults are a means for the hardware to notify the software that
it has encountered a situation it cannot handle. For instance, a page fault is in fact
an error return from a hardware LOAD or STORE primitive informing the
software paging primitive that the desired page was not found in primary memory. As a result of a fault, the state of the faulting processor is also saved and a
fault-handling mechanism is invoked. However, that faulting processor does not
necessarily leave the running state. Depending on how the fault-handling mechanism is implemented, the fault may be handled within the faulting processor
(monitor implementation) or it may require waking up another processor dedicated to handling that sort of fault (parallel processor view).

Suggested Reading and Classics

On fixed partition paging algorithms:

Belady, 1966.   On OPT and the search for good algorithms.
Belady *et al.*, 1969.   On the FIFO anomaly.
Mattson *et al.*, 1970.   The classic on stack algorithms.

On variable space paging algorithms:

Chu and Opderbeck,1972.   On the PFF algorithm.
Franklin *et al.,* 1978.   On anomalies in variable space algorithms.
Denning, 1968a.   The classic on the working set model.
Denning and Schwartz, 1972a.   On properties of the working set model.
Prieve and Fabry, 1976.   On the VMIN algorithm.
Denning and Slutz, 1978.   On the GWS.

On paging algorithm implementations:

Fotheringham, 1961; Kilburn *et al.,* 1961, 1962.   On Atlas, one of the first virtual memory systems, and its loop detector algorithm.
Daley and Dennis, 1968 and Bensoussan *et al.,* 1972.   On the Multics virtual memory.
Corbato, 1969.   On a CLOCK–FINUFO implementation.
Morris, 1972.   On a WS implementation in MANIAC.
Bobrow *et al.,* 1972 and Murphy, 1972.   On the PFF implementation in Tenex.
Whitfield and Whight, 1973.   On the Emas WS implementation.
Redell *et al.,* 1980.   An example of the use of virtual memory in a personal computer.

On program restructuring for virtual memory:

Hatfield, 1972

On cache management techniques:

Conti, 1969
Smith, 1978a

On scheduling–paging interactions:

Denning, 1968b.   The classic on thrashing.
Rodriguez-Rosell and Dupuy, 1973.   An IBM WS dispatcher implementation.

Further Reading and References

Surveys and bibliographies:

Denning, 1970.   An early but excellent survey.
Aho *et al.,* 1971.   An early survey of theory.
Denning, 1979b *or* Denning, 1980.   An excellent review of the history of virtual memory techniques.
Smith, 1978b.   A comprehensive bibliography.

On some theoretical aspects of paging:

Brawn and Gustavson, 1968.   An early look at the effect of program structure on locality.
Denning, 1972b.   On attempts at modeling program behavior.

Part 5

HIGH-LEVEL MECHANISMS

Chapter VII

File Management

1. Introduction

Before we start discussing the topic of file management itself, let us relate it to lower level mechanisms seen so far.

As described in Chapter IV, I/O management is really divided into two levels: device control at the low level, which was discussed to some extent in Chapter IV, and I/O control at the high level. For communication devices, I/O control software is often referred to as communication control or network access method, and it implements a network architecture. For peripheral storage devices, the equivalent level of software is called *file access method,* and it *manages the file system.*

In Chapter V, we started with the assumption that memory is flat (one-level), unstructured, and infinite. We proceeded to explain how this hypothetical one-level memory can be given a segmented structure. Then, in Chapter VI, we explained how the illusion of a virtually infinite memory can be simulated with multiple levels of memory. More specifically, Chapter VI described a segmented multilevel virtual memory. However, it left two problems unanswered:

1. *Name to uid mapping.* It was said earlier that users address segments by means of uids. However, we carefully avoided explaining how this can be achieved; it is not as simple as it sounds. When users write source programs that reference other program or data segments, they use *symbolic names* (sqrt, reflist, etc.), not uids, to refer to these other segments. Yet according to the segmentation model developed so far, object programs can name one another only by uid. Thus, somewhere the system must keep information that allows it to map symbolic names into uids. This is one function of a file system: a naming function, to be explained in Section 2.

2. *SST management.* At the end of Chapter VI, we said that the SPT is so small that it requires a multilevel management mechanism of its own, but we

carefully avoided saying that the problem is in fact the same for the SST. The SST typically is also too small to contain the descriptors for all segments in the world at the same time. Thus parts of it must at time reside in secondary storage. How this can be achieved is also not as evident as it sounds. This is a second function of a file system: to offer a means for remembering the VTOC or *home addresses* of the file maps of passive segments that cannot be held in the SST. This addressing function will be described in Section 3.

In addition to the naming and the addressing functions just mentioned, a third function of the file system is to ensure the integrity of information. This function has two aspects: first, to make regular copies of all disks to tapes, so that even a catastrophic system failure such as a fire in the computer room cannot cause the loss of all on-line data; and second, particularly in data base systems, to organize the transfer of information between main and peripheral storage so as to guarantee that a system crash cannot leave any segments (or even a whole data base) in an inconsistent state on the disks. Mechanisms for preserving the integrity of data will be discussed separately in Sections 5 and 6.

A fourth function of file systems is data protection against unauthorized access. This aspect of file management is discussed separately in Chapter IX, as part of a comprehensive treatment of protection issues in operating systems.

Finally, file systems typically perform a resource accounting function. The sum of all space used up by the segments of a user is charged against a resource account attached to that user. This allows system administrators to bill each user for the space used by his segments on disks. Beyond mentioning the function, we will not enter into any detail of resource accounting in this book.

Notice that the concept of a file system may be irrelevant in certain real-time systems such as process control systems. Since these systems are usually programmed only once and for all, and implement a fixed algorithm for controlling some industrial or laboratory procedure, they may not offer a file system, properly speaking. In fact, some may not even have secondary storage. They do not need to create and delete segments dynamically. Thus, they do not require the concept of uids.

2.   Naming Function: Catalog Structures

Let us consider first the name to uid mapping function of file systems. A file system is constituted of software programs managing a set of one or more data structures, called *catalogs* or *directories*. These catalogs may be implemented in many different ways. One possibility, which we will assume here, is that catalogs are implemented as paged segments.

The first function of catalogs is to serve as repositories for mappings between symbolic names found in source programs and uids of corresponding segments, further referred to as files in the context of a file system. Hence, when a program must be executed, it is possible to translate the symbolic names of subroutines and data structures it uses at the source level into segment uids meaningful to the hardware at the object level.

2.1.   Flat File System

The most elementary type of file system is called a *flat* file system. Such a system is composed of one huge catalog binding symbolic names to uids as pictured in Fig. 46. The operation of such a system is trivial. It lists all existing files under their names and for each one gives the corresponding uid that object programs should use.

Flat file systems are very primitive but very simple to implement, which is why they are found on most first generation personal computers and even on minicomputers meant to be used as single-user/single-application systems.

2.2.   Home Catalogs

The trouble with a flat file system is that it presents the risk of name conflicts due to duplication in multiuser systems. If Smith and Jones both want to have a file called SQRT, a conflict will arise, because the flat file system obviously cannot contain the same name twice.

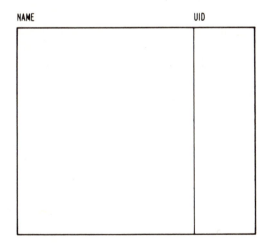

• SHORTCOMINGS: NAME DUPLICATIONS

Fig. 46. A flat file system.

To solve the conflict, the idea of one *home catalog* per user is introduced, as in Fig. 47. With this solution, every user can name his modules as he likes without risk of duplication of names in his own catalog. The symbolic names used by a user are translated in the context of his own catalog.

2.3.   Network File System

In solving one problem, the home catalog idea has introduced another one. Now that everybody has his home catalog, how can people share files? How can Smith name Jones's ALPHA file? One solution to this problem is to allow a *network* of catalogs. For instance, Smith and Jones can exchange, outside the system, the uid of a catalog where they agree to put files they want to share, as in Fig. 48. They can each refer to the shared files by using network path names starting from their own home catalog (e.g., COMMON.ALPHA). Or Smith can record the uid of Jones's catalog under some suitable name in his own catalog, so he can refer to it via some path name. In general, any connectivity structure between the catalogs may be envisioned. Even cyclic catalog structures may be constructed.

2.4.   Hierarchical File System

In addition to requiring that uids be passed outside the system to initialize sharing, the network idea also introduces a new problem, that of *lost objects*. Smith and Jones, each on his own without telling the other, could decide that they no longer need to access the shared files and assume the other still wants them. Thus, they could both erase the name and uid of the shared catalog from their home catalog. This would result in making the catalog inaccessible to anyone, since nobody would have its uid any more. Of course, a reference count system could be kept in the shared catalog to know when it can be deleted. However, this would not work if cyclic catalog structures become detached from

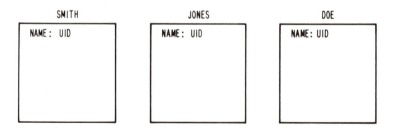

• SHORTCOMINGS: NO SHARING

Fig. 47.   Home catalogs.

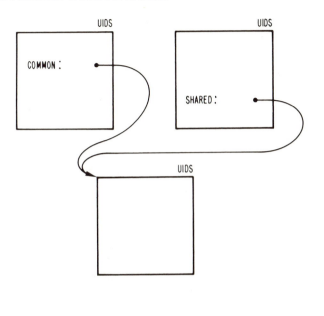

• SHORTCOMINGS : "LOST OBJECTS"

Fig. 48. A network file system.

all home catalogs. A periodic garbage collection program could purge all lost objects from the system, but this is an awkward and expensive solution to a more fundamental problem.

Thus, the idea of a *hierarchical* system (Fig. 49) is preferred. In this system, there is one master catalog that need not have a name but contains the uids of all home catalogs. It is referred to as the *root catalog* of the file system. Users can share files by exchanging their tree names and storing these tree names in lieu of uids in their home catalog under any symbolic name they want. The "lost object" problem is solved because every file has an owner. The uid of a file is contained only in the catalog of its owner. Other users refer to the file indirectly by *tree name* or *path name*. When the owner deletes the binding name–uid from his catalog, the file is also deleted (and not lost). Other users will be notified of the deletion because the path name they own for the file can no longer be resolved into a uid and will cause an error message to be returned if they try to find the file. The same would be true if the file were renamed by its owner.

Hierarchical file systems have been pioneered in Atlas, Multics, Unix, and Tenex, among other systems. They are now common on many commercial systems, including IBM's PC-DOS 2.

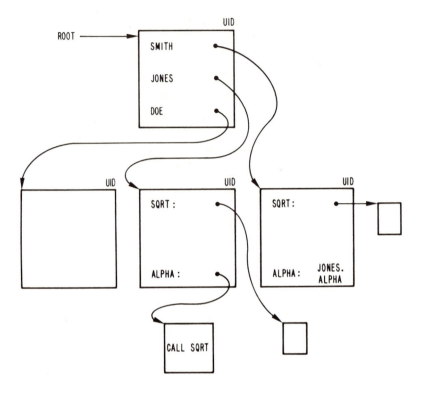

● SHORTCOMINGS: ACCIDENTAL BINDINGS

Fig. 49. A hierarchical file system.

2.5.   Referencing Catalogs

Although we are approaching the end of the series of catalog structures, the hierarchical file system is not quite sufficient yet: it also suffers from one problem. In Fig. 49, both Smith and Jones have a program called SQRT in their home catalog. The two SQRT programs might perform completely different computations. When Smith and Jones call a subroutine named SQRT, the name SQRT is mapped into different subroutines for each of them. So far, so good. Now assume that Smith has borrowed Jones's ALPHA program and executes it. Also, assume that ALPHA calls a subroutine named SQRT. According to the logic developed so far, the call should result in picking Smith's SQRT. Yet, in writing his ALPHA module, Jones probably did not know about Smith's SQRT and certainly meant ALPHA to call his own SQRT. By picking Smith's SQRT, the program might go astray. This is called an *accidental binding*. It is due to an excess of modularity in interpreting names.

The solution to this problem is to introduce the concept of a *referencing catalog*. When a program *A* references a file *B*, the link from *A* to *B* should be translated by looking for a file named *B* first in the referencing catalog, i.e., the catalog containing *A*, and then in the home catalog of the user executing *A* only if no *B* can be found in the referencing catalog (Fig. 50).

2.6.   Substitution Catalogs

In fact, we have overcorrected the previous problem. We have assumed that the program called SQRT in Smith's catalog never had anything to do with the SQRT in Jones's catalog. This may be true most of the time. However, in certain cases, two modules bearing the same name in different catalogs might indeed perform the same function (e.g., square root) but according to different algorithms. It may be the case that when Smith calls ALPHA, he knows ALPHA calls a subroutine named SQRT but he does not like the SQRT supplied by Jones

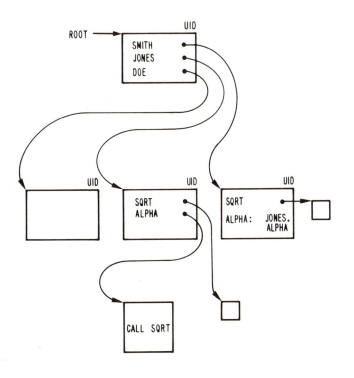

● SHORTCOMING : NO SUBSTITUTION

Fig. 50.   Referencing catalogs.

or is developing a new one and wants to use his version. With the referencing catalog concept developed above, Smith could not substitute his SQRT for Jones's! This is called an *irreversible binding*. It is the result of a lack of modularity in interpreting names.

Thus, we introduce the concept of a *substitution catalog* (Fig. 51). Every user is entitled to define one catalog as his present substitution catalog and to file in that catalog any file he means to substitute for files that he knows are referenced inside programs that he borrows from colleagues. When a file with name X is referenced by some program and must be located in some catalog, the file system searches first in the substitution catalog of the requesting user to allow for substitution. If the file is not found there, it is looked up by default in the referencing catalog. If this search fails, X is finally looked up in the home catalog of the requesting user.

So far, we have established that a file named X must be searched for sequentially in three catalogs: the substitution catalog, the referencing catalog, and the home catalog. In practice, if X is not found there, it can then be searched for in a

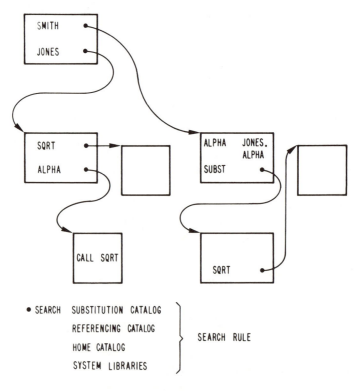

Fig. 51. Substitution catalogs.

set of catalogs called the system libraries, which are used to store standard programs that most users will want to use. If a file called X cannot be found in any catalog, an error message is returned to the user to notify him that his program tries to call a module that does not exist.

A set of catalogs that have to be searched in sequential order as explained above is called a *search rule*. The search rule described above is not the only possible one. It may not even be the best one. In fact, if Smith has an SQRT in his substitution catalog and borrows a program from someone else, not knowing that the borrowed program contains a call to an SQRT, he falls back into another accidental binding problem. Thus, substitution catalogs are a mixed blessing. The main intent of this discussion is to point out that many different search rules, all with their advantages and their problems, can be designed. The purpose of a search rule is to steer the translation of a symbolic name into a system-wide tree name that will unambiguously lead to the uid of the desired file.

3. Addressing Function

Having described the naming function of a file system, we now discuss its addressing function, namely the function allowing the operating system to completely purge from the SST the home or secondary storage addresses of passive segments.

We stated earlier that there may be so many segments in a system that the SST entries necessary to record their home addresses cannot all fit in main memory. On the other hand, these entries cannot simply be removed from the SST and copied out anywhere to secondary storage. If this were done without care, segments would get lost, because once their SST entry was in peripheral storage there would be no way to retrieve them, since a uid alone is not enough to locate a segment and the address of its file map in the VTOC is stored in the SST entry now ejected to an unknown place in peripheral storage.

Of course, one could arrange to have an SST in main memory and an SST' in peripheral storage, at an address permanently recorded in the SST. Active segments could be described in the SST and passive segments in the SST'. While such a scheme would conceptually hold and would avoid losing segments, it is impractical: In a real system, there can be so many segments that hash-searching the SST' for the uid of a given segment could take very long, since the SST' is in secondary storage and searching it for any single uid could take multiple disk accesses.

A scheme is necessary whereby it is possible to directly find the home or VTOC address of the file map of a passive segment, given its uid. The most obvious scheme consists of storing this address together with the uid in a place where all users must look up the uid anyway, i.e., in the file system. Thus, aside from its naming function (binding of names to uids), the file system also has an addressing function that consists of playing the role of the SST for passive segments, i.e., binding uids to home addresses.

Of course, the problem that plagued the SST now affects the file system. If segments are never to be lost, the file system must be stored in a location always recorded in the SST. For the hierarchical system described earlier, this means permanently recording the address of the root catalog in the SST. From that root catalog, it is then possible to retrieve any file in the system.

Notice that, when a system is halted, all segments are of course deactivated. The SST becomes empty and in fact vanishes as soon as the hardware memory is powered down. Thus, the root of the file system must reside at a constant known location in peripheral storage so that it is possible to reconnect a newly initialized system to it by creating an SST entry from nothing.

4. File Access Mechanisms

Having described the naming and addressing mechanisms embodied in a file system, it is now time to turn our attention to so-called *file access mechanisms*. File access mechanisms are the mechanisms that manage the allocation of space to files on peripheral storage devices and allow user programs to refer to these files. File access mechanisms will be described in the context of hierarchical file systems. However, what will be said would also hold for any other flavor of file system.

While the description of addressing, virtual memory, and file systems we have given so far is conceptually correct, we have swept some important implementation issues under the rug for simplicity. It is now time to unveil these issues and to address their solution.

Files versus segments. We have used the word file almost interchangeably with the word segment. A file has been described essentially as a segment in the passive state. This is indeed so in so-called direct-access file systems, but in all other types of file systems, called indirect-access systems, files and segments are two completely different objects that are accessed in their own way.

Virtual memory size. We have let the reader believe that segmentation and paging allow all users to view the entire file system as a shared virtual memory composed of an essentially infinite supply of automatically paged segments. Again, this view holds in direct-access systems but is overly simplistic and beyond the capabilities of indirect-access file systems: the supply and size of segments is usually too small to access all files directly as paged segments.

Support of uids. Finally, we have left the reader with the impression that user object code directly uses uids to address segments. While conceivable in principle, this design is difficult to achieve in practice for several reasons:

1.   If uids are to be unique over all time, they must contain somewhere between 32 and 64 bits, which, when added to the size of word offsets (e.g., 16–24 bits), is a size fairly large to store in address, base, or index registers and in object programs.

2.   Also, the efficient hash-search of one uid in the SST that may contain several hundred or thousand entries would require special associative search circuits that are complex, fast, and thus expensive, even with today's technology. This would be in a sense putting all of the SST in a big SAM device.

3.   Finally, now that we have seen that passive segments are not even described in the SST, it is clear that if a user references a passive segment, there would be no way to retrieve that passive segment with just its uid. The segment first must be activated, which requires the VTOC home address of its file map. This address is stored in the catalog entry with the symbolic name and the uid. However, the user presents the symbolic name only when he first translates it. Once he has looked up the name in the file system and has received the uid, he no longer uses the symbolic name.

In the following, we first discuss direct-access file systems, where files are indeed the same thing as passive segments and virtual memory is by definition large enough to address as much data as a user ever needs in practice. We shall explain how the difficulty of implementing uids can be circumvented. Then, we will turn our attention to indirect-access file systems, where files and segments are distinct objects, and where virtual memory is not unlimited in practice.

Note that we discuss direct-access systems first because they are conceptually simpler and very closely fit the virtual memory model we have developed so far. However, from a chronological point of view, such systems were introduced last because of the sophisticated paging, segmentation, and file management mechanisms they require.

4.1.   Direct-access File Systems

a.   Filing Disks

In *direct-access* file systems, disk space is managed by block allocation, the size of a block being equal to the size of one virtual memory page, as suggested in our discussion of virtual memory in Chapter VI. Though different schemes are possible, disks are typically split into two parts: the VTOC and the paging area. Such an implementation is found in the present version of the Multics system, although the original design was different (Bensoussan *et al.*, 1972). It is also found in the Unix system, where the VTOC is called the i-list of the disk (Ritchie and Thompson, 1974).

As explained at the end of Chapter VI, the VTOC contains one file map per file (segment) residing on the disk. That entry contains the list of the addresses on the disk of the various blocks (records, pages) composing the file.

b.   User Address Spaces

To circumvent the uid implementation problem, one defines *user address spaces* that are distinct from the system address space and are indexed by *segment number* instead of being addressed by uids. User address spaces operate as windows on the system address space. Each user process sees its own address space.

Segment numbers are best regarded as local abbreviations for uids. The system contains for each user process a private abbreviation lexicon, hereafter called its *Name Table* (NT), which is indexed by segment number and maps these segment numbers into the tree names, the uids, and the VTOC home addresses of only those segments needed by that user process, as shown in Fig. 52. The NT of a user process defines its private address space. It is an abbreviated (cache) version of the file system, since a NT entry contains exactly the same information as a catalog entry, but the whole NT describes only a subset of all the files described in the file system, namely that subset currently used by the corresponding user process.

With direct-access file systems, the size of a NT is such that the user has enough room for as many segments as he is ever likely to want to use at the same time (e.g., many hundreds or thousands). Every time he wants to use a new file, the user names it. The system then uses the name of the file to search the file system, obtains the uid and home address of the file, allocates a segment number to the file, and records the uid and home address under that segment number. This is called opening the file.

Then, the user accesses the file by segment number rather than by uid. The mapping to uid is performed via the NT. If the uid is found to be missing in the SST, the system can go back to the current user's NT to retrieve the VTOC home address of the passive segment, activate it, copy its file map from the VTOC entry to a free PT in the SPT, and add the uid to PT address mapping in the SST.

c.   Address Space Implementation

This design solves the problem of retrieving the VTOC home address of a file, given the segment number of that file. It also avoids the disadvantage of seeing uids in object programs and index registers. However, it does not yet avoid the need to refetch entries from the SST by hashing, every time the SAM must be reloaded. And in addition, as it is described so far the design introduces another level of indirection in the address interpretation mechanism: a segment number to uid mapping.

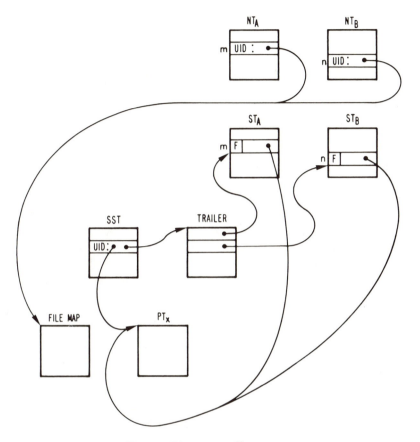

Fig. 52.   Direct-access file system.

The latter problem, indirection, can be circumvented by changing the format of the SAM. Rather than storing uid to page table address mappings in the SAM, we can store segment number to page table address mappings. In doing so, the effect of the extra level of indirection will be felt only when the SAM is loaded. Notice that this implies that the SAM be cleared every time a new virtual processor is dispatched, since segment numbers have processor dependent meanings.

However, the former problem is not yet solved, i.e., searching for a uid in the SST every time the SAM must be reloaded. To correct the problem, instead of keeping the direct mapping between segment numbers and page table addresses only in the SAM, which is small for cost reasons, we also keep it in memory, in a table called the *Segment Table* (ST). Every user process has an ST. While it runs, its ST is pointed to by a hardware base register. Every time a segment number is not found in the SAM, the SAM is reloaded from the ST. The ST is also indexed by segment number. It plays at the same time the role of extension to the SAM and of cache for SST entries. It is not as fast as the SAM because it is in main memory, but it is faster than the SST because it is smaller and indexed by segment number rather than by hashed uids. With this mechanism, it is necessary to resort to hashing a uid into the SST only to initialize an ST entry the first time a user needs it. This is sufficiently infrequent that one can afford to do it in software and avoid the need for expensive associative search hardware.

Now, the management of the ST poses new problems. How should entries be initialized there? And how should they be deleted?

d.   Segment Connection

Let us consider the initialization first. Upon request by the user, the system opens a file by initializing the NT entry for it. The ST entry for it remains blank. Upon the first attempt to reference the segment number of the newly opened file, the hardware fetches the corresponding entry of the ST, notices that is is not initialized, and generates a *segment fault.* *

Upon a segment fault, the address space (NT) manager is invoked. Using the segment number that caused the fault, it looks up the identity of the opened file in the NT of the user process that caused the fault and finds the uid and the VTOC home address of the corresponding segment. It then invokes the segment (SST) management mechanism and gives it the uid and the home address. If the segment is already active, its *PT address* is returned. Otherwise, the home address is used to retrieve the segment's PT and activate it. Upon return from the segment manager, the PT address is stored in the ST and control is given back to the user process. The segment is said to be *connected.*

e.   Segment Disconnection

Now, consider the more complicated problem of deleting an ST entry. In a system where users are allowed to share the main memory copy of a file, many users may have a private ST entry connected to the PT of a segment. Thus, when a user decides to close a file, the file cannot be blindly deactivated since other users may be connected to it. One solution, used in the Unix system, consists of

---

*This event is not to be confused with what was called a segment fault in Chapter VI, which corresponds to a user referencing a passive segment. In the present system, referencing a passive segment cannot occur at address interpretation time, as will be seen in the next paragraph. Thus, it does not require any fault mechanism. On the other hand, the new concept of segment fault does not necessarily imply that the segment is passive, as will be seen also in the next paragraph.

keeping a count of connected users in each SST entry and deactivating the file only if the connected count reaches zero.

In other systems, such as Multics, where the SPT management algorithm may spontaneously decide that a segment has not been used for a long time and should be deactivated, even if users are still connected to its PT, there must be a way to know which users are connected to it, if any. This mechanism is provided by a list of backward pointers, called a *trailer list,* from an SST entry to every ST entry connected to the corresponding PT. This rather cumbersome architecture results from the need to store segment number to page table address mappings in STs, thereby disseminating system information among several users.

The foregoing description is by no means the only way to make files accessible to user processes. It is only one design among many possible ones. This particular design is characterized by the fact that the user, through his address space, *directly* accesses the files cataloged in the file system. Paging is done directly from the file system disks.

f.   Summary

Direct-access file systems demand that the virtual memory seen by the system as well as the address spaces seen by the users be large enough to access as many files as may ever be simultaneously necessary. This means that there must be a virtually inexhaustible supply of very large segments, i.e., very many segment numbers in each address space.

User address spaces are implemented on top of the file system, and the file system is itself on top of the virtual memory. The entire file system represents a universal virtual address space where segments are addressed by uid. User virtual address spaces are implemented on top of that virtual address space, using the same disk access mechanisms, but showing segment numbers instead of uids.

The whole paging (or swapping) mechanism is inside (below) the file system. It manipulates directly the master copies of files stored in the file system. This architecture is very attractive because it represents an economy of mechanism: all disks are treated alike and are used for paging. This implies that paging traffic is spread across all disks in the computer system. This architecture is not found very often however. It will now be compared to a more classic design.

4.2.   Indirect-access File Systems

Pursuing our study of file access mechanisms in reverse chronological order, we come to *indirect-access* file systems. This type of design uses separate disks, and separate disk access mechanisms for the user virtual address spaces and the file system.

a.   Separate Filing and Paging Devices

User address spaces are supported by one ST in each user process. The virtual
memory mechanism is underneath only the user address space mechanism. The
file system uses a completely separate disk access method on its own disks.
When a user opens a file he also copies it from the file system disks to the virtual
memory disks. This results in PTs pointing to disk records on volumes different
from those containing the records pointed to by the file maps of the file system
disks, as shown in Fig. 53. Thus, all paging traffic is restricted to the virtual
memory disks. Two different sets of programs are necessary to manage the two
pools of disks.

However, these disadvantages are counterbalanced by advantages. Indirect
file access leads to more robustness in the face of system crashes. Because the
virtual memory and the file system are on two separate sets of disks, the long-
term (file system) and short-term (virtual memory) storage devices are clearly
kept apart, so that falling back to a consistent system state after a hard- or
software crash is easier. The parts of the system potentially affected by a crash
are more easily identified. For instance, if a crash occurs at a time when no file is
in the process of being transferred between the two sets of disks, then every file
is certainly in a consistent state. If a file is being transferred, only the integrity of
that file is questionable, whereas in the direct-access architecture, any file that is
opened at the time of the crash is potentially affected and a careful examination
of the SST and SPT must be undertaken to salvage the content of main memory
as far as possible.

Since filing and paging devices are separate, there is nothing to prevent the file
access software from implementing contiguous space allocation on its disks,
although paging disks are subject to block allocation. Yet another possible allocation scheme is block allocation, but with threaded block lists instead of
indexed file maps.

b.   Absence of Uids

It should be noted that such indirect-access file systems, in general, though not
by definition, do not support sharing in primary memory except for system
programs and common utilities. Thus, when two users open the same file, they
each get their own copy of it. The file system offers the possibility of locking
opened files so that two users will precisely not open the same file simultaneously, which would lead to trouble for writable files.

Since there is no objective of sharing files in main memory, the only concept
of sharing is at the file system level. This type of sharing is based on the use of
file names that are commonly understood by all users. Thus, there is no need for
uids in such systems. Indeed, it may be useful to remind the reader that the whole
concept of uid was introduced in Chapter V not only to avoid static relocation of

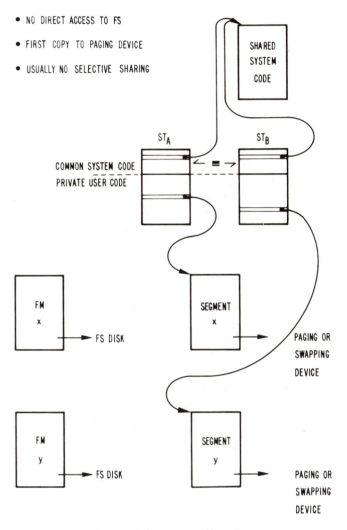

Fig. 53. Indirect-access file system.

subroutines but also to allow sharing in primary memory. In the absence of this desire to share in main memory, it is unnecessary to implement the whole uid machinery, which results in simpler file access software.

Each user process is given a ST that directly maps segment numbers into PT addresses, as in the direct-access design. However, there is no concept of an SST, no need to have back pointers to individual STs, and even no need to have any NT, since the purpose of the NT was to be able to retrieve the home address of a segment, given its segment number—a problem that has gone away now that every user is in explicit control of the activation and deactivation of his segments.

c.   *Restricted Virtual Memory Size*

Since files and paged segments are stored on different disks in indirect-access systems, virtual memory disks consume space in addition to file disks to store currently opened files. Thus, indirect-access systems cannot provide each user with a virtual memory of essentially unlimited size, as this would mean duplicating the amount of filing disk space for paging disks.

The virtual memory is larger than the real memory and paging is automatic, but the virtual memory size is nowhere near as large as in direct-access file systems. While direct-access systems can easily offer virtual memories in the range of hundreds of gigabytes (namely as many as can be addressed with aids in the entire file system), indirect-access systems typically offer virtual memories in the range of megabytes. Such systems do not give the user the illusion that all files in the world can be viewed through his segmented virtual memory at the same time.

One implication of this space limitation is that indirect access systems cannot afford to consume one entire virtual memory segment per program or data file. Instead, to economize virtual memory space, small files may be packed several to a segment in virtual memory.

While this is certainly a drawback for software development, it is an advantage for business data processing. Indeed, avoiding static relocation is a mixed blessing. When programs composed of many little procedures and data structures are being developed, they are often recompiled. In such a case, avoiding static relocation is desirable to save time, as explained in Chapter V. However, in the everyday life of a business data processing system, software development in far from being the main concern. Good performance is what counts. To achieve it, it is preferable to statically relocate many small procedures that are used very often and always as part of the same program than to map them each into a different segment, which would cause a lot of internal fragmentation and reduce the locality of reference of the program.

A second and more important difference concerns large files. In data base systems, the data base management software usually fits in the virtual memory. However, the data base itself may be many megabytes larger than the available virtual memory. Thus, the data base programmer can count on the virtual memory mechanism to page the code segments in and out automatically. But he cannot depend on virtual memory to manage the data. Data management is the programmer's responsibility. Concretely, the programmer must explicitly invoke the file access method to import and export relevant portions of his data base into and out of his virtual memory as appropriate.

d.   File Organizations

To this end, the file access method must be prepared to support at least the most classic access patterns that the programmer might require.

Sequential file access. The most classic file access pattern is the sequential one. If it is known that a file will be used exclusively sequentially, which is true in many cases, the file access method may decide to allocate disk storage for it in a contiguous fashion so as to minimize disk access time when reading or writing the file. In addition, the file access method may anticipate read operations and read the file ahead of the user program to further improve performance. The same is true for write operations. Access methods supporting such patterns are often called *queued access* methods. Sequential access may be performed on a character-at-a-time basis, or on a record-at-a-time basis. In the former case, one talks of a file stream access method. In either case, the access method buffers entire disk blocks for the user program, reading and writing them as needed.

Random file access. At the other extreme of the spectrum of access methods, we find random access patterns. If it is known that a file will often be accessed at random, the access method will preferably use block allocation of space for it, allowing the user program to read and write individual disk blocks or logical records at random. If the logical records are indexed in sequential order, the access method may easily compute the number of the disk block containing a particular logical record, given the index of that record, and the number of records per disk block.

Indexed sequential file access. If a data base file is accessed randomly but logical record indices are not in packed sequential order, the file allocation technique just described will waste a lot of space. To remedy the problem, the access method keeps an index table for the file. By hashing the index of a particular logical record into the index table, the access method can then find the address of the disk block that supposedly contains the desired record. In case the record is not found there, hash bucket overflow techniques must of course be used to continue the search.

A remark is in order about systems that do not support any virtual memory. In such systems, since there is no virtual memory, there cannot be a distinction between file system disks and paging disks. Direct access to files is clearly excluded. Indirect file access is the rule, and the file system must support one or more of the above file organizations.

5.   File Backup

Of all file systems functions, those dealing with *file integrity* are often played down as secondary to addressing and naming. Yet data integrity is fundamental to the everyday operation of the system because users directly depend on it and are vividly aware of it (or its lack) in case of system crashes, as any personal computer owner who once lost a diskette worth of data would readily witness. Thus, one cannot insist enough on the importance of the data integrity aspect of file systems. The description of techniques for *file backup* is the objective of this section.

5.1. Physical Backup

Violent or natural catastrophes, such as fires or flooding, can immediately wipe out a whole computer center. Besides these possible but rare accidents, the most frequent equally radical failure that can affect files stored in a computer system is a disk head crash. Such accidents occur as a result of a violent mechanical shock (e.g., quake or explosion) affecting a disk drive, a sudden power failure on a disk drive, or the penetration of dust inside a normally sealed disk pack. In the first two cases, heads that are normally hovering a few micrometers above the disk surface may "lose altitude". In the latter case, a piece of dust may find its way into the narrow disk–head gap. In any case, the disk surface is usually carved by the disk head beyond repair, causing the loss of many data records if not the whole disk.

Recovery from any of the above damages usually calls for complete replacement of the affected disks. However, with the damaged units went all the information they contained. When new units are installed, they must be reloaded with all the information that used to be on the defective units.

This of course assumes that this information is available from backup copies of the failed units. In order to be able to reload a virgin disk as fast as possible to bring it up to a carbon-copy state of a failed disk, the most classic technique consists of regularly making "carbon copies" of all disks onto tapes. "Carbon copies" is used to mean physically identical copies of the originals. Thus, at regular intervals, all disks are dumped physically, cylinder by cylinder, surface by surface, and sector by sector, onto tapes. These tapes can then be reused later if necessary to reconstruct identical physical images of any disk onto a new virgin disk unit.

Of course the backup tapes as well as the tape containing the software for performing a reload operation should be kept in a safe location, away from the computer center, so that a fire or flooding of the center cannot affect them as well.

Because the physical dump process operates across file boundaries to capture a snapshot of a complete disk, it may take a substantial amount of time and is necessarily disruptive, i.e., it cannot occur while there is activity on the disk. In practice, this implies that physical dumping must occur when the system is not in operation, at night, and not too frequently, typically once a day to once a week.

These very restrictions limit the usefulness of physical dumping. Indeed, if the last available physical dump of a disk is between a week and a day old, many updates made to the disk between that last backup and the time of a crash will be missed by the reload procedure.

On the other hand, there are many kinds of failures, besides the radical ones we have just described, that can be repaired with less expensive but more dynamic dumping procedures. Both to satisfy the needs of these less radical failures and to complement physical dumping (i.e., to bring a physically reloaded disk up to date), logical dumping techniques are recommended.

5.2.   Logical Backup

Contrary to physical backup, which is performed on a spatial basis, cylinder by cylinder, surface by surface, and sector by sector across file boundaries, logical backup is performed on a conceptual basis, file by file. While physical backup needs to capture snapshots of entire disks, therefore requiring that all disk activity be frozen while dumping takes place, logical backup captures snapshots of only one file at a time, thus requiring that activity cease only on that file.

In other words, logical dumping can proceed in parallel with normal operation. Not being disruptive, logical dumping of a particular file can take place much more often than physical dumping of a whole disk. Logical dumping is typically performed by one or more background processes that continuously scan the entire file system. Such processes will systematically dump to tape any file that has been modified either since it was last dumped or since some fixed amount of time has elapsed. Both policies can be found in existing systems, sometimes complementing one another, as in Multics, for instance. Either requires that the file system keep information regarding when each file was last dumped and last modified. Using either method, a file may be dumped logically anywhere between a day and an hour after having been modified.

As suggested in Section 5.1, logical backup can be used to complement physical backup by first reloading a damaged disk from a physical dump and then bringing that disk up to date on a file-by-file basis using logical dumps of individual files that have been modified since the physical dump was taken.

In addition, logical dumps can be used in case of smaller failures. For instance, if a system crashes for some hard- or software reason not affecting the disk as a whole, some file may find itself left in an inconsistent state, requiring that it be refetched from the latest logical dump tape. Logical dumps can also be used to recover from individual user mistakes. If a user has by accident deleted a file he really meant to keep, he can recover the latest version of it from logical dump tapes.

Not only can logical dumping be performed while the system is in normal operation, but retrieval of a dumped file can also be performed during normal operation, which is not easy for physical reload.

While logical dumping may seem to be the final answer to all problems, it is not. In certain systems, most notably data base systems, failures must be as rare as possible, the time needed to recover must be as short as possible, and the probability that a file may be damaged—even if it is recoverable—in the course of a crash must be minimized. To this end, some special disk management techniques may be used that enhance the integrity of disks and files. They are discussed next.

6.   Disk Management for Data Integrity

6.1.   Atomic Stable Storage

Imagine a file system where a critical disk record that has just been updated is written back to permanent storage "in place", i.e., the updated version is written back on top of the old version, thereby erasing it. Clearly, if the system crashes for whatever reason while the write-back operation is taking place, the record will be damaged, since the new version has not had time to be written out completely but the old version is already partially erased by the incomplete new version.

One technique for guaranteeing the integrity of the record is called *atomic stable storage*. With this technique, stable storage, i.e., the disk, is made to look as if it were atomically modifiable. When it is updated, the update operation looks as if it happens either successfully or not at all, without any bad side effects. Achieving atomic stable storage really requires two disk records per logical data record. The two records should be allocated preferably on different disks to prevent their both being affected by one head crash.

When writing out a logical record, the following algorithm is used (Fig. 54). First, the modified logical record is written out to one physical record and immediately read back in and compared to the main memory copy. This operation is retried several times until either what is read in matches what was written out, or it can be asserted that the physical disk record is damaged and non-writable. (In the latter case, another record can be chosen or an operator action is required.) If and when the first operation succeeds, it is applied similarly to the second physical record implementing the logical record.

Now, when reading a logical record, as long as the two physical records implementing it are identical, the logical record is considered to be up to date. If both physical records are readable (no CRC check) but different, it is assumed that the system crashed after writing the first one but before writing the second one. The second record is updated from the first one. If either physical record is found illegible (e.g., CRC check), the assumption is that the system crashed while writing the bad record. That record is thus reinitialized from the other one. If the first record is reinitialized from the second one, the latest update to the

```
SIMPLE - WRITE ( B , ADDR )    NTRIALS = 0 ;
                               WHILE  NTRIALS< N DO            {
                                   WRITE ( B , ADDR )
                                   B' ◄— READ ( ADDR )
                                   IF COMPARE ( B , B' ) DO RETURN ( TRUE )
                                   NTRIALS = NTRIALS + 1 }
                               RETURN ( FALSE )

SAFE - WRITE ( B , B₁ , B₂ )   UNLESS SIMPLE - WRITE ( B , B1 ) DO RETURN (ERROR 1)
                               UNLESS SIMPLE - WRITE ( B , B2 ) DO RETURN (ERROR 2)
                               RETURN ( OK )

SIMPLE - READ ( ADDR , B )     B ◄— READ ( ADDR )
                               IF CORRUPTED ( B ) DO RETURN ( FALSE)
                               RETURN ( TRUE )

SAFE - READ ( B , B₁ , B₂ )    CODE 1 ◄— SIMPLE - READ ( B₁ , B )
                               CODE 2 ◄— SIMPLE - READ ( B₂ , B' )
                               IF CODE 1 AND CODE 2 AND COMPARE ( B , B' ) DO
                                   RETURN ( TRUE )
                               IF CODE 1 DO
                                   RETURN ( SIMPLE - WRITE ( B , B₂ ))
                               IF CODE 2 DO      {
                                   B ◄— COPY ( B' )
                                   RETURN ( SIMPLE - WRITE ( B , B₁ ))
                                                 }
```

Fig. 54.   Atomic stable storage.

logical record is lost but the logical record is restored at least to a consistent state, even if it is not the latest state.

The atomic stable storage technique is restricted in two ways by definition:

1.   It is applicable to selected critical records of the file system, like directory blocks or file maps, but it would be too expensive to use for entire files. This would indeed require having enough disk storage to contain all files twice.

2.   The technique is applicable only to records with internal consistency constraints but no external consistency constraints. In other words, if the balance of all the accounts of a bank agency could fit into one record, the technique could be applied to that record. Since, all accounts will never fit into one record, transferring money from one account in one record to another account in another

record cannot be guaranteed atomic by the above technique. Although both account records may be correct according to our above readability rule, the system may have crashed after subtracting money from one and before adding it to the other, which is clearly not acceptable.

6.2.   Shadow Pages

When several records having integrity constraints between them can be grouped into a file that has no integrity constraint with other files, the *shadow paging* technique can be applied.

With this technique, when a file is opened for updating, the file map (its PT) is activated (loaded in main memory). (In the case of an indirect-access file system, the file pages are copied from the filing disks to the paging disks.) While the file is being updated, the system marks every updated page of the file as modified.

Later, when the file is deactivated, pages that have not been modified are not written back to the filing disks. Pages that have been modified are written out but not to their original disk addresses. Instead they are written to newly allocated places, called shadow pages, as shown in Fig. 55. The file map residing in main memory is updated accordingly. Only when *all* updated pages have been written out to their disk shadow is the modified file map written out too.

Typically, the file map is updated in place. Thus, to be absolutely safe, it should be updated with the atomic stable storage technique. However, many systems implementing the shadow page technique, assuming that the probability of failure in the middle of a file map update is negligible, simply overwrite file maps in place.

Shadowing does offer a good measure of file integrity in that if the system crashes after some shadow pages have been written out but before the file map has been updated, the update will be lost in the crash but the file will be left in its latest consistent state before the crash since shadow pages are not cataloged in the old file map preserved on disk.

Page shadowing presents two limitations by definition:

1.   With time, it degrades the performance of sequential file access. When a sequential file is initially created, its records are best allocated in sequential order on the disk so as to minimize disk access time. However, as the file ages and goes through many update operations, every operation destroys the nice sequential allocation a little at a time.

2.   While shadowing guarantees to a large extent the atomic update of individual files, it does not guarantee the atomic update of a disk as a whole. Indeed, shadowing requires that new pages be allocated and old pages be released from the disk map. Thus, as a result of a file update, not only the file but also the disk map must be updated. As the file and the disk maps cannot be written out to disk at the same time, a system crash may cause the file map and the disk map to be inconsistent about the allocation state of certain records.

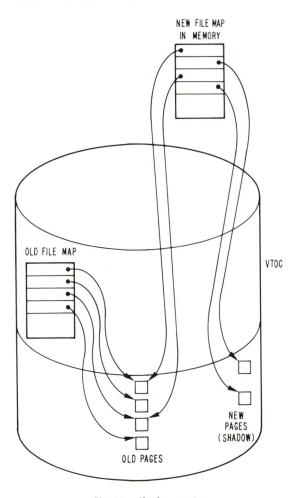

NEW FILE MAP
IN MEMORY

OLD FILE MAP

VTOC

NEW
PAGES
(SHADOW)

OLD PAGES

Fig. 55.   Shadow paging.

6.3.   Salvaging Disks

Disk salvaging is a procedure aimed at repairing inconsistencies such as those described above, in files, file maps, or disk maps that have been damaged following a system crash. The essence of the procedure is described hereafter first in the case of systems using shadow pages and then in the case of systems updating pages in place.

In some systems, disk maps are small enough to be kept in main memory during normal operation. In other systems they are too large and must be paged in and out as needed. In either case, part of the disk map on disk may differ part of the time from the portion in main memory. Furthermore, except for data base systems, where special precautions may be taken, no distinction is made in the disk map between permanent and shadow pages, and disk and file maps are written out asynchronously. As a result, a system crash may occur after a disk map reflecting a shadow allocation has been written out but before the shadow pages become permanent. Alternatively, it may crash after a file map is written out, but before the disk map reflecting the release of old pages is written out. In either case, the disk map will show records as allocated while they belong to no file. In the former case, shadow pages are allocated but not attributed to any file yet. In the latter case, old pages no longer belong to any file but are not yet released.

Thus, when restarting the system after a crash, it may be necessary to perform what is called *salvaging* or rebuilding the disk. This consists of recomputing the entire disk allocation map from the file maps. All disk records are initially marked as free in the rebuilt disk map. All file maps are then scanned one by one, marking all file pages as allocated in the disk map.

In systems that update pages in place, salvaging is more delicate. In indirect access file systems, a modified file is vulnerable while its pages are being written from the paging disks back to the filing disks, that is, while it is being closed. A crash may leave such a file "half" updated. However, until such time, the latest file version is safe because paging disks play a bit the role of shadow storage.

In direct access file systems that update pages in place, salvaging is even more complex. Basically, any file that is open for writing at the time of a crash is potentially damaged. The system must keep track on disk of which files are open, so it can purge them following a crash, rebuild the disk maps by scanning the remaining "good" file maps, and finally reload the "bad" files from earlier logical dumps. In some systems, after certain soft crashes, special software takes over operations and safely writes out those portions of the SPT, SST, and files that have been spared by the crash in an attempt to simplify salvaging. In some systems too, files that are known to be temporary are allocated in separate directories so the system knows it need not worry about their integrity.

In certain systems such as Tripos (Richards, 1979) or the Alto operating system (Lampson, 1979), enough redundant information is maintained, linking file maps to their pages, linking pages together, and linking them back to their file maps, for inconsistencies to be corrected by a complete physical scan of the disk.

6.4. Version Storage

With the decreasing cost of storage and emerging optical storage technologies, a few recent systems, mainly research prototypes (Svobodova, 1981), have proposed a new technique for preserving file integrity, which avoids the lack of sequential allocation and the disk map integrity problems of shadow paging. This technique, called *version storage,* consists of treating permanent storage as append-only or write-once storage, which optical disks are anyway. Thus, new versions of files are constantly added to the system, and old versions are never overwritten. This avoids the sequential file problem in that new versions of sequential files can be stored sequentially as well. The disk map update problem is cured in that pages of old files are never released anyway, while pages of new versions may simply be wasted if a crash occurs after they are allocated and written out but before the corresponding file map is written out.

6.5. Atomicity in Data Base Systems

All the disk management techniques seen above were designed primarily for and are particularly applicable to data base systems. However, regular filing systems may also use such techniques and would do well to implement them in the future.

Following are some more remarks on data integrity in data base operating systems. These remarks are specific to data base systems and irrelevant in time-sharing or personal computer operating systems. The essential difference between the latter and the former from a data integrity point of view is a matter of the volume of data. In regular operating systems, the largest logical unit of information whose integrity is at stake is a file, and files are typically in the range of kilobytes to megabytes. In data base systems, the logical unit of information may be the whole data base, which typically spans over many files and represents tens to hundreds of megabytes. The data integrity techniques seen so far are quite adequate to preserve the integrity of individual files but fall short of guaranteeing the global integrity of entire data bases, composed of multiple files, possibly spread across several computers in a distributed system.

a. Serializability

In Chapter II, when we discussed multiprocessing issues, we introduced the concept of serializability. Serializability is a property that many data base trans-actions (queries and updates) must have, whereby although they are carried out in parallel, they must look as if they are being carried out one after the other, i.e., they must look as if each is seeing a consistent snapshot of the data base. Serializability of a transaction guarantees its *atomicity*. Seen from other transactions, the effects of an atomic transaction appear to be indivisible. Serializability is only one of the two components of atomicity. It deals with the parallelism of transactions.

Achieving serializability was said to require a two-phase locking protocol, where all necessary locks are acquired during the first phase, during which no lock may be released, and all locks are released in a second phase. We then explained how deadlocks can arise between two or more transactions following a two-phase locking protocol. We suggested that in certain cases, the probability and the cost of deadlocks could be minimized by prelocking all necessary data base records before real work starts, i.e., by reducing the locking phase of the protocol to one point in time.

b. Recoverability

Now, we come to the second facet of atomicity, called *recoverability,* which deals with the reliability of transactions, requiring that the second phase of the protocol be reduced to one point in time, as explained below.

A transaction is said to be atomic, as suggested earlier, if either it succeeds or it fails without leaving side-effects, i.e., either it completes and leaves the data base in a consistent state, or it aborts (crashes) and goes away without leaving any visible trace of its existence in the data base.

When considered in the presence of parallelism, atomicity means serializability of transactions. In the presence of failures, it means recoverability of consistent states for the data base. Atomicity is not only a term that has different meanings in the two different contexts. It is also a term that relates parallelism to error recovery: serialization through a two-phase locking protocol cannot ignore recoverability.

Because of parallelism, a transaction should never unlock a record before it has *locked* all the records it needs (two-phase locking), otherwise it would expose that unlocked record to parallel transactions and yet be forced to abort because of a later deadlock. Now, adding the possibility of crashes, the transaction should never unlock a record before it has *locked* and *updated* all the records (and file maps) it needs. Indeed, even if it has acquired all the locks it needs, thus knowing it can no longer be deadlocked, it may still crash, which would also abort it, and should also return the data base to its state before the transaction start. This supports our earlier statement that the unlocking phase cannot start until all the work is completed and updated records have been safely written out to disk, i.e., this phase must be punctual in time.

6.6. Committing Data Base Transactions

Now the problem is that the system (or systems in the case of a distributed data base) may crash after all the work is complete and *some* records belonging to different files on different machines have been written out safely, but before *all* records have been written out. Atomic stable storage or shadow pages alone will not solve the problem in such a case. The transaction cannot take the risk of crashing after having updated some but not all of the modified records on disk. There must be one point in time before which the transaction can safely abort without leaving visible traces and after which it must be recoverable, i.e., after which it must be possible to force its successful completion. This point is called the *transaction commit point.*

While it is important to explain the essential difference between regular operating systems and data base systems from a data integrity point of view, it would
be inappropriate in this general volume on operating systems to go any further
and discuss the details of advanced techniques for data integrity in (distributed)
data base systems. For the interested reader, we will just name and briefly sketch
three of the most common techniques.

Intentions lists. The first technique uses what is called an intentions list or
commit record. This is a small data structure, by definition fitting inside one disk
record, associated with the transaction. The record describes the state of the
transaction (in progress, committed, or aborted) and points to the old *and* new
versions of all the files or logical records currently locked by the transaction.
Every file or record lock contains a pointer to the transaction's commit record.
When the transaction has completed its work, it writes out all updated records
and files to disk, without releasing their locks. Then, it updates its commit record
to indicate that it has reached its commit point. This takes a single disk access.
Finally, it substitutes the new files for the old ones in the data base catalogs, and
it releases all the locks. If the transaction crashes before committing, no harm is
done since new files do not yet appear in the catalogs. If it crashes after committing, it can be restarted to completion any number of times since the commit
record indicates what files have to be updated and the new versions are safely on
disk.

Undo–redo logs. A second technique uses what is called an undo–redo log.
Updates to the data base are done in place. However, before doing an update,
enough information to undo or redo it is recorded in a log file and forced out to
disk. The commitment of transactions is also recorded on the log. In case of a
crash, the log can always be inspected to undo aborted transactions or redo
commited ones.

Two-phase commit protocol. The last technique is aimed specifically at distributed systems. It assumes that either the commit record or the log technique is
used on each machine involved in the distributed transaction. The problem is that
all commit records or logs must be coordinated across machine boundaries. To
do so requires what is called a two-phase commit protocol. Some machine,
usually the one where the transaction was issued or started, is declared coordi-
nator of the transaction. It holds the master commit record. The master record
points to all slave records, and vice versa. When the master is ready to commit
the transaction, it sends all participants an order to prepare to commit. This tells
them to force all their updated records out to disk. They are expected to respond
positively to the prepare order, but they may unilaterally respond negatively or
not respond at all (in case of crash). This is the first of two phases: the prepara-
tion. When the master has received positive acknowledgments from all participating systems, it forces its own commit record out to disk in one disk access

and then informs all participants. This is the second phase: commit. If any system crashes before or during the first phase, no harm is done since all systems can query the master record and discover that the transaction did not commit and can be abandoned. If a crash occurs after the commit point, all is safe since all files and commit records have been written out to disk. The transaction can be restarted any number of times and forced to completion.

Suggested Reading and Classics

On file system implementations:

> Meyer, 1970; Pamerlee, 1972. IBM's CP67/CMS flat file system.
> Daley, 1965, 1968; Bensoussan, 1972; Organick, 1972, Chapter 6. The Multics hierarchical file system.
> Ritchie, 1974. The Unix hierarchical file system.
> Rees, 1975. The Emas hierarchical file system.

On file system integrity:

> Stern, 1974. Techniques for file archival on Multics.
> Lampson, 1979. File integrity by redundancy in the single-user Alto system.

On distributed file systems and file servers:

> Swinehart, 1979; Paxton, 1979. On WFS.
> Israel, 1979 or Sturgis, 1980. On DFS.
> Birrell, 1980; Dion, 1980. On the Cambridge file server (CFS).
> Dellar, 1980. On a local network page server.
> Mitchell, 1982. A comparison between CFS and DFS.
> Svobodova, 1981. On the Swallow file server and its potential for optical storage.
> Fridrich, 1981. On the Felix file server.
> Svobodova, 1983. A comparative discussion of file server designs.

On file integrity issues in distributed systems:

> Bernstein, 1981; Kohler, 1981. Surveys of concurrency control techniques.
> Reed, 1983. On version storage techniques.

Further Reading and References

On reliability:

> Randell, 1975
> Randell, 1978
> Randell, 1979
> Astrahan, 1976; Blasgen, 1976; Gray, 1981. Reliability in the System R data base.

On file organization:

> Dodd, 1969

Chapter VIII

Addressing and Naming

At the beginning of Chapter V, we assumed a one-level random access memory. Data in such a memory are referenced by absolute address. However, as data and programs are created and deleted in such a memory, holes appear that are hard to reuse and waste memory space. Thus, remaining programs must be recompacted. This makes absolute addresses unattractive in practice because they are reusable and cannot be assigned permanently to programs.

To remedy the problem, uid-based segmentation was introduced. Uids can be tied permanently to files because they are expendable and, unlike absolute addresses, are not reused. However, it was pointed out that human users refer to programs by names rather than by uids.

Thus, a set of catalog structures was proposed to keep track of inactive segments, called files, by name. The hierarchical file system structure was introduced as avoiding name duplication and lost object problems, while offering sharing and even selective sharing among users.

Then, uids were shown to pose certain implementation and manipulation problems. The SST needed to support uids was shown to be too small to hold descriptors for all segments at the same time. Solving these problems required the introduction of user address spaces, based on segment numbers, as a necessary shorthand for uids.

In the end, one problem remains to be solved: bridging the gap between source programs that use symbolic names and object programs that need segment numbers. The file system, as a repository for all names, and the concept of search rule provide the semantic basis for performing this name to address translation, but the mechanism for implementing the translation has not been discussed yet. This mechanism, called *linking,* is described in the Section 1. Section 2 presents a comparative study of linking mechanisms. Section 3 explains, by means of an illustrative example, how these different linking mechanisms compare in practice. Section 4 offers a summarizing perspective of naming and addressing in operating systems. The four concepts discussed above, segmentation, file system, user address space, and linking, all deal with naming problems, that is, problems concerned with binding names to other names—e.g., symbolic names to segment numbers (linking), segment numbers to uids (address spaces), names to uids (file systems), and uids to addresses (segmentation). Their relation will be summarized in one diagram.

1.   Linking

The file system provides the vehicle for mapping symbolic names into uids (and secondary addresses), while the user address space provides the vehicle for mapping segment numbers into uids (and primary PT addresses). The missing element is the linking mechanism, which is the mechanism for mapping symbolic names to segment numbers in such a way that both the symbolic name and the segment number point to the same segment, i.e., to the same uid, thereby allowing sharing on a uid basis.

   Notice that a native linking mechanism is a facility proper to programmable systems. Dedicated systems, such as process control systems, are linked completely off-line, usually on another computer where the software is developed and the system generated.

   The particular linking mechanism described here as an example addresses the case of systems where sharing or even selective sharing of programs and data in primary memory is desired. This example is chosen because such linking mechanisms are among the most complex and therefore present some of the most interesting design challenges. As the design is presented, it will be clear what simplifications would occur in a less sophisticated case and what price is paid for the higher functionality in the present case.

1.1.   Links

In the SST, every segment is named by a uid. In the world of source programs every program module is named by a symbolic name (e.g., SQRT, ALPHA, SORT, MAIN—LIB). When a source program is compiled or assembled, the resulting object module acquires a uid. The problem to be discussed here is the following: When a source module A refers to a module B by symbolic name, how can the object A refer to the object B by a segment number denoting the uid of B?

   When a source procedure is compiled or assembled, the language processor translates every symbolic reference encountered in the source by a reference called a *link* in the object module. At the time of the translation, the link contains, at least conceptually, the symbolic name used in the source module. In practice the link is actually empty and the symbolic name is stored in some definition section together with a reference to the link to which it corresponds.

Before execution, a program called a *linker* is invoked to translate symbolic names into segment numbers, and store the segment numbers in the appropriate links.

In any system where sharing executable code in main memory is not an objective, the links reside in the text of the object module they belong to. However, where main memory sharing is an objective, this simple design is unacceptable. If the links of an object module were in its text, all the users wanting to share the same object module would be forced to use the same links. Yet segment numbers have private, user-dependent meanings. Thus, they cannot be shared. To avoid sharing them, it is necessary to pull them (just like any normal working storage) out of the text of object modules into a place where they can be translated independently by each user.

This could be done as follows. Language processors generate pure objects. A pure object is composed of reentrant object code and a separate *linkage area* or *linkage section*. Reentrant object code means code that contains no working storage and no links and is not self-modifying. Such code can be executed by several users at a time without risk of conflicts. All the links are collected in the linkage area and the object code refers to them indirectly. When a user wants to use an object module, he can make his own copy of the linkage area and have the linker translate it according to his own search rules and into his own segment numbers. Since the translated links may be used heavily, on every external reference made by the program, it would seem desirable to load the translated copy of the linkage area into dedicated processor registers, called linkage registers, at run-time. The object code could then refer to a link indirectly by referring to the linkage register that contains it. This is represented in Fig. 56.

1.2.   Linkage Areas

While this architecture is logically correct, it presents one problem. An object module may have a variable and potentially large number of links, while a processor has a fixed number of linkage registers. Thus, it appears that the translated links must reside in memory in spite of the performance penalty. All the links are collected in a translated linkage area (distinct from the original linkage area generated by the language translator), and only one linkage register is required to point to the linkage area at run-time. Thus, an executing object module can refer to its links indirectly through the linkage register (Fig. 57).

1.3.   Linkage Tables

Another problem arises now. Every object segment has its own linkage area. Thus, if a user executes a large computation involving many object segments, he will need many linkage registers, perhaps more than the processor has. Again, we solve the problem by pushing the linkage registers back into memory in an

- SHARING OBJECT CODE → CODE MUST BE REENTRANT

→ LINKS OUTSIDE CODE
- IN PROTOTYPE LINKAGE SECTION
  BEFORE TRANSLATION

- IN LINKAGE REGISTERS
  AFTER TRANSLATION

EXECUTING PROGRAM

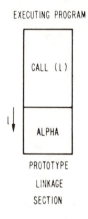

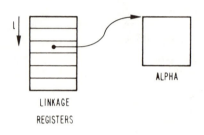

- SHORTCOMINGS : LIMITED NUMBER OF LINKAGE REGISTERS

Fig. 56. Linkage registers.

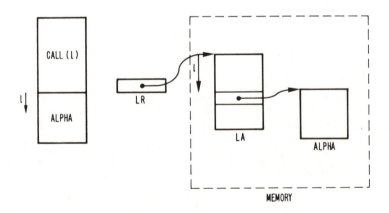

- SHORTCOMINGS : AFTER TRANSFER TO ALPHA, HOW IS LR SET TO POINT TO ALPHA'S
  LINKAGE AREA ?

Fig. 57. Linkage areas.

area called the *Linkage Table* (LT). For every segment, there is one entry in the LT, with an index number equal to the number of the corresponding segment, that points to the appropriate linkage area. And we require that processors have only one linkage register, called the LT pointer. Thus, an executing module can refer to its links by referring indirectly to the LT pointer, picking the right linkage pointer out of the LT, and following it to the linkage area (Fig. 58). The value of the LT pointer of a user process is part of the state of that user process.

1.4.   Linkage Registers

Now comes the last problem. In order to reference its working storage or any other procedure module it might call, an object module must make three memory references: to the LT, to its linkage area, and finally to the storage itself.

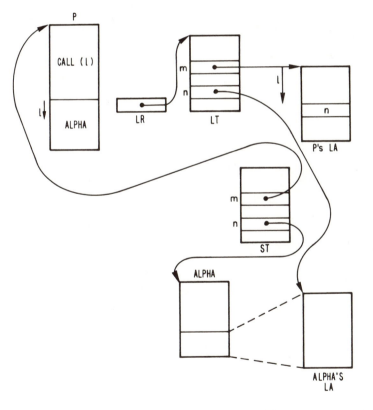

• DRAWBACK : 3 LEVELS OF INDIRECTION

Fig. 58.   Linkage tables.

This design is most inefficient. To speed things up, we reintroduce the idea of having several (4, 8, 16, etc.) programmable *linkage registers* in every processor. Thus, when a module is entered, it should first use the register pointing to the LT to load its linkage pointer into a linkage register and then use that linkage register to load the most frequently used links into other available linkage registers. In doing so, many references will be saved during normal operation (Fig. 59). These linkage registers play the role for linking that the SAM plays for segmentation and the PAM for paging. However, there is no need for these registers to be associative and managed by a LRU algorithm, because the compiler can decide which link to put into which register by program better than a demand mechanism could by guessing.

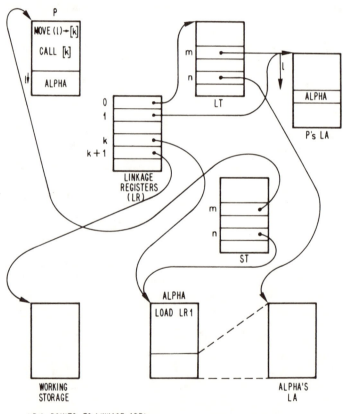

LR 1 POINTS TO LINKAGE AREA

REGISTER k IS USED TO POINT TO HEAVILY USED SUBROUTINE ALPHA

REGISTER k + 1 IS USED TO POINT TO SOME WORKING STORAGE SEGMENT

Fig. 59. Linkage registers revised.

The linking architecture and associated hardware described above correspond in principle, if not in every detail and in the terminology, to the mechanism found in the Honeywell Multics system. This design is extremely powerful in that it allows main memory sharing of programs. However, this feature has not been achieved without cost. It should be kept in mind that most linking mechanisms are not as sophisticated and thus can be much simpler than the one presented here.

2.   Linkers

The above description showed primarily what data structures were necessary to support the linking operation in the particular case of a system offering uid-based segmentation for main memory sharing. Now, it is desirable to understand not only what data structures are necessary but also how the linker operates, what type of linkers exist, what their respective characteristics are, and how simple their operation can be in comparison to what was suggested in the foregoing example.

It was said earlier that main memory sharing is regarded as a fairly sophisticated feature not offered by most systems. The hardware and software necessary to support the concept of uids are relatively complex and expensive. Accordingly, one cannot blindly say that main memory sharing is an advantage without qualifying the sort of objectives one has in mind for the computing system. The same sort of argument can be made for linkers.

In this section, we will study a succession of linking mechanisms, each more sophisticated but also more expensive and complex than its predecessors. We will not talk about advantages or disadvantages of linking schemes, but rather about their abilities to perform certain functions that may be desirable in some system environments and undesirable in others. The linkers to be described will be discussed from two different points of view: (1) the point in time at which they are invoked to perform their task in the program development process; (2) the type of addressing hardware that they assume or require.

Let us first review the program development process. The process involves six operations, which are presented in an order not necessarily reflecting their order of execution:

Translation. In all cases, the first operation considered here is the translation of the source program into an object program.

Linking. Linking allows combining several object modules (files, segments) into one larger module, thereby resolving intermodule references, as explained earlier.

Allocation. Allocation is the operation by which it is decided where a program will be located in the user address space or logical address space. In systems offering addressing hardware such as base-and-bound registers, segmentation, or paging, the allocation operation does not deal with mapping into main memory addresses, but with assignment of virtual or relocated addresses, as seen by the user program.

Relocation. As defined in Chapter V, relocation is the operation consisting of adding the offset of the program in the address space where it will be run to internal references it may make, to account for the fact that the logical address space in which it was translated is different from the address space into which it will run.

Loading. Loading is the operation whereby space is allocated in the *main* memory and the program is brought in.

Execution. Finally, execution is the last step, concluding the development of the program.

The point of the following sections is to study when the various linkers are invoked between compile-time and run-time. Figure 60 summarizes their respective features.

2.1.   Early Systems

a.   Compile-and-go

In primitive computer systems, from the early days of computing and compiling, when only absolute addressing was known, a typical mode of operation was known as *compile-and-go*. In this mode of operation, compile-time and run-time can be viewed as equal, at least from a macroscopic point of view. The mode is characterized by the absence of linking. And for all practical purposes, one cannot talk about any relocation. The compiler is given one program that must include all subroutines and data areas. The compiler is responsible for allocating addresses in the user address space, which also means in memory here, for directly loading the generated code at the right place, and for starting execution. This is a very simple but very rigid scheme. It is rigid because it precludes saving precompiled modules in the file system and linking them later and it forces recompilation before every execution.

b.   Load-and-go

To remedy this situation, the next generation of compilers was designed so that the compilation and the execution were separate. The compiler is responsible for allocation and generates a so-called absolute object module that is stored away in the file system, or more commonly punched out on cards. Then a so-called *absolute loader* fetches the deck from the file system or the card reader and loads

PROCESSING MODE	LINKING	ALLOCATION	RELOCATION	LOADING	APPLICABLE ADDRESSING
COMPILE-AND-GO	—	CT = RT COMPILER (BATCH)	—	CT = RT COMPILER (BATCH)	ABSOLUTE
LOAD-AND-GO	(USER)	CT COMPILER	(USER)	<RT ABS. LOADER	ABSOLUTE
BINDERS	CT≤ <RT BINDER	CT≤ <RT BINDER	CT≤ <RT BINDER	<RT ABS. LOADER	ABSOLUTE BASE-AND-BOUND VIRTUAL
LINKAGE EDITORS	CT≤ <RT LINK. ED	<RT REL. LOADER	<RT REL. LOADER	<RT REL. LOADER	ABSOLUTE BASE-AND-BOUND VIRTUAL
LINKING LOADERS	<RT LINK. LOADER	<RT LINK. LOADER	<RT LINK. LOADER	<RT LINK. LOADER	ABSOLUTE BASE-AND-BOUND VIRTUAL
OVERLAYING LOADERS	@RT OV. LOADER (CALL)	@RT OV. LOADER (CALL)	@RT OV. LOADER (CALL)	@RT OV. LOADER	ABSOLUTE BASE-AND-BOUND
DYNAMIC LINKERS	LINKER (FAULT)	LINKER (FAULT)	SEGMENT (FAULT)	PAGING (FAULT)	VIRTUAL
INTERPRETERS	CT=RT (INTERACTIVE)	CT=RT (INTERACTIVE)	CT=RT (INTERACTIVE)	CT=RT (INTERACTIVE)	ANY

CT = COMPILE-TIME   RT = RUN-TIME

Fig. 60. A comparison of linkers.

it in memory at the absolute address specified by the compiler. One can start talking about linking and relocation in the sense that several object decks can be submitted simultaneously to the loader, placed in main memory, and executed as part of one large program. However, the operations of linking modules to one another and relocating them with respect to one another are the responsibility of the programmer, who must sprinkle his code with declarative statements telling the compiler what the absolute addresses of separately compiled modules must be. Thus, the function is there but is carried out manually.

2.2.   Common Mechanisms

a.   Binders

We now turn our attention to solutions that are more modern, offer true linking and relocation, and are still applicable in today's systems. The first solution consists of decoupling allocation, linking, and relocation from both compilation and execution. The compiler produces relocatable object modules. Loading is of course still coupled with execution. In such a case, a *binder* is responsible for allocation, linking, and relocation. From several relocatable object modules it produces an absolute load module, which can be loaded individually by an absolute loader. The mechanism is clearly relevant to absolute addressing machines. However, in such machines it suffers from the fact that once a program has been bound, it can be loaded in only one place in memory. Binders are more interesting for other types of machine.

Consider machines with base-and-bound registers. A binder can be used to generate load modules that in an absolute addressing machine would be executable only if located at address zero. However, with a BBR the very same programs can be located anywhere in memory, provided the BBR is set accordingly. Thus, binding is an interesting mechanism in such systems.

In machines offering a demand paged virtual memory and an indirect-access file system, binding is a valuable idea as it allows packing program modules contiguously, without any fragmentation in the virtual memory space. In such systems, each user sees his own address space. All address spaces are identical. Thus, one can choose some conventional address in all address spaces, where all user programs start. A program bound to start at that fixed address would have to be loaded at that address in an absolute addressing machine, but actually can be located anywhere in a virtual memory system, thanks to the relocation mechanism. This is exactly the solution adopted in the IBM VM/SP operating system. Of course no absolute loader is necessary. Loading is taken care of by the virtual memory.

Finally, in machines with uid-based segmentation, binding is useful to increase program locality. As mentioned in Chapter V, one of the objectives of uids is sharing, the other being to avoid relocation. Avoiding static relocation is desirable for software development, but detrimental to program locality as it spreads many small segments over a large area of virtual memory. Thus, it is undesirable for high-performance data processing. Binding several small segments into a big one improves performance in a uid system. As in the previous case, an absolute loader is not necessary thanks to the virtual memory.

b. Linkage Editors

Binders are of interest for systems with relocation hardware. However, they still leave something to be desired for absolute addressing systems. A better thing there is *linkage editors*.

With linkage editors, only linking, which is the sole function of a linkage editor, is separate from compilation and execution. Allocation, loading, and relocation are performed by a so-called *relocating loader* and are delayed until execution time. This separation of linking from the other function allows the linkage editor to tie together several small modules into a large one that is still relocatable, contrary to the case of binding. This offers the property that it is possible to take linked modules and to further link them to other modules. In addition, linked modules can always be loaded at any address, which is desirable in an absolute addressing machine. Of course, having retained this flexibility is paid for at the price of a relocating loader and a linkage editor that are invariably more complex than an absolute loader and a binder, respectively. Linkage editors are also used in demand paging virtual memory systems, such as IBM's MVS.

c. Linking Loaders

It is possible to gain even more flexibility, at some additional cost, of course, by resorting to *linking loaders*. With linking loaders, allocation, linking, loading, and relocation all are delayed until run-time. The added flexibility resides in the ability to change any individual module of a program without having to relink it explicitly before execution. Linking is delayed until the latest moment before execution. The added cost is that every time a program needs to be executed it must be relinked first, since there is no linked version of it around. This may be quite expensive. Thus, as we go down the list of linker types in the order in which we presented them, we observe that they become more and more flexible for the programer, but more and more complex and expensive from the operating system point of view, which was to be expected.

d. Overlaying Loaders

For systems without virtual memory, even more power is conceivable. The drawback of the previous solution is that it requires loading *all* the modules and data structures composing a program into memory at the same time, prior to any execution. In certain cases, this is most of primary memory. In other cases, the complete program may not even fit in memory.

To remedy these problems, the idea of an *overlaying loader* is used. The idea allows delaying the allocation, loading, linking, and relocation of *individual* modules until the very moment when they are needed. An overlaying loader can be driven by the compiled object code of the modules and/or by the user requesting the execution of the modules of a program. When the user has completed execution of one subset of the modules, called one overlay, execution stops, the results yielded by the partial program are saved in a small storage area, the program modules that are in memory are erased, and a new set of modules is "laid over" the first one, thereby reoccupying the same memory locations. Execution of the new overlay can then proceed.

2.3.   Advanced Mechanisms

a.   Dynamic Linkers

While the overlaying technique is quite an improvement over others for systems without virtual memory, it is complex. Organizing a computation in sections that can be laid over one another and coordinating the transfer of partial results between overlays is no trivial task. Fortunately this task is eliminated in systems with very large virtual memories.

With virtual memory, program modules (procedures and data) can be named by virtual addresses (i.e., segment numbers can be allocated) without actually consuming any primary memory. Actual loading can take place later on a page fault. Thus, it is possible to translate symbolic links without loading all modules of a program into memory at the same time. This is how binders and linkage editors operate in virtual memory systems.

One virtual memory linking technique goes even further than anything seen so far. It is called dynamic linking, the first and best example of which was designed in the Honeywell Multics system. *Dynamic linkers* not only delay the linking as a linking loader would, but they even delay it as an overlaying loader would, i.e., until the actual call to the individual module. Furthermore, linking need not even be requested explicitly. It is performed on demand, like paging or segmentation, which is why it is only worth considering in a virtual memory system. Dynamic linking has been implemented in Multics (Organick, 1972) and Emas (Millard *et al.,* 1975).

Every symbolic link contains not only a symbolic name but also a flag. When a user executes a module and needs to follow a link, he trips on the flag if the link has never been used and translated before. By tripping on the flag, he causes a processor exception called a *link fault*, which results in his computation being temporarily suspended. The dynamic linker is then invoked to translate the link, turn off the flag, and restore the computation state that existed just before the fault.

Considering how much goes into translating a link—using the search rules to retrieve the link target, allocating a segment number, and patching the link in the linkage area—linking can be a fairly involved and expensive task. In practice, when a user executes a program, he does not usually execute every single subroutine, mathematical module, error-handling procedure, or bit-crunching tool contained in the closure of all modules of the program. Instead, he follows one computational path through only a few modules of the closure. This means that only a few of the links inside the closure are actually used. Since it is fairly expensive to translate a link, it is nice not to translate those links that a particular user does not use.

Dynamic linking does not require the a priori search of all modules of a closure for all links of the closure. Also, during program development, the user can drive his program along selected computational paths, explicitly avoiding other, unfinished ones. Thus, he need not supply the modules that would be needed along these other paths, as the linker will never even notice that they are missing.

b.   Interpreters

For the sake of completeness, it seems desirable to mention that all above scenarios were developed under the assumption that one has a classical compiler and not an interpreted language, such as APL or BASIC. Interpreters for such languages again make compile-time and run-time coincide, not only macroscopically but even microscopically. Translation proceeds one instruction at a time and execution of that instruction follows immediately. There are no stored object programs or load modules, though one can talk of linking, loading, allocation, and relocation. All functions are performed within the interpreter. While the coincidence of run-time and compile-time may remind us of the compile-and-go technique, the analogy stops there. Compile-and-go forced recompilation before every execution for lack of a better solution, while interpreters allow this coincidence as a service to the interactive user, to help him develop and test programs one instruction at a time.

3.   Linking in Practice

It is interesting to review the impact of segments, pages, user address spaces, and linkers on the program development process. To this end, let us consider the various steps a user has to go through on a primitive eight-bit microprocessor system and compare them to what can be done on a large general purpose time-sharing system of the most sophisticated type (Fig. 61). Let us assume that a main program module P calls a subroutine Q containing a loop. Let us further assume that the programs are not written in a language, such as APL or BASIC, that is interpreted and would make all following operations invisible to the user on any system, small or large.

   1.   In both cases, the first step is to write the source code and to compile it until it is at least syntactically correct.
   2.   The next step is the linking of the two modules together. For the microprocessor, this involves first merging P and Q into a common logical address space. Q is mapped into the addresses following P, which requires some internal relocation. Then follows the proper linking operation, namely the translation of P's reference to Q into the address of Q. For the large system, linking can be done on demand, assuming a dynamic linker, and will actually follow address allocation.
   3.   For the microprocessor case, having linked the two modules together, it is necessary next to decide where they will be located in the user address space. This is the address allocation phase. On a typical microprocessor with contiguous space allocation, this involves *explicitly* deciding where the linked program modules will sit. On a large system, this involves simply allocating a segment number to each module, which is done *implicitly* at the request of the linker as it tries to translate links into segment numbers.
   4.   Then, one must relocate the two modules, i.e., adjust the internal references they contain to the actual addresses to which they will have to refer in the user address space. In the microprocessor case, this involves adding the value of the base address of $P-Q$ to the internal loop address of Q and to the link between P and Q. In a large system, relocation is not necessary since there is segmentation to automatically relocate references relative to the base of segments.
   5.   Finally comes the loading of P and Q in the main memory. This calls for an absolute loader in the microprocessor case, while the demand paging mechanism of the large system will take care of loading automatically.
   6.   Only then can the program be executed.

   Thus, in the microprocessor case, the user must explicitly invoke the compiler, then the linker, which typically invokes the memory management mechanism to request address allocation, invokes a loader, invokes a relocation subroutine, and finally performs the linking. In the large system, the user also calls the compiler. He can then directly ask for execution of the main routine of the program. As he will trip on the missing segments, pages, and links, the rest of the work will be done by the system on demand. As the linker discovers that P and Q are to be linked it will ask the system to allocate segment numbers. Segmentation and paging then take care of relocation and loading. However, one cannot stress enough the hardware and software price that has been paid for achieving such apparent simplicity in the eyes of the user.

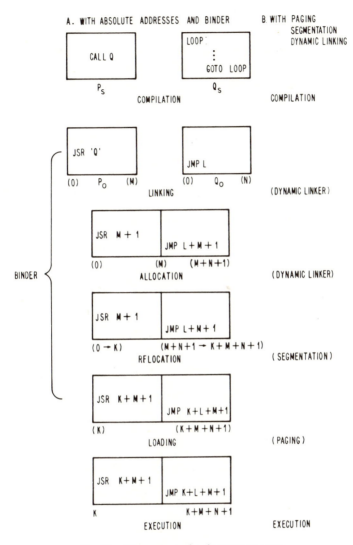

Fig. 61.   The program development process.

4.   Naming and Addressing Synthesis

The various types of names and addresses encountered in operating systems can be summarized as follows.

1.   The system offers a segmented address space where segments are named by uids, which are system-wide numerical names.

2.   Source programs refer to these segments by using symbolic names, which are local, human-oriented ones.

3.   In order to allow linkers to map symbolic names into uids, the concept of a tree name is used. A tree name is a system-wide human-oriented name that is easily derived from a symbolic name by use of a search rule.

4.   In order to allow object programs to conveniently address segments, the concept of a segment number is used. A segment number is a machine-oriented (numerical) local name that is bound to a uid by the NT.

All this is represented in Fig. 62. A segment number to tree name binding may be added to the NT to allow users to recall what segment number corresponds to what file. However, this binding plays no role in the addressing mechanism.

It appears that objects (files or segments) can be referenced by identifiers that can be classified into local or universal, and human-oriented (names) or machine-oriented (addresses), giving a total of four possible combinations. In addi-

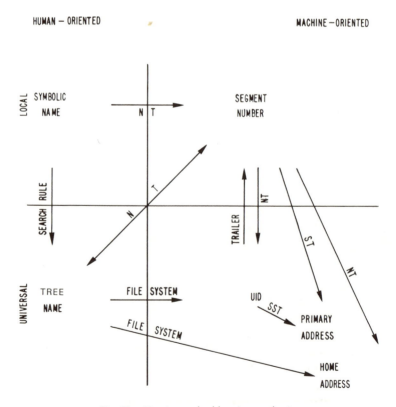

Fig. 62.   Naming and addressing synthesis.

tion, all forms of identifiers, except uids, are of the reusable type, meaning that they are not expendable, must be reallocated at times, and cannot be permanently tied to files or segments.

Figure 62 also shows that every arrow binding one type of identifier to another is marked by the name of a structure or table. This table represents the context in which the two types of name are bound. Binding contexts are fundamental to relate identifiers to other identifiers or to objects. Most tables in an operating system can be viewed as binding contexts. For instance, the UPT binds user process identifiers to their NT, ST, and LT and, while loaded, to a corresponding virtual processor identifier. The VPT binds the identifier of running virtual processors to a physical processor. The LT of a process binds the object modules used by the process to their linkage areas, and the linkage areas bind the external references made by modules back to segment numbers of other modules.

Notice that most tables bind identifiers to other identifiers that are in turn bound to lower level identifiers. However, one eventually reaches a level of identifiers that are no longer bound to anything but directly denote actual objects. This is the case of a disk block address or a main memory page address, for instance. We will limit ourselves here to pointing out this pervasive binding concept between identifiers and other identifiers or objects. It will be investigated more systematically in Chapter X to develop a structural model for operating systems.

As can be seen in Fig. 62, there are direct connections between segment numbers and physical addresses, and between tree names and physical addresses. The reader is therefore entitled to wonder why we still need uids at all, since they can be by-passed both from the naming and the addressing sides. Uids are still needed for the following reasons.

If we did not have uids, it would be impossible to implement the SST. And therefore, it would be impossible to selectively share segments in main memory. Indeed, the uid is used as a key to be hashed into the SST to find out whether or not a segment is active. If we did not have uids, we could never connect a user to the same copy of a segment already used by some other user.

One is of course entitled to question the value of selective sharing of segments in main memory, and very rightly so, since many systems do not allow such selective sharing of segments. In fact, such sharing seems to be of little value in general: selective sharing of segments in primary memory has rarely been observed in systems where it is supported. In all systems, there are of course public (fully shared) segments. However, these do not warrant having a uid system, because they are permanently active as integral parts of the basic facilities every user sees. They bear fixed segment numbers in every user address space and are directly connected to shared PTs.

Selective sharing of segments in main memory is perhaps most valuable in data base systems, where it avoids having to make a copy of a segment that could be shared in main memory as long as its simultaneous users make sure to lock the specific records they use.

Notice that in Unix a restricted form of selective sharing is achieved even without uids. The system allows selective sharing of (non-writable) code segments. Such sharing is accomplished by means of the equivalent of a SST, called a text table. While a SST, as described in Chapter V, maps uids into home or memory addresses of segments, the Unix text table just maps home addresses to memory addresses. A home address, consisting of a disk device identifier and a so-called i-number, is really an index into the i-list (VTOC) of the disk where the segment is to be found. This home address plays the role of the uid in our SST as the basis for sharing.

The essential difference between a home address and a true uid is that it is not unique over all times. When a segment is deleted, the home address of its i-node may be reused for another segment. Thus, if a copy of a home address could remain in the system after the corresponding segment has been deleted, it could accidentally become bound to a new segment occupying the same disk i-node. To prevent this problem, Unix never lets users see home addresses. Home addresses are stored only in catalog entries. Every i-node contains a counter indicating how many catalog entries point to it. The segment (file) can be deleted only when that counter reaches zero.

What other argument is left in favor of uids? Uids allow more than just sharing in primary memory. They allow sharing in general with a level of safety that no other mechanism can provide, because they are expendable and not reusable. Where uids do not exist, the only way for a user to express his desire to share access to a file of another user is to name that file by tree name. However, this may present certain problems: the name change problem, the version change problem, and the segment migration problem.

The name change problem occurs when the owner of a file suddenly decides to change the name of that segment. When he does so, a borrower of the segment is unable to find the segment for which he has only the old name. If uids are implemented, the borrower can, at least in well-designed systems, first try to use the tree name and then, if this name cannot be resolved, try the search again by using uids instead of symbolic names, assuming he knows the right uids.

The version change problem occurs if the owner of the segment replaces it with a segment by the same name but containing an incompatible program or a differently formatted data base from what the borrower expects. In a uid system the borrower can be warned in time that there has been a version change and that inconsistencies may present themselves, again assuming he knows the right uid.

The segment migration problem occurs in some systems, where segments occasionally need to migrate from one disk to another for better balancing disk load. In such cases, the use of uids is an escape hatch to inform any user having opened a file with a given uid and thus having stored the file's home address in his NT that this home address no longer hosts the file with the given uid and that the file should be refetched from the file system to reset the NT to the right values. This of course assumes that file maps of inactive segments, in the VTOC, are labeled with their uid.

Thus, uids make the sharing of files in general, and not just in primary memory, immune to name changes, version changes, and disk address changes—a potentially important property, particularly for distributed systems, where name, address, and version changes can be frequent and pose many synchronization problems.

Naming and addressing issues in distributed systems are more complex than in shared-memory systems for at least three reasons:

1. There exists at least one more level of indirection between an object name and the object itself. Translating the object name into a uid and an address is not sufficient. The address must further be translated into a route from the source of the reference to the actual location of the object. This requires that the communication access method and the whole network software behind it support a routing function. We will not discuss this topic any further here.

2. In distributed systems, the problem of implementing system-wide or universal names/uids takes a new dimension to account for the existence of several physical machines that typically each have their own naming domain and conventions. In order to guarantee that names on different machines remain universally unambiguous, one usually resorts to additional levels of naming hierarchies. Where a tree name is usually sufficient to uniquely identify an object in a single file system, the tree name must be concatenated with a machine name and perhaps even network names to uniquely identify the resource in a distributed system. Similarly, where a time-stamp uid is usually sufficient to unambiguously denote one object in a shared-memory system, it must be concatenated at least with a machine serial number to remain unambiguous in the context of distributed system.

3. Finally, the very fact that objects are scattered around in a network often requires that catalogs mapping object names into their uids, their addresses, and routes to them be distributed too, i.e., partitioned and replicated in potentially complex ways. This in turn raises issues such as catalog consistency and object migration (Lindsay, 1981; Birrell *et al.*, 1982), which require potentially complex catalog management software.

Suggested Reading and Classics

On naming issues in operating systems:

Presser, 1972. A survey of linker and loader techniques.
Organick, 1972. Dynamic linking in Multics (Chapter 2).

Millard, 1975. Dynamic linking in the Emas system.
Saltzer, 1979. A comprehensive discussion of name resolution issues in operating systems.

On naming issues in distributed systems:

Shoch, 1978. On the meaning of names, addresses, and routes.
Watson, 1981. On naming in distributed systems.
Saltzer, 1982. On name and address resolution.
Lindsay, 1981. On naming objects in a distributed data base.
Birrell, 1982. On the Grapevine electronic mail system.
Solomon, 1982. On the CSNET name server.

Further Reading and References

Bensoussan, 1972
Daley, 1968
Dennis, 1966. More on Multics naming and addressing.

Chapter IX

Protection and Security

1.   Assets and Threats

Computers, like any major invention, carry with them both threats and promises. One of these threats affects man's privacy. As the basis for modern information systems, playing the role of keepers of information about people and on behalf of people, computers offer both a powerful and a ominous tool for manipulating such information in more—or less—desirable ways than were possible with the manual information systems of yesterday's paper world. The objective of this chapter is to put the issue of *protection* and *security* of computerized data in perspective and to explain the means operating systems can and should implement to limit or thwart potential threats to the assets they guard.

The first issue to discuss when analysing the problem is, When is protection necessary? Protection of information in a computer system is necessary when two conditions are met:

1.   The computer contains information assets worthy of protection, e.g., data about private citizens or programs representing an asset to the company owning them.

2.   There are potential threats. The information must at times be stored, processed, or transported in an environment where it will be confronted with potentially hostile agents (people or programs).

If either of the two conditions is not met, there is no need for any protection mechanism inside the computer. Indeed, if the information belongs to the public domain and can easily be reconstructed, there is no need to protect it. Similarly, if it is confidential but belongs entirely to one company and never has to leave the premises of the company, the owner may simply run the computer in a locked environment where only authorized people will be allowed.

The next question to ask is, What should information be protected against? or in other words, What are the various threats to information? There are three recognized types of security attacks:

1. There is the obvious case of information theft. The owner of some confidential information does not want this information to be released to unauthorized people. For instance, a discharged bank employee might want to cause damage to the bank by publishing a statement of account of all the customers of the bank, thereby violating their privacy while embarrassing the bank.

2. There is the less obvious case of information modification. The owner of some valuable information may be very dependent on the accuracy of this information and want it to be protected against malicious changes. For instance, a frustrated bank employee, without stealing or divulging any information about bank accounts might do even more damage to the bank by introducing deliberate errors into the bank's accounting records, or by surreptitiously crediting minute amounts of money to his own account over a long period of time—an often encountered case.

3. Finally, the least obvious threat is a denial of use of the information. Our same bank employee may decide to introduce a "bug" into the bank's system such that it will effectively cease to provide the information it keeps as expected, which could make the information just as good as destroyed.

2.   Non-technical Protection

Before discussing the actual means for protecting information inside a computer, it may be worth pausing a bit to review the context outside the computer and see what means of protection exist there and what measure of protection they afford.

1. The first type of non-technical protection measure is legal protection. Legal protection comprises the set of laws and assimilated regulations that state what is valuable information and what constitute violations of the security of such information. Legal protection is the most elementary type of protection. It only states what is permitted and what is not and may eventually state what penalties are associated with what violations of the rules. However, it will never provide any solution to the problem of discovering that a violation has occurred, much less to the problem of proving it, certainly not to that of preventing it.

2. The second type of protection is called surveillance. Surveillance includes all measures and devices aimed at identifying occurrences of violations. This may range from closed-circuit TV systems in the computer room to more subtle tricks like imbedding purposeful though harmless errors in private information. By knowingly falsifying a manifest though unimportant bit of information about oneself (e.g., a middle initial) when providing an agency with a personal record, one can monitor the use of that record by the agency by watching for the manifest

sign in other records one discovers about oneself (e.g., address labels of bulk advertisement mailings). Surveillance techniques do offer a handle on discovering instances of violations. However, they do not yet provide any means to prevent these violations.

3. The next step in the gradation of these complementary non-technical protection devices is the physical protection of the computer installation. Physical protection denotes that set of measures meant for the prevention of physical attacks against the computer. This includes an extremely wide variety of mechanisms.

The most obvious example is the physical control of access to computer centers by armed guards or by locked doors and magnetic badge readers.

Another important example is the set of rules for disposal of waste produced by the computer. Listings (punched cards or paper tapes where they still exist) should be shredded before being disposed of to prevent hostile agents from stealing information from trash containers on the sidewalks. Magnetic devices should be erased many times before being reused to prevent subsequent users from deciphering their residual magnetization. A printer ribbon should always be removed from the device after use to prevent a third party from reading the marks left on it by the impacts of the hammers, daisy-wheel, or type-ball. Trays of listings or cards should never be left unattended in a public area, etc.

Less obvious but important, iron nets functioning as Faraday cages are often cast in the walls of computer rooms to prevent radiation of electromagnetic devices from being picked up by sensors outside. In at least one case, this measure even worked in reverse in favor of the computer center. The Faraday cage prevented radiation of a nearby radar from penetrating the computer room and causing computer failures due to transmission errors on the high-speed links between the units, as had been observed before the installation of the net.

3.   Technical Protection Objectives

Section 2 has discussed what non-technical mechanisms are available outside the computer to achieve various degrees of security. The remainder of this chapter will discuss technical protection mechanisms found inside computers.

The following constitute a few basic principles that govern the design of any technical protection mechanism and should always be kept in mind when trying to understand the ideas behind a mechanism.

Simplicity. Any mechanism should be kept as simple as possible. Complexity is a guaranteed way to build a leaky mechanism. The more complex a system is the harder it will be to convince oneself that it is indeed information-tight and intrusion-proof.

Attractiveness. The mechanism must be attractive to the users so that they will be encouraged to use it. In general, the owner of the computer and keeper of the information is not the actual user or programmer who will drive the system. Thus, users may not care about security as much as the information owner. They may be tempted to take shortcuts and circumvent the protection mechanism if that will make their life easier. Hence, for it to be effective, the mechanism must not get in users' way. For instance, every record should be private by default, with a possibility to make it accessible to a wider group of people if necessary, otherwise the employees might leave them all public out of laziness. Any objective where protection demands a conscious decision and act from the user is doomed to miss its target. Similarly, any system which requires the user to give a password for every operation that he performs will be rejected as cumbersome.

Open design. The effectiveness of the mechanism must reside in the existence of secret codes, keys, passwords, access lists, etc., but not on the secrecy of the design of the mechanism itself. Secret codes, etc., can always be changed if they have been exposed, whereas a secret design cannot. And it would be grossly underestimating the ingenuity of potential intruders to believe that they could never find out the secret underlying a design. There is nothing as appealing to a compulsive computer hacker as a system penetration exercise aimed at finding hidden loopholes in a kernel design.

Matched power. The power of the protection mechanism should be matched to the value of the information to be protected and to the means of attack of a potential intruder. This argument leads to a more general and very important principle: The whole point of technical protection is to guarantee that the computer is not the weakest link in the chain of protection mechanisms around the information. This means that a computer is only one element among many involved in a global information system. It is only a substitute for the file cabinets of yesterday. Thus, one should not attempt to make it safer than those file cabinets, unless this is trivial. There is no point in installing a very expensive protection mechanism in the computer if a night operator is corrupt and will accept bribes.

4.   Technical Protection Means

We are now in a position to classify technical protection means inside a computer or a system of several computers. They are divided in two main categories: (1) peripheral means and (2) central means.

Peripheral means deal with the protection of computer information outside the main computing complex, i.e., on peripheral devices or communication lines tying these devices to the central machine(s). Peripheral protection is itself composed of encryption measures and authentication measures.

Encryption covers all techniques dealing with the secret coding of information while it transits over communication lines or is stored on remote media such as magnetic tapes or disks.

Authentication deals with the set of measures aimed at identifying a user at a remote terminal so as to determine what he should be allowed to access inside the machine once he starts working.

Central protection deals with the protection of information in the main computer. It is itself divided into access monitoring, access control, inference control, and flow control.

Access monitoring is the electronic equivalent of surveillance. It is the set of mechanisms whereby the computer system can keep track of who accesses what pieces of information at what times. Such monitoring may later reveal accidental or malicious protection violations, just as in the case of surveillance. Access monitoring will not be further discussed in this book.

Access control is the basic component of central protection. It covers all mechanisms, software and hardware, of which the purpose is to ensure that previously authenticated users access only the files they are authorized to manipulate according to some control structure.

User programmable control is a more sophisticated form of access control allowing a user to specify much more than just who can read and/or write which of his files. For instance, if a user owns a data base from which statistics may be extracted, user programmable control allows him to specify exactly what statistics may be extracted without at the same time requiring that he declare any of his data as directly readable by any other user.

Flow control is a more refined and advanced form of access control. It is the set of mechanisms designed to prevent users from acquiring information indirectly. With plain access control a user may stipulate who is to have access to which of his files. However, any of the so authorized users are assumed trustworthy in the sense that they will not copy the file they have access to into another file that they make accessible to a third party. Flow controls are a way to prevent authorized but untrustworthy users from passing information on to persons not originally authorized. Flow controls are of particular interest for military information systems.

5.   Peripheral Protection

5.1.   Encryption

As defined earlier, encryption is the technique used to secretly encode and decode the information which has to transit over unsecured communication channels or to be saved onto unsecured media. The basic principle of encryption is sketched in Fig. 63. In the case of communication lines, each end of the line is terminated by a cryptography device, often called a crypto box. Both ends of the line, e.g., a computer and a user, or two computers, insert in the crypto box a previously agreed upon secret key. There is one secret key per user. The key consists of a bit string of some length. On the human end of a link, the key is inserted in the form of a magnetic badge that the crypto box can read. On the machine end of a link, the key is supplied electronically by the computer, which must have a copy of all user keys in some well-protected internal file.

Any information, called *cleartext,* entering the link at either end undergoes a reversible mathematical transformation, which is a function of the key. The design of such a transformation is a whole science by itself and was born long before the first computer in the context of message cryptography, of which the first traces date back to classical history. It is beyond the scope of this book to discuss this topic; specialized works can be consulted for this purpose.

- IDEALLY : ONE-TIME PAD = INFINITE KEY

- PRACTICALLY : SYMMETRICAL SYSTEM (E.G.,DES)

- POSSIBLY : ASYMMETRICAL SYSTEM (E.G.,PKS)

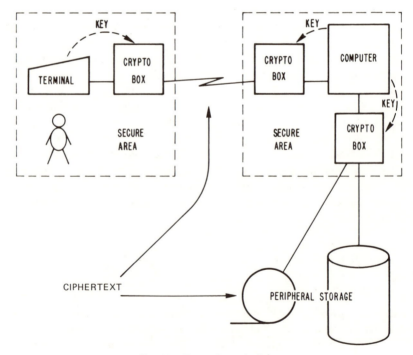

Fig. 63. Encryption principle.

While travelling across the link, information is thus in an illegible form, called *ciphertext,* so that a potential intruder, even armed with the best eavesdropping equipment to tap the lines, could not make any sense out of the garbled bits he reads.

At the other end of the link, the other crypto box, having a copy of the same key, performs the inverse mathematical transformation and regenerates the cleartext.

The same principle applies to storage media, except that the same box is involved in both the encoding and the decoding of the information before and after storage, respectively.

The problem consists of finding a key and an encoding scheme that cannot be broken by any guesswork or mathematical tools. It has been shown that the only theoretically unbreakable code is one where the key has an infinite length, or at least a length equal to that of the message to be transmitted or stored. This is called a one-time pad. Practically, only finite keys can be used on blocks of clear text of finite length. Thus, the key must be reused cyclically. One can show mathematically that over large statistical samples of ciphertext, and given the language, natural or computer, of the cleartext, one can establish a correlation between certain patterns of ciphertext and certain patterns of cleartext based on a matched frequency analysis of the occurrence of the patterns in typical samples of the ciphertext and cleartext. This can then lead to deducing the key.

Thus, all *block codes,* or finite-key codes are in principle unsafe. In practice though, one can design codes that are so sophisticated that cracking them according to the above theory would demand so much time and money that the result would not be worth the effort and would be useless by the time it is available.

a.   The DES Algorithm

In practice, one block coding technique, proposed by IBM and later adopted with some modifications by the U.S. National Bureau of Standards as the *Data Encryption Standard* (DES), has gained widespread acceptance in the commercial world. Its attractiveness lies in that there is, at least in the open literature, no published solution to crack it. In addition, it can be implemented with large-scale integrated circuits, making its use convenient, inexpensive, efficient, and commercially viable.

One criticism of the DES, or any code based on a secret key, is the fact that the two partners in a communication system must have securely exchanged the secret key prior to using it. In many cases, this can be done safely. A user can walk to the computer center and agree on a key with the security officer of the system, or he can send a copy of the desired key by mail. However, if he is in a remote and hostile country, he may not be able to visit the computer center or to rely on the secrecy of the postal service.

b. *PKS Algorithms*

Thus was born the idea of looking for an encryption system that does not require any secure key exchange. The idea is that there should be not one but two corresponding keys for any user. One of the keys is and remains secretly kept by the user, while the other is officially published in something as public as a telephone directory. Such a system is called a *public key system* (PKS). The two keys are mathematically related but not identical and not derivable from each other.

Thus, a message encoded by a user under his own secret key can be decoded by anybody but will guarantee to that person that the message was really sent by the sender, since only the sender has the secret key necessary to encode something that will decode properly under the public key. Conversely, a message encoded by a user under some public key can only be decoded by the user possessing the matching secret key.

Thus, by superposing the two mechanisms, a user can encode a message under his secret key and then under his partner's public key, so that only the partner will be able to decode the message and will at the same time know for sure that the message truly came from the originator. Thus, we have a two-way authentication mechanism here.

The whole question, of course, is to find a mathematical trick that allows building two such matched keys without making it possible for anyone to deduce a secret key from a public one. Theory has produced several schemes that fulfill the requirements, of which at least one has withstood cracking so far (Rivest *et al.*, 1978). However, no such mechanism has been implemented, because the hardware required for such calculations, in particular at the speed at which they ought to be performed, is still beyond the capabilities of technology. There is little doubt, however, that this problem is only of a temporary nature.

5.2. Authentication

As stated earlier, authentication is the set of techniques whereby a computer can identify a remote user or vice versa. Historically, *one-way authentication*, i.e., authentication of a user by a computer, has been predominant, but there has been a realization lately that it is insufficient and that two-way authentication may be desirable in certain cases.

a. *One-way Authentication*

Passwords. The most frequent means for achieving one-way authentication is the use of a *password*. The user is requested to supply some previously agreed upon secret password to the computer. Passwords present three problems:

Storage. The passwords of all users must be safely stored in the computer. This is usually achieved by using the password or a function thereof as a key to encode some known message including the name of the user. The user name and the resulting encoded message are stored on a disk file. Every time the user gives his password to the system, the known message is reencoded with it and compared to the stored encoded version. Thus the password itself is never stored in the computer.

Exposition. In order to be used, a password must be typed on the remote terminal where the user sits. This typing is a source of exposition of the password. On a printer terminal, the password will be typed on the paper and pressed into the ribbon. On a display terminal, the password will be posted on the screen if only for a few seconds. In any case, the user should make sure that nobody is looking over his shoulder while he types the password in. On a printer terminal, one can make the password invisible by overwriting it with random characters. However, one must make sure to do the overwriting before and not after for maximum security. Furthermore, one must make sure that the random characters are always the same from one session to another or it would be possible to superpose the papers of several sessions and to look through them to a powerful lamp, which would reveal the password in black on a gray background. With certain terminals, one can avoid the problem. On a field-formatted display terminal, one can mask the password field so that the password will not show on the screen. On any echo terminal, one can inhibit the echoing of the password so it will not show on the terminal. On other terminals, one can always use *one-time passwords,* but the danger is then that the user may fail to keep track of where he stands in his list of agreed passwords and lock himself out of the system. Furthermore, the user must keep a written list of the prearranged passwords, which leads us to the third problem of passwords.

Memorization. In order not to forget his password(s), the user may be tempted to write it down. In doing so, he runs the risk of having his piece of paper lost or stolen, and the password compromised. To avoid this trap, many users tend to pick passwords that are easy to remember. However, this is not without risks. Experience has shown that passwords that are easy to remember are also easy to guess or to find out for someone else. A spouse's nickname, a telephone number, a license plate, a birth date are all easily checked pieces of information. Of course, one can start skipping letters or spelling backwards, but if a user can think of such tricks, so can an intruder, as long as the tricks remain trivial. If they do not, then the memorization problem reappears. Ticking off words in some word list has a similar problem, where the list is hard to guess but the place of the tick mark is also hard to remember, and writing the ticks brings us back to the paper copy problem. This goes to say that choosing a word that is easy to remember and not to guess is not trivial. Writing some familiar text in a grid and picking columns in the grid based on the system name and the time of year

presents the advantages that the password is easy to reconstruct if not to remember, it is very hard to guess considering the number of parameters involved
in the choice of the grid and its columns, and the trick can be transported
unchanged through many years and over many systems. Some systems offer as a
solution to the memorization problem the possibility of generating words that are
meaningless but are easy to pronounce.

Non-forgeable Identifiers. A better authentication technique is based on the
use of *non-forgeable identifiers* such as fingerprints or voice patterns. While
such techniques present advantages that passwords do not have, they still have
defects. Identification is not always correct. Unauthorized users may be accepted
while authorized ones are rejected. In addition, such techniques remain experimental and thus are expensive and not generally available on commercial
systems.

On top of everything, passwords as well as non-forgeable identifiers present
the disadvantage that in order to be transmitted, they have to be reduced to
electrical pulses on the line. At that stage, any intruder can tap the line, record
the signal, and play it back electrically at a later time.

Furthermore, both techniques provide only for one-way authentication. Thus,
it is always possible for an intruder to cut a communication line during the night
and plug in his own computer, pretend to be the computer that the user actually
expects to talk to and thereby ask the user for his password, gently collect it, and
send out an error message saying that the computer is going down because of
some software problem; and finally, to reconnect the sectioned line and walk to
some real terminal, where the stolen password can be used without problem.
This situation, called *masquerade*, can only be avoided by two-way authentication, whereby the user is sure he is talking to the computer he means to talk to.

b.   Two-way Authentication

Two-way authentication rules out the exchange of passwords by definition, since
no partner can trust the other to begin with. A simple mechanism for two-way
authentication avoids both the problem of masquerading and the problem of
having to transmit any secret identification.

The system is based on encryption. When sitting down at his terminal, the user
first turns off the crypto box so that cleartext is sent on the lines. After sending
his name in cleartext, he and the computer turn on their respective crypto boxes
with the appropriate key. The system then sends its identification with the date
and time. (If this identification does not decode properly on the user terminal,
then the computer is a fake.) Then the user repeats his name with the date and
time. (Again, if they do not decode properly on the computer side, the user is not
who he claims to be.) The date and time are necessary to make sure that the

messages are actually generated now and are not the playback of a wiretapping recorded in the past by an intruder. The intruder could not make any sense of the information, since it is encrypted, but he could cause damage to user files by playing back today something recorded yesterday (e.g., debiting a bank account with the same amount twice).

Based on the above mechanism, an elegant scheme has been designed (Needham and Schroeder, 1978) for allowing two-way authentication in a distributed system, where users are not even required to have agreed in advance on encryption keys with each and every potential host machine they may want to work with. The only requirement is that all users and hosts have agreed on one encryption key each with a mutually and commonly trusted authentication computer.

Under these assumptions, the mechanism represented in Fig. 64 can be used for authentication of a user A by a computer B he wishes to use. User A sends a cleartext message to the authentication computer, stating his own identity, the identity of the computer B he means to communicate with, and a unique identifier I for the message (e.g., a time-stamp). The authentication computer replies to that message by sending back to A a message encrypted under A's key, so only

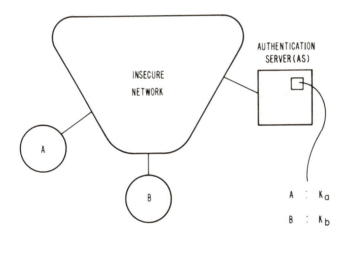

$$A \rightarrow AS : (A, B, I)$$

$$AS \rightarrow A : (B, I, K, (A, K)^{K_b})^{K_a}$$

$$A \rightarrow B : (A, K)^{K_b}$$

Fig. 64. Two-way authentication.

A can see it and at the same time be sure that only the authentication computer could have sent it. That message contains the name of *B*, the session identifier *I*, a newly generated encryption key *K* to be used in the future session with *B*, and a message encrypted under *B*'s key containing the name of *A* and the encryption key *K*. *A* decrypts the whole message from the authentication computer and forwards the portion encrypted under *B*'s key to *B*, thereby informing *B* of his own identity (*A*) and of the key (*K*) that should be used for the communication.

The unique identifier *I* serves the same purpose as the date and time exchanged in the two-way authentication scheme described earlier. It authenticates to *A* the encrypted message returned by the authentication computer. If that message did not contain *I*, it could have been generated by an intruder, masquerading as the authentication computer by playing back an older message. If *A* accepted this message, he would let himself be tricked by the intruder into using key *K*, which the intruder may somehow have figured out in the meantime, making the session unsafe.

The message forwarded to *B* is encrypted under *B*'s key by the authenticator so only *B* can decipher it to get *K* and at the same time be sure that it really comes from *A* and that *K* was really generated by the authenticator, since only the authenticator could have generated the message.

6.   Central Protection

Having discussed peripheral protection mechanisms for data encryption and communication authentication, we turn our attention to central protection mechanisms found inside the processor–memory complex to enforce access control. To put the subject in the right perspective, it must be said that many systems, particularly small systems, e.g., first generation eight-bit microprocessors, do not include any central protection mechanism. Among those systems that do support some protection, one can distinguish four levels of sophistication:

1.   The first and most primitive type of access control is encountered in systems providing *complete isolation* between its users, i.e., systems that allow each user to build his own information system in total isolation of everybody else's system without any possibility of communicating or sharing information and programs between subsystems.

2.   The second type of system provides *controlled sharing*, where each user can specify who can access his files in what way (reading, writing, execution).

3.   The third type of system offers *user programmable* protection. Users have the ability to control in software not only whether their files should be readable and writable but in what way they should be read and written. For instance, a user might specify that his census data base can be read to establish statistics

about the population but not to extract specific records from it. This demands user programmable controls, of which inference controls are a particular example to be discussed for illustration.

4. Finally, there are systems offering *flow control* mechanisms to contain the propagation of information beyond users explicitly authorized to see it.

Notice that the various levels of protection are found in very different systems:

1. Most simple or early systems offer only total isolation, because it is relatively easy to implement.

2. Most commercial time-sharing systems offer controlled sharing mechanisms.

3. User programmable mechanisms are found only on a few experimental machines or specialized systems, though systems with user programmable controls are about to become available commercially.

4. Flow control mechanisms exist only in systems built specifically for the military.

Before attacking the description of any mechanism, it is desirable to review the fundamental concepts and some of the terminology used in protection systems to help the reader understand subsequent explanations.

When talking about the protection among users in a computer, one usually regards each user as being named inside the computer by a so-called *principal identifier*. The principal identifier is a computerized form of name associated with the computation (process) of the user after that user has been authenticated.

After a user is authenticated, his process is installed in a sealed environment, called a *domain* (Lampson, 1969, 1974a), associated with its principal identifier. The domain is defined as the set of access permissions available to the user. If those rights constitute a set that is mutually exclusive with the sets found in other domains, one is dealing with a total isolation system. On the other hand, if some rights point at files or segments also denoted by rights in another domain, then the system is at least of the controlled sharing type.

When a computer is multiprogrammed between multiple users, there must be a protected way for it to hop from one domain to another, i.e., from one process to another. In total isolation systems, the computer may not carry any information with it when hopping from one domain to another. In other systems, some well-controlled amount of information may be carried over while hopping. The computer can travel from one domain to another by passing through well-defined holes in the domain walls, called *gates*.

Evidently, the concepts of principal identifiers, domains, and gates are constructions of the mind. In any particular computer they have to be realized by some mix of hardware and software. This is to say the hardware and software involved in the realization of these sensitive protection devices are themselves very sensitive. The hardware and software mechanisms supporting the protection of the system constitute the security kernel of the system. Tampering with the kernel can lead to a melting of the whole protection mechanism. Thus, the kernel of the system must itself be protected by the very mechanisms that it implements.

6.1.   Complete Isolation

Complete isolation is the simplest protection mechanism that can be implemented, as it requires only a base-and-bound addressing architecture (Fig. 65). It is implemented on all base-and-bound systems, as well as on systems such as the IBM VM/SP, which allows (at least in its original version) no sharing at all between the virtual memories of different users. Sharing of information is allowed only at the level of virtual disks, called minidisks.

In such a system, the area of memory denoted by the BBR is nothing else but the user domain. If the user attempts to access something outside his domain by writing a program that would try to spell the address of some external word, the hardware will trap the fraudulent reference and block it.

Of course, if the user could load any value he wanted in the BBR, he could potentially allow himself to reference the whole memory. Thus, the register must be protected. This is done by wiring the hardware in such a way that the register can be modified only when a hardware bit in the processor is set to one. That bit is called the master/slave, control/application, supervisor/user, or privileged/normal *mode bit*.

Now the problem is pushed back one level: the entity to protect is now that bit, for if the user could change it he could overwrite the register and expand his domain in violation of access authorizations. This is where the concept of gate appears. The hardware of the computer is so designed that all the instructions that cause the mode bit to flip from zero to one at the very same time force the computer to cease executing the program of the user and to jump to some fixed address where a kernel or supervisor program has presumably been loaded. Thus, the user program loses control of the processor, which now executes a program contained in the kernel. These instructions are the hardware embodiment of gates between any user domain and the kernel domain. On many systems, such gate calls are called supervisor calls (SVCs). Most forms of interrupts and faults can also be viewed as gates.

The kernel is of course carefully designed to behave in a well-controlled and strictly enforced way. The processor management mechanism loads the BBR only with values taken from VPT entries describing the addressable domains of legitimate virtual processors. When loading the register, the kernel resets the mode bit to zero, so that the user finds himself confined to his own domain. Kernel software never loads the register with a random bit string supplied by a user. It also never leaves the mode bit on when returning control to a user

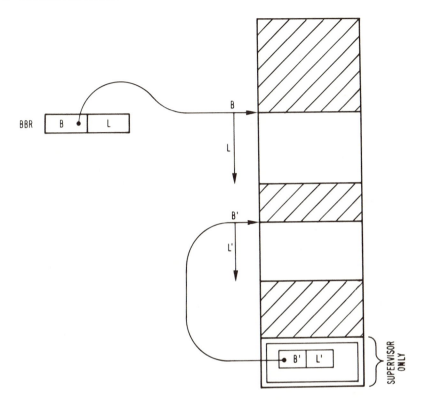

Fig. 65.   Complete isolation implementation.

domain. The mode bit is the kernel's self-defense mechanism. The programs and tables of the kernel are themselves in an area of memory that belongs in no user domain, so no user can modify them.

6.2.   Controlled Sharing

The next level of access control mechanism offers controlled sharing, i.e., the ability for each user to specify who can read, write, execute, etc., his information. While complete isolation protection operates at the level of complete address spaces, controlled sharing has traditionally been implemented at the level of files. For each of his files, a user can define who has read and/or write access.

a.   Access Control List Systems

One mechanism offering controlled sharing is based on the use of *access control lists*. While pure access control list systems are impractical and have never been built, they help us understand other systems by comparison. Thus we discuss them now.

With an access control list system, users may not be allowed to access every file in the system, but they can at least address any of them, because they are all in the same universal address space. Thus access control is exercised below the level of addressing.

Consider the pure segment addressing architecture as it was originally presented in Chapter V (Fig. 66). This architecture offered a universal address space based on uids. As we described it, a user program just has to utter the uid of a particular segment to address and therefore access it. In our original description, there was no protection. Now imagine that to each entry in the SST we add an access control list. This list names all users authorized to access the segment described by the SST entry, together with bits defining the *access rights* or permitted *access modes* (e.g., read/write) of the user to the segment.

In addition, assume that processors have a special register that contains at all times the principal identifier of the user currently running on it. Every time the

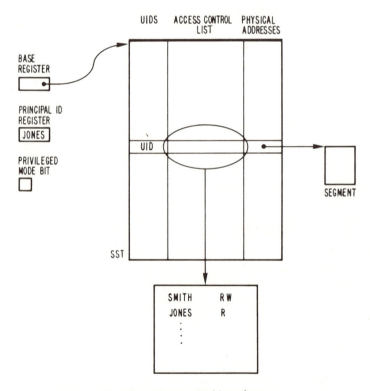

Fig. 66. Access control list system.

user presents a uid to the SST for addressing, the SST is checked to see if the principal identifier of the running program is in the access control list of the corresponding segment with the right access mode.

Clearly, since the principal identifier register is as critical to system protection as the BBR was in complete isolation systems, it is protected in the same way. It can be changed only in supervisor mode, and entry into supervisor mode is coupled with transfer of control into the kernel code. The kernel is designed so as to add permissions to access control lists only as directed by the owner(s) of the corresponding segments. The SST itself is protected by an access control list giving write access only to the privileged principal identifier corresponding to the kernel.

One advantage of access control lists is the accountability they offer: one can find out at all times who has access to what file. A second advantage is that propagation of access permissions can be very tightly controlled. An access control list not only says who can access a file, but also who can modify the list itself.

An access control list system as we have described it is, however, impractical. Not only does it assume a pure uid addressing architecture, which was said in Chapter VII to present several problems in practice, but it assumes that every access to the SST is validated. Since an access control list may have a variable length and is content-addressed by principal identifier, searching it to validate each access would be too time-consuming.

b.   Agency Systems

A second controlled sharing protection mechanism uses the idea of an agency. *Agency systems* are a very practical idea found in most time-sharing systems today. The following description corresponds fairly closely to the Multics implementation of an agency.

While access control list systems allow users to address everything although they cannot access everything, agency systems allow users to name anything but not to address anything. They put access control not below addressing, as access control list systems do, but above addressing and below naming. Thus instead of seeing a universal address space, every user is given his own address space. He can name any file he wants, but he can only address those in his address space. Opening a file in the address space is controlled by the system, which plays the role of permission agency.

Instead of the pure segmented architecture envisioned above, consider now a segmented architecture with segment numbers, as described in Chapter VII, where every user has his own address space materialized by a private ST.

In an agency system, the concept of access control list is still present. However, access control lists are not associated with segments in the SST, they are associated with files in the file system. In addition to containing the uid and the home address of a file, a catalog entry also contains an access control list for the file. Instead of searching the access control list every time the file is addressed, as in an access control list system, an agency system searches the list only when the user tries to open the file to map it into his address space (ST) under some segment number. The ST defines the user's domain.

If and only if the search is successful will the system allow the file to be opened. This operation is materialized by installing in the user's ST, under a newly allocated segment number, a pointer connecting the segment number to the page table of the corresponding segment. In addition, the format of the ST is somewhat extended to contain access mode bits (read/write/execute/ . . .) to qualify the just granted permission. Thus a ST entry, which in our original description in Chapter VII merely contained a pointer, now embodies a permission. It is called a permission *ticket* for the corresponding file. The system realizes controlled sharing in that different users may get different tickets for the same file.

The agency approach to controlled sharing has been implemented in Multics (Saltzer, 1974) and in Unix (Ritchie and Thompson, 1974), for instance. In Unix, the access control list resides in the i-list (equivalent of the VTOC) together with the file map, as part of the i-node. Furthermore, it is simplified in the sense that it contains only three entries. These define access rights for the file owner, for members of the same project as the file owner, and for everybody else. Access rights cannot be defined for an isolated individual other than the owner.

An implementation of an agency system is shown in Fig. 67. Agency systems, like access control list systems, require that the processor be equipped with a principal identifier register to validate access against access control lists. The processor also contains a privilege bit, representing the kernel's self-defense mechanism, and a BBR pointing to the user's ST. [Multics implements actually not two but eight increasingly privileged modes, called rings (Schroeder and Saltzer, 1972). They are numbered from 0 to 7, 0 being the most privileged one. These different levels of privileges are used to introduce a finer control of privileges inside the Multics kernel itself and among different levels of user software.]

Protection is enforced as follows. As seen in other systems, the BBR can only be changed if the privilege bit is on, and any instruction that turns the bit on also transfers control to the kernel, acting as a gate. The kernel has its own ST (i.e., its own domain, not shown in Fig. 67) and manages the BBR in a safely controlled fashion. A ST is itself protected against fraudulent changes by the user: The first ticket in it points to itself and contains a read-only right. Thus, the user cannot write into his own ST. Only the kernel has a write ticket for the ST of each user.

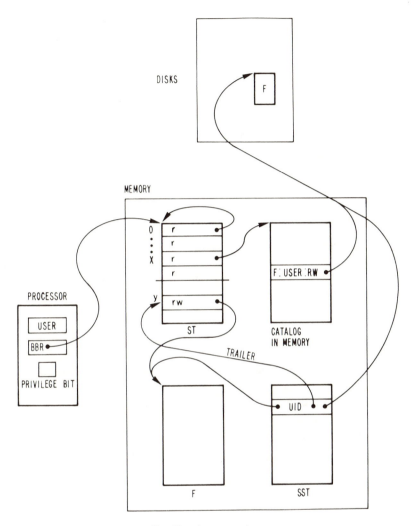

Fig. 67. Agency system.

Now consider what happens when a user removes from some access control list the name of another user who has currently opened the file. This *access revocation* should be effective immediately. Yet the user who has just lost permission has already successfully accessed the file. To fix the problem, revocation of access should disconnect the user from the file he has opened. When the system changes an access control list, it should use the uid of the file (found in the catalog entry) to search the SST. If the file is active, the corresponding

entry in the SST will contain the trailer list introduced in Chapter VII, which can
be used to disconnect all users from it. Users will then have to reconnect themselves, and the user who lost access will not be allowed to do so.

The methods used in and out of the memory are duals of each other. Inside
memory, every user is associated with a list (ST) of files he can access. Outside
memory, every file is associated with a list (access control list) of authorized
users.

Agency systems have the same advantages as access control list systems,
without the implementation problems. The ticket mechanism is very easily
grafted onto the existing addressing hardware and does not cause any significant
overhead at run-time.

c. *Capability Systems*

Access control list systems enforce protection strictly on the basis of access
control lists. Agency systems enforce it through a combination of access control
lists and permission tickets. Now try to imagine a system where there are only
tickets and no access control lists. (Ignore implementation aspects for now.)
Such a system is called a *capability* system, and the tickets are called capabilities
(Dennis and Van Horn, 1966).

The implication of a pure capability system is that there are no access control
lists and no agency to get permissions from. A user cannot name a file and ask
the system to give him a capability for it. All the user can name is what he has a
capability for, and vice versa. Thus a capability is a sort of protected name and
protected address at the same time. While access control list systems put access
control below addressing, and agency systems between addressing and naming,
capability systems put it above naming.

Putting access control below addressing, access control systems offer a universal address space. Putting access control between addressing and naming, agency
systems offer a universal name space (the file system) but per-process address
spaces. Putting access control above everything, capability systems make an
address space as such a fairly vague concept. The address space or domain of a
user is defined by the set of capabilities he has. However, these capabilities do
not have to be concentrated in one ST. They may and in practice are sprinkled
throughout his files.

The whole point of capability systems is that the domain of a user process can
change over time. The granularity of protection, which is an entire process in
other systems, can be as small as one procedure in capability systems. In the
linkage section of a procedure, using capabilities directly instead of segment
numbers referring to tickets indirectly in effect turns the linkage section into the
address space and name space of the procedure. While executing that procedure,
the user can only access the domain of the procedure, in ways prescribed by the
procedure. A procedure entry point is in effect a gate into the procedure domain.

Since a user cannot get capabilities for shared files from the system, he must be able to get them some other way. This can be done simply by protected copying. A user willing to permit another user to share one of his files asks the system to copy the original capability he has into a file of the other user. Thus, contrary to systems using access control lists, the passing of permissions occurs not through updating access control lists but through plain copying of capabilities. As a result, capability systems suffer from a problem not found in access control list systems: the lack of accountability. It is not possible to determine by simple examination of a list who has access to a particular file. If a user has given a capability for one of his files to a colleague, the colleague may have passed the capability on to many more users, without informing the original owner. As a result, the original owner, not knowing who has access to his file, cannot take permissions away. Some systems have been designed that allow the owner to restrict the copying of his capabilities by colleagues who received them and make revocation possible. Such systems are, however, fairly complex and cause overhead at run-time.

The key to protection enforcement in capability systems resides in the protection of capabilities themselves. Users may not create or tamper with capabilities. Capability systems come in two flavors: partitioned and tagged.

In *partitioned systems,* capabilities are grouped into special segments often called *c-lists.* Each c-list is like a small segment table. Turning linkage sections into c-lists, as suggested above, assumes a partitioned architecture. The Hydra (Wulf *et al.,* 1974), Medusa (Osterhout *et al.,* 1980), and StarOS (Jones *et al.,* 1979) systems built at Carnegie-Mellon University fall in this category. So do the CAP system (Needham and Walker, 1977) built at Cambridge University and the Plessey 250 (England, 1974), one of the first commercial capability systems, used in real-time communication applications.

In *tagged systems,* capabilities need not be segregated in special c-lists. They can be embedded in any data segment. However, to distinguish data from capabilities, every memory cell contains a tag bit that is set only for capabilities. The Burroughs B6700 system is a tagged machine.

Both in partitioned and in tagged systems, words of memory known to contain capabilities cannot be written into with ordinary store instructions, which prevents users from manufacturing capabilities. Capabilities can only be copied from other capabilities that were manufactured by the system in the first place. Manufacturing original capabilities when new objects are created requires executing in privileged mode, as in other protection mechanisms.

d. Capability System Implementation

The foregoing section has described capability systems in principle. However, nothing has been said about their implementation. Three problems must be clarified:

1.   The implementation of capabilities as protected addresses.
2.   The significance for the file system of capabilities as protected names.
3.   The meaning of linking in a capability system.

Let us consider each problem in turn.

Capability Implementation.   The mechanics of access control list systems could be explained easily in terms of the universal uid-based addressing mechanism described in Chapter V, because access control list systems fit naturally in a universal address space. The mechanics of agency systems could be grafted as easily on the revised segment-number-based addressing mechanism introduced in Chapter VII, because agency systems assume per-process address spaces. However, capability systems suggest address spaces that are neither universal nor per-process. The concept of capability does not fit any addressing model developed so far.

Going back to our uid-based addressing model of Chapter V, one could envision capabilities as being protected uids, with additional read and write access permissions (Fig. 68). By presenting such a sealed uid to the addressing hardware, a user could address the corresponding object. This would achieve a true capability system. However, we have seen in Chapter VII that such uid-based addressing is impractical, as it would require implementing the SST as a large and fast associative memory, which is beyond today's technology. Furthermore, if the search fails in the SST, the uid alone would be insufficient to retrieve the passive object from the file system.

A possible alternative, used in the Plessey 250 for instance, consists of using

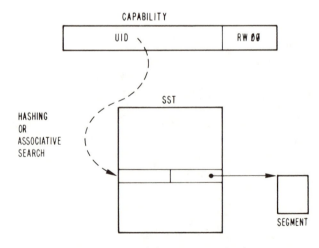

Fig. 68.   Capability as protected uid.

SST indices instead of uids in capabilities. However, this creates an extra level of indirection in addressing. To by-pass this indirection, before a capability is used it is loaded into a register, where it is translated into the corresponding memory address (Fig. 69).

With either implementation, a new problem is raised, however. In agency systems, a ticket is confined to the ST of a process, which is destroyed when the process is terminated. Thus tickets never migrate to the file system. They stay only in main memory. The situation is radically different with capabilities. Capabilities are not confined to one table. They can be copied into any c-list in a partitioned architecture or to any segment in a tagged architecture. And these c-lists and segments may have a permanent existence in the file system. Thus capabilities do migrate to the file system with deactivated files. However, the SST indices contained in capabilities do not have a permanent existence. When a segment is deactivated, its uid is removed from the SST, making the SST index invalid. Thus, one must allow capabilities to migrate but not SST indices, which implies that migrated capabilities cannot contain SST indices.

It follows that, in practice, capabilities require not one but two implementations, known as in-form (e.g., SST index) and out-form. A capability is converted from out- to in-form when it is first used to reference the corresponding object. It is converted back to out-form when the c-list or segment containing it is written back out to file storage.

The next question to be answered, naturally, is about the out-form of capabilities. Basically, the out-form must have a permanent existence and allow easy conversion back to in-form. Giving it a permanent existence can be achieved with a uid, but a uid alone is insufficient to retrieve the designated

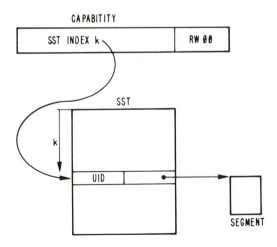

Fig. 69.   Capability as SST index.

object from the file system and activate it, when converting the capability to in-form. Remember that, in our earlier description of file systems, to allow retrieval of inactive segments catalog entries contained uids and (home) disk addresses.

Building on this model, one possible solution for out-forms is to concatenate a uid with a home address (Fig. 70). The home address allows retrieval and activation of the object. The uid allows validation of the capability in case the object has been deleted and the home address reused by an object with a different uid.

This is the solution adopted in iMAX, the operating system of the Intel iAPX-432 processor (Kahn *et al.*, 1981; Pollack *et al.*, 1981; Cox *et al.*, 1983). An in-form capability contains a 24-bit memory address, while an out-form capability contains a 40-bit disk address, a 24-bit uid, and a 16-bit redundancy code for error detection. The 40-bit disk address is itself composed of a 24-bit VTOC index and a 16-bit disk name. (The 16 bits actually point to a name stored

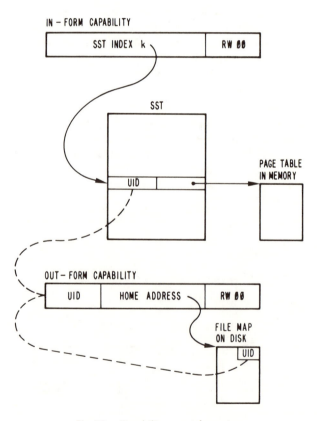

Fig. 70. Capability as catalog entry.

in a name table on the disk containing the capability.) The probability that two disks with identical names will have objects with identical uids, located at identical addresses is assumed to be negligible. Thus, capabilities are truly unique worldwide, which allows disks to be ported across systems without the risk of endangering the protection of information.

File System. The second issue of capability implementation is the nature of the file system. From the above discussion, it becomes clear that a capability is a protected name. Indeed, it contains functionally the same information as is found in traditional file systems in a named catalog entry. Then what is the meaning of a catalog in a capability system?

Since a capability fulfills the role of a catalog entry, c-lists in partitioned architecture systems are nothing else but catalogs. In tagged architecture, the equivalent of catalog entries is not confined to "catalogs", since capabilities can be found anywhere. In tagged systems, the distinction between catalogs and plain files is irrelevant.

More important, we stressed earlier the interest of hierarchical file systems, where each file is denoted by one and only one catalog entry. In capability systems, by definition, there can be multiple capabilities pointing to the same file, which results in a network file system, raising the lost object problem evoked in Chapter VII. In such a file system, users each have a home catalog, from which they can reach whatever objects are reachable in the network by indirection through capabilities.

In the iMAX system, the lost object problem is solved by reference counts and regular garbage collection for active objects, and by the concept of ownership for passive objects. With ownership, only one among all capabilities denoting an object has the ownership permission bit turned on. When that capability is destroyed, the object is also destroyed, leaving potential other capabilities dangling, a fact that software must be prepared to cope with.

Linking. Finally, we come to the problem of linking. We suggested earlier that where links contain segment numbers referring to tickets in an agency system, they directly contain capabilities in a capability system. Suppressing the indirection through segment numbers makes addressing more efficient. However, it make links less flexible. Since a procedure can refer to other objects only by capability and not by name, it is impossible to translate links into different objects for different uses. All procedures must come bound to the objects they reference. All users must use procedures as they come and cannot substitute their own subroutines and data in them.

Personalizing working storage and arguments when the same procedure is invoked by different users can be done in different ways. In partitioned systems (e.g., CAP, Hydra), there is a special c-list for passing capabilities for arguments, so that procedures need not be bound permanently to their arguments, which would be total nonsense.

Personalizing links is more difficult if one insists on not using an agency mechanism. In CAP, there is a per-process, per-procedure c-list for that purpose. Necessary links must be initialized as capabilities before a procedure is invoked. These capabilities must be obtained from other c-lists accessible to the user. In iMAX, links are more dynamic. They are regarded as special indirect objects containing names. The names are turned into capabilities on a per-user basis when first translated. The capabilities must also be within the domain of the calling user before translation. When a link is converted to out-form, it remains translated. It cannot be converted back to a name.

6.3.   User Programmable Controls

a.   Sealing and Amplification

Complete isolation mechanisms keep users totally apart from one another. Controlled sharing mechanisms allow them to share (read or write) access to data in a controlled way. The next level of sophistication in access control mechanisms is user programmable controls, which allow the users to control much more than just the selective readability and writability of data.

Imagine that a university keeps a large data base of all employees and students on its main computer and wants to allow sociologists or other researchers to collect statistics on the university population from that data base. This scenario implies that the university must share access to the data base with the interested researchers. Of course, the university does not want the data base to be damaged accidentally or maliciously by anyone. So it will make the data base writable only by employees of the personnel department, not by the researchers. Researchers need only read access to collect statistics.

However, giving them full read access would allow them to extract any individual record from the data base and to find out about the salary, the medical history, or the criminal record of any university member. Thus, some sort of more sophisticated technique than read permission must be found. User programmable controls are needed.

Such controls will allow the university people to specify that the researchers are only allowed to read certain (anonymous) fields of each data base record and not the whole data base. These controls require that the university write a complete data base management system (DBMS) specifying exactly what type of data base query is permitted and what is not.

The DBMS is given a principal identifier as if it were a user. In the catalogs of the file system, the data base is marked as readable and writable by the principal identifier of the DBMS. It is also marked as "sampleable" by the authorized

EXTENDED CAPABILITY

IN / OUT — FORM	TYPE DBMS	SAMPLE , X , Y , Z

Fig. 71.   Extended capabilities.

researchers. The sample right means that any authorized researcher may receive a capability for sampling the data.

Capabilities are more sophisticated in this system than in controlled sharing systems. In addition to containing the address and the rights for the object they denote, they also contain a type field (Fig. 71). For normal segments, the type field is set to zero, meaning that the hardware can interpret the mode bits as read or write rights.

However, if the type field is not zero, the hardware will refuse to either read or write the segment. Such capabilities are said to be *sealed*. The only thing that can be done with such an "extended type" capability is to pass it to a domain whose principal identifier matches the capability type field. Thus, our data base capabilities are marked of type "university DBMS".

Gate instructions must exist in the hardware of the computer to allow a user to request that control be transferred to a given domain (not just to the kernel domain) together with given capabilities. This allows authorized researchers to cause the computer to start executing the DBMS system on their behalf. The DBMS then takes the sealed capabilities it has received and sets the type field to zero and the mode bits to read, an operation called *amplification*. Amplification is allowed only because the principal identifier matches the type field of the sealed capability. The principal identifier of the DBMS is found at run-time in a register of the processor, where it has been stored when control was transferred to its domain.

User programmable controls have been implemented in Hydra (Wulf *et al.,* 1974), where extended capabilities are called auxiliary rights. Similar controls have been built into CAP (Needham and Walker, 1977), where the capabilities are called software capabilities. User programmable controls are also available in Multics, and in Unix, where they are based on special rights in access control lists. Certain programs can be filed as gates into domains under the control of user-programmed subsystems. When a user calls such a gate, the system switches the processor into the user-programmed domain and gives control to the gate program. The gate program can then authenticate the user on behalf of whom it was called and enforce user-programmed controls accordingly.

b.   Inference Controls

User programmable controls allow the personnel department of the university to define in software the exact protection they want for their data base. In the particular case of a statistical data base, the programming of these software controls is not trivial. It requires methods of inference control. Such methods are useful not only in systems with user programmable controls; they are also mandatory in any system keeping a statistical data base, even if the users are only allowed to talk to the DBMS from their terminals and are not permitted to program the system. Inference controls will be discussed here to illustrate the problem of user programmable controls. However they are not part of the operating system itself.

The problem is best illustrated by an example. Assume that our data base is well protected by the hardware of the machine and the software of the DBMS. A researcher with ill designs might want to find out the salary of the president of the university.

First of all, the DBMS should refuse to answer any direct question of the sort, or even indirect but specific questions like, What is the salary of the owner of the car with license plate *X?*

In spite of that, the intruder may carry out a so-called *overlap attack,* using legitimate queries that the system must normally answer yet will give the desired information to the intruder. For instance, it should be perfectly legitimate to ask the system about the average salary of female employees in the department of mathematics. It should also be legitimate to ask the average age of members of the university board. Then why should it be forbidden to ask the average salary of women sitting on the board? This is allowed. Unfortunately, the intruder knows that the president is the only woman on the board and thus has learned her salary! He obtained it by asking a question about two sets of people, women and members of the board, knowing that their overlap boiled down to the one person he was interested in.

The remedy to this situation is to program the DBMS so that it will always refuse to answer questions of which the final answer bears on less than some minimum query set, say 10 people.

However, our intruder has more than one trick in his bag. If the system is clever enough to see that he is trying to isolate one record within one question, it may not be clever enough to see that he is isolating the record by successive questions using a so-called *tracker attack.* Thus, he will proceed as follows. The tracking element is that the president is the only woman on the board. However, in order not to make the tracking obvious, the intruder will first ask the average salary of all women employed by the university, then the number of female employees, then the average salary of all women not on the board of directors, and finally the number of all female employees not on the board. Since each question bears on perhaps thousands of records, the computer will be happy to answer, yet from these four figures, the attacker will be able to compute the president's salary with elementary arithmetic.

Remedies to the latter type of problem are a lot harder to find. One can partition the data base into subsets such that any question is answered using only one subset, thereby making the correlation from question to question impossible, since one cannot be sure that the same subset was used to answer consecutive questions. One can also systematically round numerical answers to the nearest ten or hundred, depending on the case. One can eventually introduce faked records of inexistent persons in the data base. One can finally perform swapping between pieces of records (e.g., attribute the president's salary to another member of the board or another woman at random). However, all such techniques introduce a certain percentage of error in the answers to even fair questions.

Perhaps the most attractive solution is to set a minimum query set and to answer any question based on a random sample of the data base. This introduces small errors in the answers. However, they are statistically quantifiable. From the attacker's point of view, the answers are unusable, because they represent small errors on large numbers of samples but since his tracker attack is based on the subtraction of large sets, the small errors cumulate and result in astronomical error margins on the individual records he might be tracking.

6.4.   Flow Controls

All protection mechanisms seen so far are so-called *discretionary* in the sense that what a user does with information he has obtained legitimately from someone else's file is left at his discretion. He should keep it for himself for ethical reasons, but the computer will not prevent him from copying it into another file that he makes public.

Yet, there exist information protection requirements in the human world that are *non-discretionary*. Most notably in the military domain, if a file is classified "top secret", even an officer with a "top secret" clearance should not pass it on to another officer with a lower level of clearance.

Systems have been built that enforce such non-discretionary controls by guaranteeing the *confinement* of the classified information to the domain where it belongs. This is not to say that a cleared user could not cause the information to be printed and then give the printed listing to some uncleared user. Such a threat falls outside the realm of the computerized information system. All that is desired here is to prevent this illegal declassification from happening inside the machine, where it might be impossible to detect.

Two types of solutions have been proposed for such a problem. Both assume that every file in the system is cataloged with its complete classification, that the ST is expanded so that each capability contains the encoding of the classification of the file it describes, and that every register of the computer is expanded to contain an encoding of the classification of the information item it contains. Every time a register is loaded with some information out of any file, the register inherits and becomes tagged with the classification of the file.

1. In the first solution, called the *high-water mark* technique, every time the register content is stored back into some file the classification of that file is upgraded to the classification of the register, if it is higher. The name of the technique comes from the fact that the files are classified at the level of the highest classified item they contain. That high-water mark remains even after the water has receded (i.e., after the item has been removed). The problem with this approach is that all files tend to be overclassified pretty soon if many people are malicious or careless.

2. In the second solution, called the *no-write-down* system, an attempt to store a register in a file of lesser classification is rejected by the hardware.

It should be noted that even the no-write-down system is not totally tight. Even if all read/write communication channels are blocked in the downward direction, there are many so-called *covert channels* in a computer. Such channels could be exploited by attackers to get at classified information.

The best known example of covert channels is time-dependent channels. A time-dependent channel is a channel which allows observation of the variations with time of some characteristic of the computer system that is of public knowledge. Consider, for instance, the disk traffic of the computer. The disk traffic is a measure of the frequency with which the computer must access its disks to fetch or retrieve a file. The heavier the disk traffic is, the longer one has to wait to access a file on disk and, in general, the longer one has to wait to get any job done on the computer. Thus, disk traffic has observable effects.

An attacker could write a program that sorts the records of a data base, a second program that has imbedded in it a Morse code table and spends all its time reading and writing some disk file it does not even use, and a third program capable of monitoring the disk traffic of the system. Then he could advertise his sorting package without telling anyone that the Morse code program is hidden in it. A user with a top level clearance could then borrow the sorting package to sort a top-security file. But in addition to sorting the records as desired, the sorting program would look for and spy on selected records from specific data bases and call the Morse code program to generate faked disk traffic at rates dictated by the Morse code for each consecutive letter of the target records. The third program, running in an unclassified domain, would then monitor the modulation of the disk traffic pattern to decode the Morse message from outside the confined domain.

The key to the whole problem above is that the owner of the data base has used to sort it a program that he does not know—a *Trojan Horse,* as unknown borrowed programs are called when they are rigged. In fact the same sort of problem can arise even without borrowing any program. If the authorized user sorting the data base with his own program is dishonest, he can play the Morse code trick himself to transmit the data base to an accomplice in a covert way inside the machine without taking the risk of printing the data base and passing a copy to the accomplice outside the computer.

There are two ways that such problems can be avoided:

1.   The first way is always to run programs in an environment with all resources preallocated, i.e., an environment such that it is known in advance how much memory space, processor time, and disk resources will be needed so that it is impossible for a Trojan Horse to modulate any resource usage. Everything is fixed in advance. This solution, however, is costly.

2.   The other solution is to revert to program *certification*. Program certification means the line-by-line scrutiny, audit, verification, and proof that the program is harmless and performs what it claims. Complete program certification is not yet possible with today's technology. Only relatively simple programs can be certified. The task of certification is enormous, because it is not sufficient to show that the program does what it should—already quite a problem. One must also show that it does not do anything it should not. This kind of negative proof is extremely hard, because one has no handle on the problem. One does not know what to look for.

The plot described in the foregoing paragraphs may sound impossible. It may seem to border on science fiction. Many more scenarios and tricks of the same level of fantasy have been discussed, involving the most improbable channels, the weirdest ideas, and the sneakiest programs. However, let us not forget that we are talking here essentially about military systems and that anything that sounds fictitious is better than what is real, because the enemy may not yet have thought about it or thinks that you have not thought about it.

Aside from the military scenario discussed above, flow control mechanisms are also used in a somewhat different but more common scenario, called *mutual suspicion*.

In the military scenario, classified data must be confined to a closed environment so that a user with legitimate access to it cannot leak information outside the environment knowingly (maliciously) or unknowingly (as a result of borrowing a Trojan Horse program). Now imagine that the owner of some classified data wants to borrow a program to process his data, but this program itself represents an asset to its author. The author does not want to let anyone borrow that program and run it in his own environment where he could make a copy of it for later reuse. In other words, there is mutual suspicion between the author and the borrower. The former does not want his program to be freely readable by anybody, while the latter does not want his data to be readable by anybody.

The solution to the problem consists of invoking the program in a separate domain, as is done for user programmable controls in our earlier data base management example. In this case, however, the domain is used not to protect a data base, but to protect the program itself from its caller. In addition, to prevent the author of the program from stealing classified data passed to it as argument, the domain is submitted to some flow control mechanism. Thus, it cannot extract information from classified data passed to it and save it into a non-classified file that could be read by the author at a later time.

Suggested Reading and Classics

On general issues of data security:

> Turn, 1972
> Turn, 1976

Surveys of protection issues and mechanisms:

> Voydock, 1983. Discusses protection in computer networks.
> Denning, 1979a; Jones, 1979b. In-depth tutorials on principles.
> Shankar, 1977. A high-level survey of principles.
> Saltzer, 1975. A survey with references to real systems.

On password-based authentication:

> Evans, 1974. On the protection of stored passwords.
> Morris, 1979. On the dangers and limitations of passwords.

On encryption-based authentication:

> Needham, 1978. Classic on encryption-based authentication.
> Bauer, 1983. A tighter and symmetrical solution of the same problem.
> Gligor, 1979b. Encryption for object migration and authentication.
> Gifford, 1982. Advanced uses of encryption for data secrecy and signature.

On protection issues and models:

> Dennis, 1966. On hardware supported protection concepts.
> Conway, 1972. On data-dependent protection.
> Lampson, 1973. On the confinement problem.
> Graham, 1972; Lampson, 1974a. On a matrix model of protection.

On capability-based protection:

> Fabry, 1974. The classic.
> Redell, 1974b. On the issue of access revocation.
> Feustal, 1975. On tagged capability architecture.
> Gligor, 1979a. A more general view of access revocation.

On protection-related aspects of fault tolerance:

> Molho, 1970. Hardware aspects.
> Lampson, 1974b. Memory access control issues.
> Denning, 1976. A model for the containment of errors using capabilities.

On system certification:

> Millen, 1976. On a model of security for certification.
> Denning, 1977. On automated program certification.

Robinson, 1975. On the SRI secure system project.
Schroeder, 1977. On the Multics kernel redesign effort.
Walker, 1980. On the UCLA secure system effort.

On landmark implementations of protection:

Linde, 1969; Weissman, 1969. Military controls in the Adept-50.
Schroeder, 1972. On Multics protection rings.
Saltzer, 1974. On protection in Multics.
England, 1974. On the Plessey 250 capability mechanism.
Wulf, 1974; Cohen, 1975; Levin, 1975. On capability-basd protection in Hydra.
Lampson, 1976. On the capability mechanism of CAL.
Needham, 1977. On the capability mechanism of CAP.
Cox, 1983; Kahn, 1981; Pollack, 1981. On the capability operating system for the Intel 432
    microprocessor.
Jones, 1979c. The StarOS multiprocessor operating system.
Osterhout, 1980. The Medusa multiprocessor operating system.

Further Reading and References

Books and bibliographies:

Westin, 1972; Miller, 1972; Parker, 1976. On general issues.
Hoffman, 1977
Demillo, 1978
Hsiao, 1979
Anderson, 1972. An annotated bibliography.

More examples of protection issues and mechanisms:

Redell, 1974a
Evans, 1967
Fabry, 1973
Jones, 1975
Merkle, 1978

More on protection implementations:

Graham, 1968. Multics.
Lampson, 1969. BCC-500.
Needham, 1972. CAP.

On programming language supported protection:

Morris, 1973
Jones, 1978

On encryption techniques:

Feistel, 1975. On IBM's Lucifer, the precursor of DES.
Diffie, 1977. A critique of the DES algorithm.
Rivest, 1978. On a public key algorithm.
Popek, 1979. A survey on cryptography.
Kahn, 1976. An entertaining history of cryptography.

Part 6

SYNTHESIS

Chapter X

System Design

Every chapter of this volume has introduced the reader to some new mechanism or component of an operating system. Each mechanism was analyzed in some detail, existing solutions were discussed and compared, and important implementation aspects were stressed. While this step-by-step study has analyzed every mechanism individually, it has not stressed some global aspects of system design enough. As we reach this last chapter, it is time to look back at the operating system as a whole to get an idea of what it means to design one and to gain a perspective view of its organization.

1. System Interface

The first question to be addressed when designing an operating system is the definition of its external interface with applications, programmers, and users in general. To this end, it is necessary to carefully understand the mission and the functional objectives expected from the system, to extablish very detailed specifications of how it should operate and what mechanisms it should include. The mechanisms required in any particular system depend very much on whether the system should be user-programmable or not, whether it should be interactive or not, whether it should serve one or more users at a time, whether it is part of a larger distributed system or not, etc.

The external interface of a system is composed of the *system calls* (e.g., SVCs) and the *command language*. System calls are the means by which application programs communicate with the system; more specifically, they are the set of primitives that can be called by application programs to invoke the services of the operating system. The command language of the system is the language in which users communicate with the system. It allows users to express to the system what they want done and maps user requests into system calls.

1.1. System Calls and Virtual Machines

The system call interface takes a particularly interesting form in so-called *virtual machine* operating systems, such as the IBM VM/SP time-sharing system (Seawright and McKinnon, 1979; Creasy, 1981). The supervisor of VM/SP, called CP, provides each user with a virtual machine that is a true superset of an IBM S/370 real machine. Each virtual machine can thus execute *all* of the hardware instructions available to a real S/370. However, a virtual machine is only an abstraction. A real S/370 can support many virtual machines simultaneously. Each virtual machine may use only a portion of the real processor time, the real memory space, the real I/O resources.

CP multiplexes the real processor among all virtual machines by doing timeslicing in a transparent manner. In addition, it offers a set of software primitives (not available on real S/370s) that virtual machines may (but do not have to) use to communicate.

CP also controls sharing of real memory among virtual machines by offering each with a virtual memory of up to 16 MB and multiplexing pages of real memory among pages of the virtual memories. This multiplexing is totally invisible to the virtual machine (except, of course, for its effect on the apparent memory-access time).

Finally, CP multiplexes real I/O resources among virtual machines in one of two ways:

1.   Every time a virtual machine attempts to use a privileged hardware I/O instruction, CP traps the attempt, inspects the state of the requesting machine, and validates the I/O request. If the request is directed at a device that is dedicated to the requesting machine (e.g., a terminal) or at a virtual device (e.g., a virtual disk) that can be mapped onto an area of a real device (e.g., a logical volume on a real disk), CP honors the request, interpretively performs it, translating virtual device addresses as necessary, and returns control to the requesting virtual machine, as if it had done the I/O itself.

2.   Alternatively, for those virtual machines that do not want to manage their own I/O at the hardware instruction level, CP provides software I/O primitives that do not exist on real S/370 machines and offer a higher level of I/O functionality.

One essential feature of the system call interface on a true virtual machine operating system is that it must be a strict superset of the real machine instruction set, meaning that even normally privileged instruction must be executable by virtual machines. Yet virtual machines must clearly run in user mode for protection reasons discussed in Chapter IX. To resolve this apparent conflict, CP maintains for each virtual machine a virtual processor state word (corresponding to a real register called PSW on real S/370 machines), where it records the virtual mode (virtual user/virtual supervisor) in which the virtual machine is at every instant. Thus, when a virtual machine executes a privileged instruction, in effect it causes a protection violation that forces the real processor to trap to CP. Then CP can decide whether the intended effect of the privileged instruction should be allowed or not. In the affirmative, it interpretively carries out the instruction in real privileged mode on behalf of the virtual machine.

A second essential aspect of the system call interface of virtual machine systems is that the portion of the interface that is over and above the real machine hardware interface cannot be visible in any way as long as a virtual machine does not use it. Thus, for instance, CP cannot occupy any room in the address space seen by virtual machines. This implies that CP entry points supporting the extra software instructions cannot be regular procedures residing in virtual memory address spaces. They cannot be invoked by procedure calls. They are invoked, like all other CP primitives, by hardware traps corresponding to nonexistent hardware instructions on real S/370s.

With these characteristics, virtual machine operating system interfaces are particularly interesting for operating system test and development. Since a virtual machine operating system offers an interface that includes at least the real machine interface, it is possible to run an operating system inside one virtual machine that would normally run on a real machine. This allows the development and testing of new system releases, prior to installation, during normal operation, a procedure that is not possible without a virtual machine facility.

1.2. Command Languages

The other external interface of an operating system is the command language through which users can steer it. Command languages have evolved much in the brief history of operating systems. In the early days of strictly batch operating systems, command languages were called job control languages. They used rather cryptic syntax and vocabulary. Only uppercase characters were recognized, and all kinds of special symbols were necessary to delimit commands and parameters. Their expressive power was constrained by the modest interpretative capabilities of early operating systems. Ease of use was certainly neither a salient feature nor even an objective. They allowed users to request compilation, linking, loading, and execution of programs, and later, to manage permanent files.

Soon after time-sharing systems appeared, true command languages were born, with such systems as CTSS (Corbato *et al.*, 1962), Multics, VM/SP, and Unix. With these languages, upper- and lowercase characters can be mixed. Special characters have become sufficiently rare that they are no longer a nuisance. Users can define their own synonyms and abbreviations for commands. The command language interpreter provides on-line command documentation. It is sometimes called a *shell*.

More important, these systems allow the combination of commands into so-called command lists, or more commonly "execs". An exec is a stored file containing a list of commands than can be executed in sequence very time the exec is invoked. Inside execs, elementary tests and jumps can be used to determine the flow of control based on symbolic exec parameter names that are substituted at invocation time. On some systems, users can even express new concepts, such as *redirection* of standard I/O to/from files, redirection of one command's output into another command's input (called piping), and simultaneous execution of parallel commands.

More recently yet, exec language interpreters, such as the one found in the IBM VM/SP operating system, have been developed into full-blown interpretive tools with complete control structures, including recursion, powerful data typing features, macro definition facilities, and general purpose command interpreter interface, allowing their use from inside other programs.

At the same time, progress in a different direction has added another dimension to command languages: menu-driven interfaces. With this concept, a user does not even have to type command names and parameters. A menu-driven system such as the IBM SPF literally takes the user by the hand through a series of screen images that reveal step by step the various choices he can make. The user selects commands and subcommands by selection codes and functions keys, is prompted for parameters when appropriate, can ask for additional help when he needs it, and is never confronted with the exact syntax of commands. At the same time, shortcuts are provided to allow experienced users to dash through many menus in a few keystrokes if they know what they are after.

Some workstations, such as the Xerox Star, Apple Lisa, and MacIntosh have already appeared where the menu idea is pushed to its limit, in the sense that the the command language no longer requires the use of a keyboard. With just a mouse, the user points at soft keys and object names or pictures on his screen to drive the system to do what he wants.

The year is probably not very far off when we will start seeing intelligent command interpreters that will understand a fair subset of a natural language, perhaps even a spoken language.

1.3.   Interface Standardization

An important consideration in system interface design which has received far too little attention so far is standardization. Though the reasons for standardizing the system call and the command language of operating systems of a certain type (e.g., general purpose time-sharing or personal computing) are very different, there is a clear need in both cases.

Standardization of command languages would bring tremendous increases in ease of use and user friendliness. For instance, if all interactive systems in the world could agree on some common language as a standard user interface, then users could use any system indifferently, without having to learn different command languages. This would reduce the learning phase of users much in the same way that the introduction of standardized driver controls have made switching cars a trivial matter today.

In the case of system call interfaces, standardization would enhance the portability of application programs and execs from one system to another. Indeed, the use of high-level languages in application programs has made programs much more portable than they used to be. However, there always remains the problem of porting compilers, linkers, and other utilities that depend directly on the operating system interface. If that interface were standardized across operating systems, great progress would be made towards portability (Hall *et al.*, 1980). The main problem is to get everybody to agree on a common call interface. Certain existing interfaces appear to have a fair potential for standardization. For instance, the IBM VM/SP system call interface has the merit of being literally cast in hardware and thus very stable. The Unix system interface appears to be a good candidate because of its popularity and wide distribution.

2.   System Organization

Once the desired system functionality is completely understood and the external system interfaces are fully specified, the next design question to be addressed is *system organization*. System organization deals with the identification of internal interfaces between the mechanisms composing the system, and the relations holding these mechanisms into a coherent structure.

This section puts all the operating system mechanisms seen in previous chapters in perspective and provides a bird's-eye view of what a typical time-sharing system looks like structurally. We are no longer concerned with the internal mechanics of any function. We do not care what scheduling algorithm, what paging algorithm, what catalog structure, or what protection mechanism is implemented. We are concerned only with how the various mechanisms relate to one another and what implications these relations have on their execution environment.

In Sections 2.1–2.3, we will develop a set of principles pertaining to the organization of an operating system. In Section 2.4, we will see how these principles can be used to describe an example time-sharing operating system including most of the mechanisms described in the course.

2.1.   System Complexity

Knowing what typical problems and their possible solutions are in an operating system is not sufficient to construct nor even to understand one. Typical commercial operating systems of the past and even some modern ones represent huge amounts of code and data structures of a very high *complexity*. Size and complexity are undesirable, as they make the tasks of understanding, modifying, and verifying an operating system very hard. The size of an operating system is often inherent to the richness of its functionality, but the complexity is not. That complexity is the result of a lack of discipline in the implementation of these systems, as illustrated by the following examples:

1.   One frequent cause of complexity is the presence of relatively large data structures and tables that contain many pieces of often unrelated or weakly related information. These tables are manipulated by many procedures that do not know about one another and are not always related, except perhaps in the minds of their designers. Thus, by looking at a table, it is impossible to guess what procedures manipulate it. And by looking at a procedure, it is impossible to understand what it does without knowing which other procedures share access to the data areas it uses. Consequently, one does not know where to start reading the system to understand it.

2.   Another cause of complexity is the presence of seemingly endless and unstructured procedures, bearing cryptic names and meandering through long runs of code, making unclear assumptions about their environment and the presence or absence of certain events and conditions in that environment. As in the previous case, more facts than a single person can keep in mind at one time are needed to keep track of what is going on. As a result, an attempt to introduce even the most minute change into an operating system often costs days of hard thinking to understand how to make the change, where to make the change, and what the consequences of it will be for the rest of the system. These consequences are in fact invariably underestimated. More often than not, even if the changed code is correct, its mere introduction may cause the most unexpected subroutine, in the most unrelated part of the system, to fail in the most obscure fashion.

3.   A third frequent source of complexity is the programming language. Most systems of the past, and even some modern ones, are written in assembly language for efficiency reasons. While writing systems in assembly languages certainly offers performance advantages and may be necessary in certain systems, it makes such systems much harder to read and thus harder to understand and to maintain. Experience with such systems as Multics, Unix, and Burroughs's MCP has shown that the use of high-level languages should be encouraged whenever possible in order to make systems easier to deal with in all respects. First, language and compiler theory have made enough progress that code optimization can be pushed very far. Second, hardware technology has made so much progress that it becomes conceivable and even desirable to solve problems by throwing more MIPS at them, if that will help. In other words, it is better to use a powerful engine, if one exists, programmed in some high-level language than to use a conservative machine and a retrograde language: hardware should be used

to help the programmer instead of using programmer time to help the hardware. This is particularly true in a era when hardware costs are sinking whereas people costs are skyrocketing.

4.   While the list is far from exhausted, a last important source of complexity is the lack or poor quality of documentation.

Of the four causes of complexity given above, the latter two apply in general to any and all types of software. However, the former two are particularly relevant to operating systems, in that dealing with these problems is much harder in an operating system than in an application program. Application programs are designed to run with the support of the operating system providing them with nice tools such as virtual processors, virtual memory, virtual I/O devices, and nicely structured file systems. However, the operating system itself cannot depend on such primitives, since its very purpose is to implement them on a bare machine. In other words, operating system code is written to execute in a very inhospitable environment, which is why it is often so complex and makes all kinds of apparently paranoid detours in trying to implement mechanisms that sound simple in principle. The rest of Section 2 discusses principles aimed specifically at fighting these aspects of complexity.

Since about 1970, some principles have been developed about the organization of operating systems. These principles can be found in some recently designed systems, even though many other systems are still being implemented without much discipline. Knowing modern principles of system organization is absolutely key to designing systems that will be understandable and modifiable if not easily, at least more easily than in the past, even by people who were not directly involved in their design.

2.2.   Modularity

In the relevant literature on software engineering and operating system structuring techniques, a wealth of approaches, methods, and ideas, some relatively formal, others more casual, have been proposed. It would be too long and inappropriate to discuss all these techniques here, even superficially. Furtunately, while all techniques differ in their terminology, in the details of their application, and in the depth of their treatment of the problem, they all agree on the basic principles. Analysing these principles is our objective here. The key idea behind any attempt to make operating systems more understandable and easier to develop is akin to the old principle, *Divide to conquer*. However, this is more easily said than done. Division must be achieved by arranging consensus and cooperative harmony between the parts of the system. The basic issues are to decide how to partition the system into its components, further called modules, and how to arrange these modules into a coherent structure, where their interactions are well understood and under control.

Bearing in mind what was said earlier about the frequent use of large tables containing unrelated information and the difficulty in determining the role of a program in manipulating such a table, all existing structuring techniques suggest that the data manipulated inside an operating system be collected into tables, where the role and meaning of each table are as limited as possible and pertain to one and only one mechanism of the operating system. This makes the description, and thus understanding, of the function of the table as simple as possible.

Then, a *module* is the set of all procedures that deal with the management of that table. Procedures should be designed so that they are concerned with one and only one table. All the procedures participating in the management of a table are clustered around their table, so that the table is completely hidden inside them. No other procedure in the operating system is allowed to touch the table directly. The module *hides information* pertaining to the implementation of the table. Any procedure required to use or influence the content of the table must do so strictly by invocation of the caretaker procedures for the table.

We recognize here a flavor of abstract data types, as found in modern programming languages. The procedures around the table represent the operations defined on the abstract type objects represented internally in the table. This view of an operating system as manager of collections of abstract objects is often referred to as the object model for operating systems. Systems such as the Intel iMAX (Kahn *et al.,* 1981), Hydra (Wulf *et al.,* 1974), IBM System/38, and several others support this view. They are called *object-oriented operating systems.*

The question is, What are typical abstract objects in an operating system. By looking at the tables of an operating system, one realizes that these tables are the representation of objects such as virtual processors, user processes, disk records, memory blocks, pages, segments, files, and catalogs. One also notices that the SST entry representing a segment maps that segment into a collection of pages, represented by entries in the SPT. In turn, each page is mapped by the SPT into either a memory block or a disk record. Similarly, a VPT entry maps a virtual processor into a set of register images and, if the virtual processor is in the running state, into a physical processor. Thus, every table is a binding context mapping names of objects of one type into one or more names of objects of other types. At the bottom of the system, a disk address or memory address does not map into any lower level name but maps into a concrete object, a disk record or memory block.

If a programming language, such as ADA, is available and offers the concept of extendable abstract data types, it may be useful to implement the system. But even in the absence of such a language, the system should be organized around abstractions. These abstractions should be documented. More importantly, system programmers should be vividly aware of them and avoid at all cost taking shortcuts in manipulating a table, which would violate the modularity of the system and lead to the problem of local changes with unexpected side-effects. Indeed, the whole purpose of clustering small procedures around a small table is to build a context that is

1.   Sufficiently small and well defined at its interface that a single programmer can understand it all and be sure that he does not need to know anything outside the boundaries of his module to change it

2.   Completely tight, so that the programmer knows that any change he makes inside the module (e.g., in the table format) will not have any repercussions outside so long as the officially documented interface to his module is not affected.

2.3.   Structure

Having decided how to divide the system into modules, it remains to arrange for a suitable *structure* among modules. Rather than trying to explain what is meant by a suitable structure, it is easier first to illustrate what a bad structure is by an example.

Consider the paging mechanism and the processor management mechanism of an operating system. Each of them can be viewed as a module. The paging module implements pages by managing the SPT. The processor module implements virtual processors by managing the VPT. As mentioned in Chapter VI, the paging module calls upon the processor module to multiprogram the machine while waiting for a page to be imported. This is why the processor module must be resident, as it cannot itself generate further page faults.

Now imagine a design where the procedures of the processor management mechanism are stored into paged segments. In this design, the page management mechanism uses the concept of virtual processor to take advantage of its multi-programming aspects, while the processor management mechanism uses the paging mechanism to address its own code and data. The risk is that the page management module, not knowing the processor manager pages from the others, could potentially remove them from memory, leading to unresolvable cyclic page faults.

A programmer trying to understand the well-contained paging module would find nothing wrong inside it. The same would be true for his colleague looking at the processor module. Yet, in spite of the nicely bounded modules, nothing would work. The problem is that the two modules are cyclically dependent on one another. Each counts on the other's services, so that it is impossible to understand what is wrong unless one looks at both modules at the same time and realizes that they have made inconsistent assumptions.

This structural problem is due to the presence of a cyclic dependency. Cyclic dependencies must not be allowed in the system. There must exist at the very least a *partial order* among the modules of the system. In other words, there must be a hierarchy among the modules, where the ordering relation is defined by the notion of service from one module to another. A module using objects, concepts, primitives, mechanisms, or, in short, services of another module is said to be above that other module. The overall system design process must not only define the function of the various modules of the system but also arrange for a strict partial order without loops among them.

In some systems, the partial order requirement is even further restricted to a *total order* requirement, leading to a *layered* structure in the system software. Such layered structures have been discussed, for instance, in the THE system (Dijkstra, 1968b) or the Venus system (Liskov, 1972a).

This leads us to consider how *service dependencies* are materialized, and what they correspond to. Service dependencies are of two types: A module depends on another one when it uses a function of the other (1) to implement the abstract objects it manages or (2) to implement the storage and processing resources that compose its own execution environment.

A few examples are in order. The segmentation mechanism depends on the services of the paging mechanism because uids map into PT addresses, i.e., segments map into collections of pages. Thus the segment abstraction would not work if the paging mechanism did not maintain PTs properly. Or put in other words, the segment abstraction would not hold unless the page abstraction held. This is a dependency of the first type resulting from the fact that segments are made out of pages. We call it a composition dependency.

However, the paging mechanism depends on the processor management mechanism not because pages are made of virtual processors, but, in this case, because implementation of the paging mechanism itself relies on (calls) the multiprogramming primitives that operate on virtual processors. In a similar vein, the user process manager depends on the paging mechanism not because user processes are composed of pages, but because the user process mechanism uses (can trigger) virtual memory paging when addressing its non-resident internal table, the UPT. The latter two dependencies are of the second type and result from the need of the module itself to be stored in some sort of information container and to run on some sort of abstract processor. We will call them environment dependencies.

In general, service dependencies between modules can be identified relatively easily. A module is dependent on another one if its uses its services, which is manifested by one of three conditions:

1. The first module calls the second one and expects control to return with results.

2. The first module, running in the context of a virtual processor, sends a signal (P, V, BLOCK, WAKEUP, etc.) to a module in another processor and expects that other processor to return some reply signal at a later time.

3. The first module is capable of causing traps, faults, SVCs, or any other hardware event that causes control to transfer to the other module, from where it will return at a later time.

The above three manifestations of service requests are the only ways in which a module can possibly invoke the activity of and therefore depend on the service provided by another module.

An operating system design has more chances of being successful if it follows the above principles as closely as possible by imposing a discipline upon the documentation of module interfaces and accepted dependencies. The first phase of the design consists of choosing a set of abstractions that on one hand reflect the various objects that will be implemented by the system and on the other hand are sufficient to implement the operating system itself as a partially ordered structure. All the dependencies that will exist must be identified and documented. Any cyclic dependency must be avoided by choosing new or different abstractions. There is no formal method to achieve success here, only the art of system design.

Rather than spending any more time discussing the principles in a rather dry and abstract context, we will now illustrate them by reconstructing and analysing the structure of a model operating system including most of the mechanisms developed in the course of this book.

2.4. Example

As stated above, the system is organized in a hierarchical fashion. This guarantees, among other things, that it is possible to start describing it in either a top–down or a bottom–up way. In fact, all along the course, we have taken a bottom–up approach so that we needed to refer as little as possible to yet uncovered material. The top–down approach is also conceivable, but assumes that one is already familiar with operating system concepts and anticipates at least the kind, if not the details, of the underlying mechanisms. The top–down approach is preferable when designing a new system from scratch. One starts by specifying the user and programmer interfaces. Then one works downwards from there, by stepwise refinement, to specify the lower level modules. Here, we will follow the bottom–up route again, ignoring the inside of mechanisms but looking at their modularity and the way they use one another inside the system.

The following discussion refers to Fig. 72, where each box stands for a mechanism realized as a module. Inside each box are the name of the table managed by the module and the name of the abstraction implemented by the module, from which one can easily deduce the name of the corresponding operating system mechanism. The arrows between modules represent dependencies. Notice that it would have been impossible or at least confusing to represent all dependencies. Only composition dependencies have been represented. Environ-

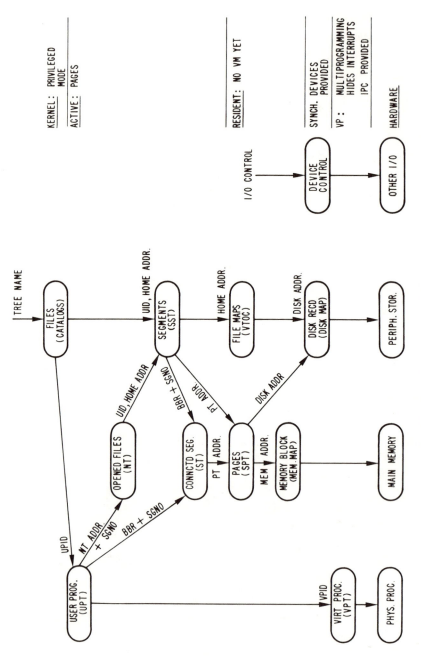

Fig. 72. Organization of a model operating system.

ment dependencies have not been drawn, but are implied by the name of the environment of modules given on the right of Fig. 72, as will be explained in the course of the following paragraphs. Each arrow is labeled with the type of identifier that is found in the table at the origin of the arrow and denotes an entry in the table at the target of the arrow, representing one or a collection of objects of the target type.

At the bottom level of the system, we find the basic ingredients or components of a system, namely its hardware, in the form of the physical processor(s), the memory, the shared storage devices that will play a dominant role in the figure, and the other I/O devices.

Immediately above the hardware is the processor management mechanism. It manages the VPT and implements virtual processors by multiplexing physical ones. All procedures and tables in the module are resident, since virtual memory is not available at that low level. And the mechanism itself must mask all interrupts, since it is running on a bare physical processor where multiprogramming is not yet available. The concepts of multiprogramming and interprocessor communication (IPC) are available immediately above this module.

With these concepts, one can organize the higher levels of the system into virtual processors and/or monitors. Technical literature contains many articles on the relative merits and drawbacks of each concept as a structuring tool. Some authors have tried to stress the duality of the concepts and their equivalence as structuring tools (Lauer and Needham, 1979). In some designs, the operating system is divided into large virtual processors (one per user), where communication among operating system modules takes the form of procedure calls between monitors. These are called procedure-oriented systems. Alternatively, a system can be organized as a large collection of small virtual processors, where inter-module communication then takes the form of interprocessor signals and messages. This is the view of so-called message-oriented operating systems.

Thus, at the next level device control modules, which are resident since they must be below virtual memory, can be realized either as monitors or as virtual processors. They build I/O programs, thereby implementing abstract I/O devices out of real ones, making the idiosyncrasies and timing aspects of specific devices invisible to the higher levels of I/O control, network access method, file system, etc. Of particular interest here is the disk control module that manages the disk map to allocate, free, read, and write disk records viewed as abstract objects by higher level modules.

Above this level, we find a set of modules, also implemented in the context of virtual processors, that reside by necessity in the resident region of main memory. First is the memory map module that implements abstract (busy/free) memory blocks out of real ones carved from the main memory paging area. Second is the paging mechanism that manages the SPT to implement pages out of disk records and memory blocks. Third is the VTOC management module that implements file maps for inactive segments out of the VTOC records of every disk. We call the abstraction it implements inactive segments or file maps.

From here on, the concept of paging is available. Thus, higher level modules can store their own procedures and tables in pages. However, one cannot yet talk of segments. Segments will come later. They correspond to uids. All we have now are pages. This is not sufficient for users, but it is sufficient for the system. Data can be stored in collections of contiguous pages and addressed as if they were segments. They are not segments in the sense that they have no uid. In fact this is desirable, since the segment deactivation function, running in the segment manager, can deactivate only segments it knows about, i.e., segments with uids. Thus the PTs in the SPT that do not implement segments with uids are never deactivated, which is exactly what is needed since they belong to the system itself. Notice that even in this environment, called the active environment, modules can still elect to implement certain tables as resident for efficiency reasons. For instance, the SST should be resident although it could be paged conceptually.

Moving up the layers, we now find the bottom part of the address space manager, which manages STs, thereby implementing connected segments out of PTs. These connected segments are the entities that the users address in hardware.

Then comes the segmentation mechanism, managing the SST to implement segments out of file maps and active PTs, i.e., collections of pages. Notice that if one stretches the concept of composition a bit, a segment, as denoted by its uid/home-address is "composed" of the connected segments pointing to the same PT, in the sense that the segment shares the PT with them and in fact views the connected segments as its components to the extent that it wants to control that sharing. The arrow between segments and connected segments is none other than the backward pointers trailer list discussed in Chapter VII, allowing the segment deactivation mechanism to disconnect any segment whose page table is ejected back to a file map in the VTOC.

All the elements are now in place to implement opened files. This is the top part of the address space mechanism, managing the NTs that implement the concept of opened files out of segments.

Opened files, together with the connected segments and the virtual processors, define the concept of user process, represented in the UPT. A user process needs an address space composed of a ST pointed to by the base register image and a NT whose identity is recorded in the UPT entry, for instance. While it is loaded a user process also has a virtual processor component.

With the user process concept and the segment concept, it is possible to implement the file system. The file system manages all catalogs to implement files out of segments. Again, understanding the file to process dependency requires stretching the notion of composition a bit. A file is not properly composed of a process. However, a file is protected by an access control list, which names authorized user processes. Thus while a file can be implemented without a process, implementing a secure file demands that the user process mechanism associate the right user process with the right ST and NT. In other words, the file system associates the tree name of a file not just with the uid/home-address of a segment but also with a list of authorized user processes.

Above the file system the privileged environment of the kernel of the system stops. Thus, it is apparent in retrospect that the tables of the system implicitly contained a picture of the structure of the system. This is not too difficult to realize. What is more complex is to appreciate the restrictions applicable to the execution environment of each module. The gradation from hardware to resident to active to segmented environment now clearly points out what module can use segments, pages, or only resident memory. Similarly, the gradation from hardware to virtual processor to user process makes explicit the context in which every module executes. This in turn restricts what events can be seen by each module. Inside the virtual processor module, all interrupts must be masked all the time. Above that mechanism, up to and including the user process module, all user interrupts must be masked. Though timer, preemption, and disk interrupts could be visible, it may be preferable to keep them masked some of the time while key system tables (SPT, SST) are locked, to minimize the length of time during which the tables are locked.

Notice that the deadlock avoidance algorithm presented in Chapter II, which requires that all locks be totally ordered, does not at all appear constraining in a system structured as explained here. Indeed, the partial ordering of the modules, which implies a partial ordering of the tables of the system and of their locks, can easily be mapped into a total ordering. Since a processor executing kernel code traverses modules in a purely ordered way, according to the partial order dictated by the system structure, and if it always unlocks the table of a module before leaving the module and returning to a higher level, locks will be claimed and released in a last-in-first-out way, which fits the deadlock avoidance scheme.

Suggested Reading and Classics

On early efforts to structure small systems:

> Dijkstra, 1968a. The THE system.
> Liskov, 1972a. The Venus system.
> Hoare, 1973. A structured paging system.

On successive contribution to the model of object-oriented organization for operating systems:

> Parnas, 1971. On information hiding.
> Parnas, 1972. On a technique for specifying modules.
> Parnas, 1972b. On information hiding as a tool for decomposing a system into modules.

Liskov, 1972b. On combining the concepts of levels of abstraction with modularity.

Liskov, 1975. On a technique for defining a module as a data abstraction.

Habermann, 1976a. An opinion on the relation between modules and software layers.

Jones, 1979a. A tutorial on the object model.

On structuring systems with monitors and processes:

Dijkstra, 1971. An early view of monitors (secretaries).

Hoare, 1974. The classic on monitors.

Keedy, 1979. Using monitors for structuring software.

Redell, 1980. On a personal computer operating system organized into inexpensive tasks.

Lampson, 1980. On the Mesa language used in the above.

Lauer, 1979. A classic and much debated paper on the duality of processes and procedures as structuring concepts.

On examples of structured systems:

Saxena, 1975. A layered paging system.

Janson, 1981. Organizing the lowest levels of virtual memory around the object model.

Lampson, 1979. On the advantages of an "open" system for personal computing.

On control languages for virtual machines:

Ritchie, 1974. On the Unix control language.

Hall, 1980. On viewing the whole system as an abstract machine through a virtual operating system call interface.

Denning, 1982. On the evolution of control languages.

Seybold, 1981. On the user view of Xerox's Star.

Ehardt, 1982. On the user view of Apple's Lisa.

Further Reading and References

On structuring systems for security:

Robinson, 1975. The SRI secure system.

Schroeder, 1977. The Multics secure kernel.

Walker, 1980. The UCLA secure Unix.

On engineering systems for portability:

Cheriton, 1979. The Thoth system.

Richards, 1979. The Tripos system.

Overgaard, 1980. The UCSD-Pascal system.

More on structuring techniques:

Parnas, 1975b. On transparency or the limits of information hiding.

Parnas, 1976. On specifying the common denominator of a family of operating systems.

Browne, 1980. On the cross-breeding of operating system and software engineering techniques.

Bibliography

Abbreviations

CACM	Communications of the ACM
JACM	Journal of the ACM
ACM CR	ACM Computing Reviews
ACM CS	ACM Computing Surveys
ACM TOCS	Transactions on Computer Systems
ACM TODS	Transactions on Database Systems
ACM OSR	Operating Systems Review
ACM CCR	Computer Communication Review
ACM SOSP	Symposium on Operating Systems Principles
IBM SJ	Systems Journal
IBM JRD	Journal of Research and Development
IEEE TSE	Transactions on Software Engineering
IEEE TC	Transactions on Computers
AFIPS FJCC	Fall Joint Computer Conference
AFIPS SJCC	Spring Joint Computer Conference
AFIPS NCC	National Computer Conference

Aho, A. V., *et al.* (1971). "Principles of optimal page replacement." *JACM* **18,** No. 1, 80–93.

Akkoyunlu, E. A., *et al.* (1975). "Some constraints and trade-offs in the design of network communications." *Proc. ACM 5th SOSP, ACM OSR* **9,** No. 5, 67–75.

Anderson, R. E., and Fagerlund, E. (1972). "Privacy and the computer: an annotated bibliography." *ACM CR* **13,** No. 11, 551–559.

Andler, S. (1979). Synchronization primitives and the verification of concurrent programs, *In* "Proc. 2nd Intl. Symp. on Operating Systems Theory and Practice." (D. Lanciaux, ed.). North-Holland, 67–100.

Apollo Computer. (1981). "Apollo Domain Architecture." Apollo Computer Inc.

Astrahan, M. M., *et al.* (1976). "System R: a relational approach to database management." *ACM TODS* **1,** No. 2, 97–137.

Baskett, F., *et al.* (1977). "Task communication in Demos." *Proc. ACM 6th SOSP, ACM OSR* **11,** No. 5, 23–32.

Bauer, R. K., *et al.* (1983). "A key distribution protocol using event markers." *ACM TOCS* **1** No. 3, 249–255.

Bays, C. (1977). "A comparison of next-fit, first-fit, and best-fit." *CACM* **20,** No. 3, 191–192.

Belady, L. A. (1966). "A study of replacement algorithms for a virtual-storage computer." *IBM SJ* **5,** No. 2, 78–101.

Belady, L. A., *et al.* (1969). "An anomaly in space-time characteristics of certain programs running in a paging machine." *CACM* **12,** No. 6, 349–353.

Bensoussan, A., *et al.* (1972). "The Multics virtual memory: concepts and design." *CACM* **15,** No. 5, 308–318.

Bernstein, P. A., and Goodman, N. (1981). "Concurrency control in distributed database systems." *ACM CS* **13,** No. 2, 185–221.

Birrell, A. D., and Needham, R. M. (1980). "A universal file server." *IEEE TSE* **6,** No. 5, 450–453.

Birrell, A. D., and Nelson, B. J. (1984). "Implementing remote procedure calls." *ACM TOCS* **2,** No. 1, 39–59.

Birrell, A. D., *et al.* (1982). "Grapevine: an exercise in distributed computing," *Proc. ACM 8th SOSP, CACM* **25,** No. 4, 260–273.

Blasgen, M. W., *et al.* (1976). "System R: an architectural overview." *IBM SJ* **20,** No. 1, 41–62.

Bobrow, D. G., *et al.* (1972). "Tenex, a paged time sharing system for the PDP-10." *Proc. ACM 3rd SOSP, CACM* **15,** No. 3, 135–143.

Brawn, B., and Gustavson, F. G. (1968). "Program behavior in a paging environment." *AFIPS FJCC Proc.* **33** 1019–1032.

Brinch Hansen, P. (1970). "The nucleus of a multiprogramming system." *CACM* **13,** No. 4, 238–241.

Brinch Hansen, P. (1971). "Short-term scheduling in multiprogramming systems." *Proc. ACM 3rd SOSP* 101–105.

Brinch Hansen, P. (1972a). "A comparison of two synchronizing concepts." *Acta Informatica* **1,** No. 3, 190–199.

Brinch Hansen, P. (1972b). "Structured multiprogramming." *CACM* **15,** No. 7, 574–578.

Brinch Hansen, P. (1973a). "Operating System Principles." Prentice-Hall.

Brinch Hansen, P. (1973b). "Concurrent programming concepts." *ACM CS* **5,** No. 4, 223–245.

Brinch Hansen, P. (1976). "The Solo operating system." *Software—Practice and Experience* **6,** 141–149.

Brinch Hansen, P. (1978b). "Distributed processes: a concurrent programming concept." *CACM* **21,** No. 11, 934–941.

Brinch Hansen, P., and Staunstrup, J. (1978a). "Specification and implementation of mutual exclusion." *IEEE TSE-***4,** 365–370.

Browne, J. C. (1980). "The interaction of operating systems and software engineering." *Proc. IEEE* **68,** No. 9, 1045–1049.

Bunt, R., and Tsichritzis, D. (1972). "An annotated bibliography for operating systems." *ACM CR* **13,** No. 8, 377–388.

Buzen, J. P. (1975). "I/O subsystem architecture." *Proc. IEEE* **63,** No. 6, 871–879.

Calingaert, P. (1982). "Operating System Elements—A User Perspective." Prentice-Hall.

Cheriton, D. R., *et al.* (1979). "Thoth, a portable real-time operating system." *Proc. ACM 6th SOSP, CACM* **22,** No. 2, 105–114.

Chu, W. W., and Opderbeck, H. (1972). "The Page Fault Frequency replacement algorithm." *AFIPS FJCC Proc.* **41,** No. 1, 597–609.

Clark, D. D., and Svobodova, L. (1980). "Design of distributed systems supporting local autonomy." *Proc. IEEE Spring COMPCON,* 438–444.

Coffman, E. G., and Denning, P. J. (1973). "Operating Systems Theory." Prentice-Hall.

Coffman, E. G., *et al.* (1971). "System deadlocks," *ACM CS* **3,** No. 2, 67–78.

Cohen, E., and Jefferson, D. (1975). "Protection in the Hydra operating system." *Proc. ACM 5th SOSP, ACM OSR* **9,** No. 5, 141–160.

Conti, C. J., (1969). "Concepts for buffer storage." *IEEE Computer Group News* **2,** No. 8, 9–13.

Conway, R. W., *et al.* (1972). "On the implementation of security measures in information systems." *CACM* **15,** No. 4, 211–220.

Corbato, F. J. (1969). "A Paging Experiment with the Multics System." MIT Press, 217–228.

Corbato, F. J., and Vyssotsky, V. A. (1965). "Introduction and overview of the Multics system." *AFIPS FJCC Proc.* **27,** No. 1, 185–196.

Corbato, F. J., *et al.* (1962). "An experimental time sharing system." *AFIPS FJCC Proc.* **21,** 335–344.

Corbato, F. J., *et al.* (1972). "Multics—The first seven years." *AFIPS SJCC Proc.* **40,** 571–584.

Courtois, P. J., *et al.* (1971). "Concurrent control with 'readers' and 'writers,' " *CACM* **14,** No. 10, 667–668.

Cox, G. W., *et al.* (1983). "Inter-process communication and processor dispatching on the Intel 432," *Proc. ACM 8th SOSP, ACM TOCS* **1,** No. 1, 45–66.

Creasy, R. J. (1981). "The origin of the VM/370 time-sharing system." *IBM JRD* **25,** No. 5, 483–490.

Daley, R. C., and Dennis, J. B. (1968). "Virtual memory, processes, and sharing in Multics," *Proc. ACM 1st SOSP, CACM* **11,** No. 5, 306–312.

Daley, R. C., and Neumann, P. G. (1965). "A general purpose file system for secondary storage." *AFIPS FJCC Proc.* **27,** No. 1, 213–230.

Deitel, H. M. (1983). "An Introduction to Operating Systems." Addison-Wesley.

Dellar, C. (1980). "Removing backing store administration from the Cap operating system," *ACM OSR* **14,** No. 3, 41–49.

DeMillo, R., *et al.* (eds.), (1978). "Foundations of Secure Computing." Academic Press.

Denning, P. J. (1967). "Effects of scheduling on file memory operations." *AFIPS SJCC Proc.* **30,** 9–22.

Denning, P. J. (1968a). "The working set model for program behavior." *Proc. ACM 1st SOSP, CACM* **11,** No. 5, 323–333.

Denning, P. J. (1968b). "Thrashing: its causes and prevention," *AFIPS FJCC Proc.* **33,** No. 1, 915–922.

Denning, P. J. (1970). "Virtual memory." *ACM CS* **2,** No. 3, 151–189.

Denning, P. J. (1971). "Third generation computer systems." *ACM CS* **3,** No. 4, 175–216.

Denning, P. J. (1972). "On modeling program behavior." *AFIPS SJCC Proc.* **40,** 937–944.

Denning, P. J. (1976). "Fault tolerant operating systems," *ACM CS* **8,** No. 4, 359–390.

Denning, P. J. (1979). "Working sets: then and now," Proc. 2nd Intl. Symp. on Operating Systems Theory and Practice, (D. Lanciaux ed.). North-Holland 115–148.

Denning, P. J. (1980). "Working sets past and present." *IEEE TSE*-**6,** 64–84.

Denning, P. J. (1982). "Are operating systems obsolete?" *CACM* **25,** No. 4, 225–227.

Denning, D. E., and Denning, P. J. (1977). "Certification of programs for secure information flow." *CACM* **20,** No. 7, 504–512.

Denning, D. E., and Denning, P. J. (1979). "Data security." *ACM CS* **11,** No. 3, 227–250.

Denning, P. J., and Schwartz, S. C. (1972). "Properties of the working set model." *CACM* **15,** No. 3, 191–198.

Denning, P. J., and Slutz, D. R. (1978). "Generalized working sets for segment reference strings." *CACM* **21,** No. 9, 750–759.

Dennis, J. B. (1965). "Segmentation and the design of multi-programmed computer systems." *JACM* **12,** No. 4, 589–602.

Dennis, J. B., and Van Horn, E. C. (1966). "Programming semantics for multiprogrammed computations." *CACM* **9,** No. 3, 143–154.

Diffie, W., and Hellman, M. (1977). "Exhaustive cryptanalysis of the NBS DES." *IEEE Computer* **10**, No. 6, 74–84.

Dijkstra, E. W. (1965). "Solution of a problem in concurrent programming control." *CACM* **8**, No. 9, 569.

Dijkstra, E. W. (1968a). Cooperating Sequential Processes. *In* "Programming Languages," (F. Genuys ed.). Academic Press, 43–112.

Dijkstra, E. W., (1968b). "The structure of the 'THE' multi-programming system." *Proc. ACM 1st SOSP, CACM* **11**, No. 5, 341–346.

Dijkstra, E. W. (1971). "Hierarchical ordering of sequential processes," *Acta Informatica* **1** 115–138, *or* "Operating System Techniques," (Hoare and Perrot, eds.). (1972). Academic Press 72–93.

Dion, J. (1980). "The Cambridge file server," *ACM OSR* **14**, No. 4, 26–35.

Dodd, G. G., (1969). "Elements of data management." *ACM CS* **1**, No. 2, 117–133.

Ehardt, J. L., and Seybold, J. (1982). "Apple's Lisa: a personal office system." *The Seybold Report* **12**, No. 10.

England, D. (1974). "Capability concept mechanism and structure in System 250." *Proc. Intl. Wrkshp on Protection in Operating Systems, INRIA, Paris*, 63–82.

Eswaran, K. P., *et al.* (1976). "The notions of consistency and predicate locks in a database system." *CACM* **19** No. 11, 624–633.

Evans, D. C., and Leclerc, J. Y. (1967). "Address mapping and the control of access in an interactive computer," *AFIPS SJCC Proc.* **30**, 23–32.

Evans, A., *et al.* (1974). "A user authentication scheme not requiring secrecy in the computer." *CACM* **17**, No. 8, 437–441.

Fabry, R. S. (1973). "Dynamic verification of operating system decisions." *CACM* **16**, No. 11, 659–668.

Fabry, R. S. (1974). "Capability-based addressing." *Proc. ACM 4th SOSP, CACM* **17**, No. 6, 403–411.

Feistel, H., *et al.* (1975). "Some cryptographic techniques for machine-to-machine data communication." *Proc. IEEE* **63**, No. 11, 1545–1554.

Feldman, J. A., "High-level programming for distributed computing." *CACM* **22**, No. 6, 353–367.

Feustal, E. (1973). "On the advantages of tagged architecture." *IEEE TC*-**22**, No. 7, 644–656.

Fotheringham, J. (1961). "Dynamic storage allocation in the Atlas computer." *CACM* **4**, No. 10, 435–436.

Franklin, M. A., *et al.* (1978). "Anomalies with variable partition paging algorithms." *CACM* **21**, No. 3, 232–236.

Fridrich, M., and Older, W. (1981). "The Felix file server," *Proc. ACM 8th SOSP, ACM OSR* **15**, No. 5, 37–44.

Gifford, D. (1982). "Cryptographic sealing for information secrecy and authentication." *Proc. ACM 8th SOSP, CACM* **25**, No. 4, 274–286.

Glaser, E. L., *et al.* (1965). "System design of a computer for time-sharing applications." *AFIPS FJCC Proc.* **27**, No. 1, 197–202.

Gligor, V. D., (1979). "Review and revocation of access privileges distributed through capabilities." *IEEE TSE*-**5**, No. 6, 575–586.

Gligor, V. D., and Lindsay, B. G. (1979). "Object migration and authentication." *IEEE TSE*-**5**, No. 6, 607–611.

Graham, R. M. (1968). "Protection in an information utility." *CACM* **11**, No. 5, 306–312.

Gray, J. N. (1979). Notes on data base operating systems, *In* "Operating Systems—An Advanced Course," (R. Bayer, R. M. Graham, and G. Seegmueller, eds.). Springer-Verlag, 393–481.

Graham, G. S., and Denning, P. J. (1972). "Protection—Principles and practice." *AFIPS SJCC Proc.* **40**, 417–430.

Gray, J., *et al.* (1981). "The recovery manager of the System R database manager." *ACM CS* **13**, No. 2, 223–242.

Habermann, A. N. (1969). "Prevention of system deadlocks. *CACM* **12**, No. 7, 373–377.

Habermann, A. N. (1972). "Synchronization of communicating processes." *CACM* **15**, No. 3, 171–176.

Habermann, A. N. (1976). "Introduction to Operating System Design." Science Research Associates.

Habermann, A. N., *et al.* (1976). "Modularization and hierarchy in a family of operating systems." *Proc. ACM 5th SOSP, CACM* **19**, No. 5, 266–272.

Hall, D. E., *et al.* (1980). "A virtual operating system." *CACM* **23**, No. 9, 495–502.

Hatfield, D. J., (1972). "Experiments on page size, program access patterns, and virtual memory performance." *IBM JRD* **16**, No. 1, 58–66.

Havender, J. W. (1968). "Avoiding deadlocks in multi-tasking systems." *IBM SJ* **7**, No. 2, 74–84.

Hoare, C. A. R. (1972). Towards a theory of parallel programming, In "Operating System Techniques," (Hoare and Perrot, eds.) Academic Press, 61–71.

Hoare, C. A. R. (1973). "A structured paging system." *Computer Journal* **16**, 209–215.

Hoare, C. A. R. (1974). "Monitors: an operating system structuring concept." *CACM* **17**, No. 10, 549–557.

Hoare, C. A. R. (1978). "Communicating sequential processes." *CACM* **21**, No. 8, 666–677.

Hoffman, L. J. (1977). "Modern Methods of Computer Security and Privacy." Prentice-Hall.

Holt, R. C. (1972). "Some deadlock properties of computer systems." *ACM CS* **4**, No. 3, 179–196.

Horning, J. J., and Randell, B. (1973). "Process structuring." *ACM CS* **5**, No. 1, 5–30.

Howard, J. H. (1976). "Signaling in Monitors." Proc. 2nd. Intl. Conf. on Softw. Eng. 47–52.

Hsiao, D. K., *et al.* (1979). "Computer Security." Academic Press.

Israel, J. E., *et al.* (1979). Separating data from function in a distributed file system, *In* "Proc. 2nd Intl. Symp. on Operating Systems Theory and Practice," (D. Lanciaux, ed.). North-Holland, 17–30.

Janson, P. A. (1981). "Using type extension to organize virtual memory mechanisms." *ACM OSR* **15**, No. 4, 6–38.

Jones, A. K. (1977). "Software management of Cm*—A distributed multiprocessor." *AFIPS NCC Proc.* **46**, 657–663.

Jones, A. K. (1979a). The object model, a conceptual tool for structuring software, *In* "Operating Systems—An Advanced Course," (R. Bayer, R. M. Graham, and G. Seegmueller, eds.). Springer-Verlag, 7–16.

Jones, A. K. (1979b). Protection mechanisms and the enforcement of security policies, *In* "Operating Systems—An Advanced Course," (R. Bayer, R. M. Graham, and G. Seegmueller, eds.) Springer-Verlag, 228–251.

Jones, A. K., and Liskov, B. H. (1978). "A language extension for expressing constraints on data access." *CACM* **21**, No. 5, 358–367.

Jones, A. K., and Wulf, W. A. (1975). "Towards the design of secure systems." *Software—Practice and Experience* **5**, 321–336.

Jones, A. K., *et al.* (1979). "StarOS, a multiprocessor operating system" for the support of task forces." *Proc. ACM 7th SOSP, ACM OSR* **13**, No. 5, 117–127.

Kahn, D. (1976). "The Codebreakers." MacMillan.

Kahn, K. C., *et al.* (1981). "iMAX: a multiprocessor operating system for an object-based computer." *Proc. ACM 8th SOSP, ACM OSR* **15**, No. 5, 127–137.

Keedy, J. L. (1977). "On implementing semaphores with sets," *Computer Journal* **22**, No. 2, 146–150.

Keedy, J. L. (1979). "On structuring operating systems with monitors," *Australian Comp. J.* **10**, 23–27, *or ACM OSR* **13**, No. 1, 5–9.

Kilburn, T., *et al.* (1961). "The Manchester University Atlas operating system—Part 1: the internal organization," *Computer Journal* **4,** No. 3, 222–225.

Kilburn, T. *et al.* (1962). "One-level storage system." *IEEE TC*-**11,** No. 2, 223–235.

Knowlton, K. C. (1965). "A fast storage allocator." *CACM* **8,** No. 10, 623–624.

Knuth, D. E. (1969). "The art of computer programming." Addison-Wesley.

Kohler, W. H. (1981). A survey of techniques for synchronization and recovery, *In* "Decentralized Computer Systems." *ACM CS* **13,** No. 2, 149–184.

Lagally, K. (1979). Synchronization in a layered system, *In* "Operating Systems—An Advanced Course," (R. Bayer, R. M. Graham, and G. Seegmueller, eds.). Springer-Verlag 252–281.

Lamport, L. (1978). "Time, clocks, and the ordering of events in a distributed system." *CACM* **21,** No. 7, 558–564.

Lampson, B. W. (1968). "A scheduling philosophy for multiprocessing systems." *CACM* **11,** No. 5, 347–360.

Lampson, B. W. (1969). "Dynamic protection structures." *AFIPS FJCC Proc.* **35,** 27–38.

Lampson, B. W. (1973). "A note on the confinement problem." *CACM* **16,** No. 10, 613–614.

Lampson, B. W. (1974a). "Protection." *ACM OSR* **8,** No. 1, 18–24.

Lampson, B. W. (1974b). "Redundancy and robustness in memory protection." *Proc. IFIP Congr.* 128–132.

Lampson, B. W. (1981). "Distributed systems—Architecture and implementation." Lecture Notes in Computer Science 105. Springer-Verlag.

Lampson, B. W., and Redell, D. D. (1980). "Experience with processes and monotors in Mesa," *Proc. ACM 7th SOSP, CACM* **23,** No. 2, 105–117.

Lampson, B. W., and Sproull, R. F. (1979). "An open operating system for a single-user machine." *Proc. ACM 7th SOSP, ACM OSR* **13,** No. 5, 98–105.

Lampson, B. W., and Sturgis, H. E. (1976). "Reflections on an operating system design." *Proc. ACM 5th SOSP, CACM* **19,** No. 5, 251–265.

Lauer, H. C., and Needham, R. M. (1979). On the duality of operating system structures. *In* "Proc. 2nd Intl. Symp. on Operating Systems Theory and Practice," (D. Lanciaux ed.). North-Holland, 371–384, and *ACM OSR* **13,** No. 2, 3–19.

Levin, R., *et al.* (1975). "Policy/mechanism separation in Hydra." *Proc. ACM 5th SOSP, ACM OSR* **9,** No. 5, 132–140.

Linde, R. R., *et al.* (1969). "The Adept-50 time sharing system." *AFIPS FJCC Proc.* **35,** 39–50.

Lindsay, B. (1981). "Object naming and catalog management for a distributed database manager." *Proc. 2nd Intl. Conf. on Distr. Comp. Syst., IEEE,* 31–40.

Liskov, B. H. (1972a). "The design of the Venus operating system." *Proc. ACM 3rd SOSP, CACM* **15,** No. 3, 144–149.

Liskov, B. H. (1972b). "A design methodology for reliable software systems." *AFIPS FJCC Proc.* **41,** No. 1, 191–200.

Liskov, B. H. (1982). "On linguistic support for distributed programs." *IEEE TSE*-**8,** No. 3, 203–210.

Liskov, B. H., and Zilles, S. N. (1975). "Specification techniques for data abstractions." *IEEE TSE*-**1,** 7–19.

Lister, A. M., and Maynard, K. J. (1976). "An implementation of Monitors." *Software—Practice & Experience* **6,** 377–385.

Luderer, G. W. R., *et al.* (1981). "A distributed Unix system based on a virtual circuit switch." *Proc. ACM 8th SOSP, ACM OSR* **15,** No. 5, 160–169.

Madnick, S. E., and Donovan, J. J. (1974). "Operating systems." McGraw-Hill.

Mattson, R. L., *et al.* (1970). "Evaluation techniques for storage hierarchies." *IBM SJ* **9,** No. 2, 78–117.

Merkle, R. (1978). "Secure communications over insecure channels." *CACM* 21, No. 4, 294–299.

Meyer, R. A., and Seawright, L. H. (1970). "A virtual machine time-sharing system." *IBM SJ* 9, No. 3, 199–218.

Millard, G. E., *et al.* (1975). "The standard Emas subsystem." *Computer Journal* 18, No. 3, 213–219.

Millen, J. K. (1976). "Security kernel validation in practice," *Proc. ACM 5th SOSP, CACM* 19, No. 5, 243–250.

Miller, A. (1972). "The Assault on privacy," Signet.

Mitchell, J. G., and Dion, J. (1982). "A comparison of two network-based file servers." *Proc. ACM 8th SOSP, CACM* 25, No. 4, 233–245.

Molho, L. (1970). "Hardware aspects of secure computing," *AFIPS SJCC Proc.* 36, 135–142.

Montgomery, W. A. (1979). "Polyvalues: a tool for implementing atomic updates to distributed data." *Proc. ACM 7th SOSP, ACM OSR* 13, No. 5, 143–149.

Morris, J. A. (1973). "Protection in programming languages." *CACM* 16, No. 1, 15–21.

Morris, J. B. (1971). "Demand paging through the use of working sets on the Maniac II," *CACM* 15, No. 10, 867–872.

Morris, R., and Thompson, K. (1979). "Password security: a case history." *CACM* 22, No. 11, 594–597.

Murphy, J. E. (1968). "Resource allocation with interlock detection in a multi-task system." *AFIPS FJCC Proc.* 33, No. 2, 1169–1176.

Murphy, D. (1972). "Storage organization and management in Tenex." *AFIPS FJCC Proc.* 41, No. 1, 23–32.

Needham, R. M. (1972). "Protection systems and protection implementations." *AFIPS FJCC Proc.* 41, No. 1, 571–578.

Needham, R. M., and Schroeder, M. D. (1978). "Using encryption for authentication in large networks of computers." *CACM* 21, No. 12, 993–998.

Needham, R. M., and Walker, R. D. H. (1977). "The CAP computer and its protection system." *Proc. ACM 6th SOSP, ACM OSR* 11, No. 5, 1–10.

Newton, G. (1979). "Deadlock prevention, detection, and resolution." *ACM OSR* 13, No. 2, 33–44.

Organick, E. I. (1972). "The Multics system: an examination of its structure." MIT Press.

Ossanna, J. F., *et al.* (1965). "Communication and input/output switching in a multiplex computing system," *AFIPS FJCC Proc.* 27, No. 1, 231–242.

Osterhout, J. K., *et al.* (1980). "Medusa: an experiment in distributed operating system structure." *Proc. ACM 7th SOSP, CACM* 23, No. 2, 92–104.

Overgaard, M. (1980). "UCSD Pascal: a portable software environment for small computers." *AFIPS NCC Proc.* 49, 747–754.

Pamerlee, R. P., *et al.* (1972). "Virtual storage and virtual machine concepts." *IBM SJ* 11, No. 2, 99–130.

Parker, D. B. (1976). "Crime by computer." Scribner's.

Parnas, D. L. (1971). "Information distribution aspects of design methodology." *Proc. IFIP Congr.* 340–344.

Parnas, D. L. (1972a). "A technique for software module specification with examples." *CACM* 15, No. 5, 330–336.

Parnas, D. L. (1972b). "On the criteria to be used in decomposing systems into modules." *CACM* 15, No. 12, 1053–1058.

Parnas, D. L. (1975). "On a solution to the cigarette smokers' problem." *CACM* 18, No. 3, 181–183.

Parnas, D. L., and Siewiorek, D. P. (1975). "The use of the concept of transparency in the design of hierarchically structured operating systems," *CACM* 18, No. 7, 401–408.

Parnas, D. L., *et al.* (1976). "Design and specification of the minimal subset of an operating system family." *IEEE TSE-***2**, 301–307.

Paxton, W. H. (1979). "A client-based transaction system to maintain integrity." *Proc. ACM 7th SOSP, ACM OSR* **13**, No. 5, 18–23.

Peterson, J., and Silberschatz, A. (1983). "Operating system concepts." Addison-Wesley.

Pollack, F., *et al.* (1981). "The iMAX-432 object filing system." *Proc. ACM 8th SOSP, ACM OSR* **15**, No. 5, 137–147.

Popek, G. J., and Kline, C. S. (1979). "Encryption and secure computer networks." *ACM CS* **11**, No. 4, 331–356.

Popek, G., *et al.* (1981). "Locus: a network transparent, high-reliability distributed system." *Proc. ACM 8th SOSP, ACM OSR* **15**, No. 5, 169–177.

Presser, L., and White, J. R. (1972). "Linkers and loaders," *ACM* **4**, No. 3, 149–167.

Prieve, B. G., and Fabry, R. S. (1976). "VMIN—An optimal variable-space page replacement algorithm." *Proc. ACM 5th SOSP, CACM* **19**, No. 5, 295–297.

Randell, B. (1969). "A note on storage fragmentation and program segmentation." *CACM* **12**, No. 7, 365–369.

Randell, B. (1975). "System structure for software fault tolerance." *IEEE TSE-***1**, 220–232.

Randell, B. (1979). Reliable computing systems, *In* "Operating systems—An advanced course," (R. Bayer, R. M. Graham, and G. Seegmueller, eds.). Springer-Verlag, 282–392.

Randell, B. *et al.* (1978). "Reliability issues in computing system design." *ACM CS* **10**, No. 2, 123–166.

Rashid, R., and Robertson, G. (1981). "Accent: a communication oriented network operating system kernel." *Proc. ACM 8th SOSP, ACM OSR* **15**, No. 5, 64–75.

Ravn, A. P. (1980). "Device monitors," *IEEE TSE-***6**, 49–53.

Redell, D. D. (1974). "Naming and protection in extensible operating systems." *MIT Lab. for Comp. Sc. Tr-***140.**

Redell, D. D., and Fabry, R. S. (1974). "Selective revocation of capabilities." Proc. Intl. Wrkshp on Protection in Operating Systems, INRIA, Paris, 197–210.

Redell, D. D., *et al.* (1980). "Pilot: an operating system for a personal computer." *Proc. ACM 7th SOSP, CACM* **23**, No. 2, 81–91.

Reed, D. P. (1983). "Implementing atomic actions on decentralized data." *ACM TOCS* **1**, No. 1, 3–23.

Reed, D. P., and Kanodia, R. K. (1979). "Synchronization with event counts and sequencers." *Proc. ACM 6th SOSP, CACM* **22**, No. 2, 115–123.

Rees, D. J. (1975). "The Emas director." *Computer Journal* **18**, No. 2, 122–130.

Rees, D. J., and Stephens, P. D. (1982). "The kernel of the Emas 2900 operating system." *Software—Practice and Experience* **12**, 655–668.

Richards, M., *et al.* (1979). "Tripos—A portable real-time operating system." *Software—Practice and Experience* **9**, 513–526.

Ritchie, D. M., and Thompson, K. (1974). "The Unix time-sharing system." *Proc. ACM 4th SOSP, CACM* **17**, No. 7, 365–375.

Rivest, R. L., *et al.*, "A method for obtaining digital signatures and public-key crypto-systems." *CACM* **21**, No. 2, 120–126.

Robinson, L., *et al.* (1975). "On attaining reliable software for a secure operating system." *Proc. Intl. Conf. on Reliable Software*, 267–284.

Rodriguez-Rosell, J., and Dupuy, J. P. (1973). "The design, implementation, and evaluation of a working set dispatcher." *CACM* **16**, No. 4, 247–253.

Rosin, R. F., (1969). "Supervisory and monitor systems." *ACM CS* **1**, No. 1, 37–54.

Saltzer, J. H. (1966). "Traffic control in a multiplexed computer system." *MIT Lab. for Comp. Sc. TR-***30.**

Saltzer, J. H., (1974). "Protection and the control of information sharing in Multics." *Proc. ACM 4th SOSP, CACM* **17**, No. 7, 388–402.

Saltzer, J. H. (1979a). Naming and binding of objects, *In* "Operating systems—An Advanced Course." (R. Bayer, R. M. Graham, and G. Seegmueller, eds.). Springer-Verlag, 99–208.

Saltzer, J. H. (1979b). Research problems of decentralized systems with largely autonomous nodes, *In* "Operating Systems—An Advanced Course." (R. Bayer, R. M. Graham, and G. Seegmueller, eds.). Springer-Verlag, 583–592.

Saltzer, J. H. (1982). On the naming and binding of network destinations, *In* "Proc. Intl. Symp. on Local Computer Networks," (Ravasio and Naffah eds.). North-Holland, 311–317.

Saltzer, J. H., and Schroeder, M. D. (1975). "The protection of information in computer systems." *Proc. IEEE* **63**, No. 9, 1278–1307.

Saxena, A. R., and Bredt, T. H. (1975). "A structured specification of a hierarchical operating system." *Proc. Intl. Conf. on Reliable Software,* 310–318.

Scherr, A. L. (1978). "Distributed data processing." *IBM SJ* **17**, No. 4, 324–343.

Schroeder, M. D., and Saltzer, J. H. (1972). "A hardware architecture for implementing protection rings." *Proc. ACM 3rd SOSP, CACM* **15**, No. 3, 157–170.

Schroeder, M. D., *et al.* (1977). "The Multics kernel design project." *Proc. ACM 6th SOSP, ACM OSR* **11**, No. 5, 43–56.

Seawright, L. H., and McKinnon, R. A. (1979). "VM/370—A study of multiplicity and usefulness." *IBM SJ* **18**, No. 1, 4–17.

Seybold, J. (1981). "The Xerox professional workstation," *The Seybold Report* **10**, No. 16.

Shankar, K. S. (1977). "The total computer security problem." *IEEE Computer* **10**, No. 6, 50–73.

Shaw, A. C. (1974). "The Logical Design of Operating Systems." Prentice-Hall.

Shoch, J. F. (1978). "Inter-network naming, addressing, and routing." *Proc. IEEE Fall COMPCON,* 72–79.

Shore, J. E. (1975). "On the external storage fragmentation" produced by first-fit and best-fit allocation strategies." *CACM* **18**, No. 8, 433–440.

Smith, A. J. (1978a). "A comparative study of set associative memory mapping algorithms and their use for cache and main memory." *IEEE TSE-***4**, No. 2, 121–130.

Smith, A. J. (1978b). "Bibliography on paging and related topics." *ACM OSR* **12**, No. 4, 39–56.

Smith, A. J. (1981). "Bibliography on file and I/O system optimization and related topics." *ACM OSR* **15**, 39–54.

Solomon, M., *et al.* (1982). "The CSNET name server," *Computer Networks* **6**, 161–172.

Spector, A. Z. (1982). "Performing remote operations efficiently on a local computer network." *Proc. ACM 8th SOSP, CACM* **25**, No. 4, 246–259.

Stephens, P. D., *et al.* (1980). "The evolution of the operating system Emas 2900." *Software—Practice and Experience* **10**, 933–1008.

Stern, J. A. (1974). "Backup and recovery of on-line information in a computer utility." *MIT Lab. for Comp. Sc. TR-***116,**

Sturgis, H. E., *et al.* (1980). "Issues in the design and use of a distributed file system." *ACM OSR* **14**, No. 3, 55–69.

Svobodova, L. (1981). "A reliable object-oriented repository for a distributed computer system." *Proc. ACM 8th SOSP, ACM OSR* **15**, No. 5, 47–58.

Svobodova, L. (1983). "File servers for network-based distributed systems." *IBM Research Report RZ* 1258.

Swinehart, D., *et al.* (1979). "WFS: a simple shared file system for a distributed environment." *Proc. ACM 7th SOSP, ACM OSR* **13**, No. 5, 9–17.

Tanenbaum, A. S. (1981). "Computer Networks." Prentice Hall.

Teorey, T. J. (1972). "Properties of disk scheduling policies in multiprogrammed computer systems." *AFIPS FJCC Proc.* **41**, No. 1, 1–11.

Teorey, T. J., and Pinkerton, T. B. (1972). "A comparative analysis of disk scheduling policies." *Proc. ACM 3rd SOSP, CACM* **15**, No. 3, 177–184.

Tsichritzis, D. C., and Bernstein, P. A. (1974). "Operating Systems." Academic Press.

Turn, R., and Shapiro, N. Z. (1972). "Privacy and security in data bank systems—Measures, costs, and protector intruder interactions." *AFIPS FJCC Proc.* **41**, No. 1, 435–444.

Turn, R., and Ware, W. (1976). "Privacy and security issues in information systems." *IEEE TC-*25, No. 12, 1353–1361.

(Unix (1978).), "Unix time-sharing system." *Bell System Technical Journal* **57**, No. 6, Part 2, 1897–2312.

Voydock, V. L., and Kent, S. T. (1983). "Security mechanisms in high-level network protocols." *ACM CS* **15**, No. 2, 135–171.

Vyssotsky, V. A., *et al.* (1965). "Structure of the Multics supervisor." *AFIPS FJCC Proc.* **27**, No. 1, 203–212.

Walden, D. C. (1972). "A system for inter-process communication in a resource sharing computer network." *CACM* **15**, No. 4, 221–230.

Walker, B. J., *et al.* (1980). "Specification and verification of the UCLA Unix security kernel." *Proc. ACM 7th SOSP, CACM* **23**, No. 2, 118–131.

Watson, R. W. (1970). "Time-sharing System Design Concepts." McGraw-Hill Computer Science Series.

Watson, R. W. (1981). Identifiers (naming) in distributed systems, *In* "Distributed Systems—Architecture and Implementation," (B. W. Lampson, M. Paul, and H. J. Siegert, eds.). Springer-Verlag, 191–210.

Weissman, C. (1969). "Security controls in the Adept-50 time-sharing system." *AFIPS FJCC Proc.* **35**, 119–134.

Westin, A. F., and Baker, M. A. (1972). "Databanks in a Free Society." Quadrangle Books.

Whitfield, H. and Whight, A. S. (1973). "Emas—The Edinburgh multi-access system." *Computer Journal* **16**, No. 4, 331–346.

Wilhelm, N. C. (1977). "A general model for the performance of disk systems." *JACM* **24**, 14–31.

Wilkes, M. V. (1975). "Time-sharing Computer Systems." American Elsevier Computer Monographs, 3rd ed.

Wilkes, M. V., and Needham, R. M. (1980). "The Cambridge model distributed system." *ACM OSR* **14**, No. 1, 7–20.

Wirth, N. "Toward a discipline of real-time programming." *CACM* **20**, No. 8, 577–583.

Wulf, W., *et al.* (1974). "F. Pollack, Hydra: The kernel of a multiprocessor operating system." *CACM* **17**, No. 6, 337–345.

Glossary

Active segment A segment currently in use, whose PT is in main memory in the SPT and whose uid is in the SST.

Connected segment A segment for which there currently exists an entry in some ST.

Disk map A per-disk table indicating which records are free and which ones are currently allocated to some file.

File map A per-file table residing in a disk VTOC, mapping page numbers into the addresses of corresponding pages on disk.

Home address The address of the map of a file on a file system disk.

Memory map A system-wide table indicating which memory blocks are free and which ones are currently allocated to some page.

Name Table (NT) A per-process table mapping segment numbers into the symbolic names, uids, and home addresses of corresponding files. It plays the role of local cache for file system catalog entries.

Opened file A file for which there currently exists an entry in some NT.

Page Associative Memory (PAM) A per-physical-processor, fast, hardware, associative cache memory used to hold the most recently used segment number–page number to page address mappings.

Page number The number of a page in a segment, which can be used as an index into the segment PT for addressing purposes.

Page Table (PT) A per-segment table residing in the SPT, mapping page numbers into the addresses of corresponding pages in central memory or in peripheral storage.

Page Table address The address of the PT of a segment in the SPT.

Passive segment A segment currently not in use, whose PT is not in the SPT, and whose uid is not in the SST.

Segment Associative Memory (SAM) A per-physical-processor, fast, hardware, associative cache memory used to hold the most recently used segment number to page table address mappings.

Segment number A number used by a process as an index into its ST and NT to refer to segments in its address space.

Segment Table (ST) A per-process table mapping segment numbers into corresponding PT addresses.

System Page Table (SPT) A system-wide table in which space is allocated to the individual PTs of active segments.

System Segment Table (SST) A system-wide table mapping the uids of active segments into corresponding PT addresses in the SPT.

Unique identifier (uid) A fairly long number (e.g., 32- to 64-bit or more) uniquely identifying a single file or segment over the entire life and scope of a system (or even a collection of systems in a distributed environment).

User process An abstract processor resulting from the multiplexing of virtual processors (VPT entries) among user computations. A user process is represented by a UPT entry. It is the embodiment of a user computation. As it evolves through a succession of virtual processor states, it causes the user computation to progress.

User Process Table (UPT) A system-wide table into which are stored snapshots of the state of all user processes not currently loaded in central memory, i.e., not running on some virtual processor.

Virtual processor An abstract processor resulting from the multiplexing of physical processors. A virtual processor is represented by a VPT entry. It is the embodiment of a computation. As it evolves through a succession of states, represented by successive snapshots of physical processor registers, it causes the computation to progress.

Virtual Processor Table (VPT) A system-wide table into which are stored snapshots of the state of all virtual processors not currently running on a physical processor.

Volume Table of Contents (VTOC) A per-disk volume table containing the map of the disk allocation state as well as the maps of all the files residing on that disk.

Index

User-programmable systems, 12
Utility software, 7

V

V, 32, 34
Variable space algorithms, 131
Version storage, 172
Virtual device, 9, 86
Virtual machines, 6, 234
Virtual memory, 10, 118, 186
  life function, 124
  locality, 123
  paging algorithms, 125
  reference string, 124
  resident set, 124
  success function, 124
Virtual processor, 9, 24, 72, 120
  ready state, 69, 70

running state, 70
states, 64, 68, 70, 73
waiting state, 70
Virtual Processor Table, 65
Virtual time, 79
VMIN, 132
Volume Table of Contents, 141
VPT, 65, 68, 72, 212, 245
VTOC, 141, 148, 245

W

Wait-die, 60
Wait-for loop, 52
Wait-wound, 61
Waiting state, 70
Wakeup, 36, 47, 70
Wakeup-waiting-switch, 38
Working Set (WS) algorithm, 131, 135, 138